William Ripley Nichols

Water Supply

Considered mainly from a chemical and sanitary Standpoint. Fourth Edition

William Ripley Nichols

Water Supply
Considered mainly from a chemical and sanitary Standpoint. Fourth Edition

ISBN/EAN: 9783337138974

Printed in Europe, USA, Canada, Australia, Japan

Cover: Foto ©ninafisch / pixelio.de

More available books at **www.hansebooks.com**

WATER SUPPLY

CONSIDERED MAINLY FROM A

CHEMICAL AND SANITARY STANDPOINT.

BY

WM. RIPLEY NICHOLS,

PROFESSOR AT THE MASSACHUSETTS INSTITUTE OF TECHNOLOGY.

FOURTH EDITION.

NEW YORK:

JOHN WILEY & SONS.

1892.

PRESS OF J. J. LITTLE & CO.,
NOS. 10 TO 88 ASTOR PLACE, NEW YORK.

PREFACE.

THE following pages contain, somewhat amplified, the substance of a course of "Lectures on Water Supply" which the author has been in the habit of delivering before certain classes at the Institute of Technology. It is primarily as an aid to engineering and other students at this and similar institutions that the book is printed. It is hoped, however, that the book will be found of service to young engineers, to persons in charge of water works, to water committees, and to others who are interested in the matter of water supply.

The aim is not to present a complete treatise on water supply for the civil engineer, nor a treatise on water analysis for the chemist, nor a treatise on mycology for the botanist, and certainly not a treatise on sanitary science for the physician, but, rather, to occupy a territory which encroaches on the fields of these and other professions and which belongs exclusively to no one alone —ground, in fact, with which all who are professionally interested in water supply must be more or less familiar.

The metric system of weights and measures is used, as well as the English; tables for the conversion of one system into the other will be found at the end of the volume. In the nomenclature of chemical substances, the old and more familiar terms are generally—although not exclusively employed—such as carbonate of soda and not sodic carbonate, sulphate of lime rather than sulphate of calcium.

The author has quoted freely from other works on the subject, and from his own earlier reports, now mostly out of print.

He would acknowledge especial indebtedness to the Reports of the Rivers Pollution Commission, and to Fischer's chemische Technologie des Wassers, and regrets that Wolffhügels Wasserversorgung did not come to hand until the manuscript was in the hands of the printer.

MASSACHUSETTS INSTITUTE OF TECHNOLOGY,
    Boston, Mass., *May*, 1883.

TABLE OF CONTENTS.

INTRODUCTORY CHAPTER.

SOLUTION.

No water which occurs in nature is pure in the strict chemical sense of the term, but all natural waters, however free from suspended particles of foreign matter which are visible to the eye, invariably contain *in solution* more or less of substances which, in their ordinary condition, are solids or gases. It is therefore important, in the beginning, to understand some of the many things which might be said of solution in general.

Solution of Solid Substances.

If some pure salt be put into water, after a time the salt disappears from sight, and becomes incorporated with the water, so that it is no longer possible to distinguish it by the eye, or to remove it by ever so fine a filter. As far as we can make it out, the change that has taken place is as follows : The ultimate particles of the salt (the molecules of the chemist) are no longer held together in a solid mass by that mutual attraction which we call cohesion, but have become separated from each other and distributed among the particles (molecules) of the water so as to form a homogeneous mixture. As far as we can perceive, it is, indeed, simply a mixture—a mixture of particles of salt with particles of water—we can discover no chemical change, we can trace no chemical action between the dissimilar substances, salt and water. This is an example of what is usually called *physical solution.* The solution differs, of course, essentially from the water. The transparency is not noticeably impaired,* but if

---

* This would not be true if, instead of common salt, we had taken a strongly colored substance like the permanganate of potash. In such a case the strong color of the solution would perceptibly diminish its transparency ; otherwise the phenomena would be as above.

much salt has been used the mobility of the water has been lessened, the boiling point has been raised, the freezing point and the temperature of maximum density have been lowered, the specific gravity, the specific heat and the electrical resistance have also been changed. If, now, the solution be allowed to evaporate at the ordinary temperature, or if the evaporation be hastened by artificially raising the temperature, the water passes off as vapor and the salt is recovered unchanged.

If a strip of zinc be immersed in ordinary muriatic (hydrochloric) acid somewhat diluted, the zinc gradually disappears, but at the same time there is a marked effervescence, due to the escape of hydrogen gas, as well as a considerable increase of temperature. There is, in fact, evidence enough that chemical change is taking place. When the action is over, we have a transparent liquid which is sometimes spoken of as a "solution of zinc," and the phenomenon is spoken of as *chemical solution*. If, however, we study the action that occurs, we find that it may be regarded as taking place in two steps: in the first place, the zinc acts on the acid to set free hydrogen gas, and to form a new compound, chloride of zinc; in the second place, the chloride of zinc thus formed dissolves in the liquid present, as did the salt in the previous example.

Using the term solution in its ordinary sense, to cover all cases of the disappearance of a solid * in a liquid, there are many cases which can be assigned without hesitation to one or the other of the two classes of actions just described, but it is by no means easy in all cases to say whether we are dealing with a simple (physical) solution, or whether chemical action also takes place. Thus, if dry oxide of sodium be put into water, it *dissolves*, that is, the solid disappears, but we are quite sure in this case that it is not the oxide of sodium which exists in the solution; in fact, the oxide of sodium combines chemically with a portion of the water to form hydrate of sodium,† and it is this hydrate, and not the oxide, which actually dissolves in the mass of the water present. Again, if dry carbonate of soda be put into water, there is next to no doubt that it combines with a

---

* The solution of gases and liquids will be considered further on.
† The chemical change which takes place is thus symbolized : $Na_2O + H_2O = 2NaOH$.

portion of the water, and that the compound which actually enters into solution has the same composition as the crystallized carbonate which contains, in addition to the elements of carbonate of soda, also a quantity of water. With regard to many solids, we are in doubt whether they dissolve simply as such, or first undergo chemical change. In cases like that of common salt, first mentioned, we can trace no such chemical change, but it is by no means certain that no chemical action takes place, and many regard the solution of salt and other similar substances as due to the same cause as that to which chemical action in general is due, manifested, however, to a slight degree.*

The term solution is applied almost exclusively to cases where the dissolving substance, the *solvent*, is a liquid; the substance dissolved may be solid, liquid, or gaseous. Every liquid can act as a solvent for certain things, although, if the liquid is of a marked alkaline or acid character, solution is usually accompanied by chemical change. Water is spoken of as the universal solvent, and more than any other liquid does it dissolve various substances without evident change. In what follows, we shall use the terms soluble and insoluble to mean soluble and insoluble in water.

Solids differ from each other very much in the facility with which they may be dissolved in water; thus, chloride of calcium, if merely left exposed to the air, readily absorbs from the atmosphere enough water to dissolve it, and is an example of a so-called *deliquescent* substance; on the other hand, sulphate of lead requires about 23,000 times its own weight of water (Fresenius), and quartz may be said to be insoluble. At a given temperature a certain quantity of water will always dissolve the same weight of a particular substance, and, as a general rule, the amount which can be dissolved increases with increase of temperature. The effect of increased temperature, however, differs greatly with different substances. Thus chloride of sodium (common salt) is more soluble in hot than in cold water, but only very slightly so; in the case of chloride of potassium, however, the amount dissolved increases regularly with the temperature, while in the case of nitrate of potassium the increase of solubility for a

* See, for instance, a paper On Solution and the Chemical Process. Hunt's Chemical and Geological Essays, pp. 448 and foll.

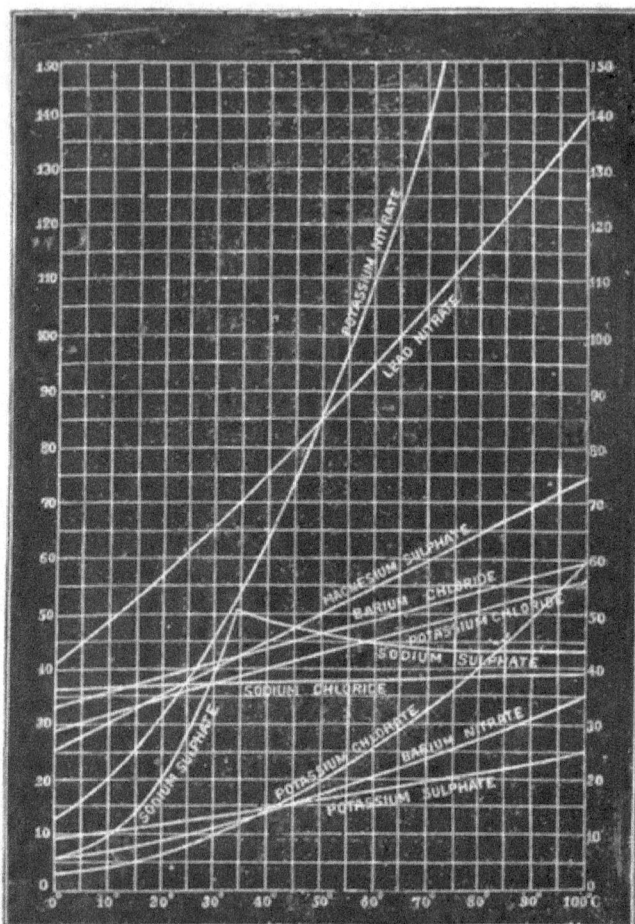

FIG. 1.— CURVES OF SOLUBILITY.

given increase of temperature is greater the higher the temperature :

		GRAMS.	DIFF. FOR 10°.
100 grams of water at	0° C. dissolve of chloride of potassium.	29.23	
	20°	· 34.70	5.47
	40°	.. 40.18	5.48
	60°	.. 45.66	5.48
100 grams of water at	0° dissolve of nitrate of potassium....	13.32	
	20°	.... 31.70	18.38
	40°	.... 63.97	32.27
	60°	....110.33	46.36

The diagram on the opposite page shows the relation of solubility to temperature in the case of a number of common salts. The horizontal lines indicate the number of parts by weight of the salt which 100 parts by weight of water will dissolve at the indicated temperature.

There are some remarkable exceptions to the general rule that a larger amount of a substance can be dissolved in a given quantity of hot water than in the same quantity of water at a lower temperature. Sulphate of lime is one of these exceptions. This substance occurs in sea-water and in other natural waters, and, by virtue of the fact that its solubility decreases with increase of temperature, it gives much trouble in steam-boilers by separating out from the water and forming a coherent scale. The following table shows the solubility of sulphate of lime in sea-water at temperatures above 103° Centigrade.

TABLE I.—SOLUBILITY OF SULPHATE OF LIME IN SEA-WATER.*

Temperature in Degrees		Pressure in Atmospheres.	Sea-water Saturated with Sulphate of Lime		
Centigrade.	Fahrenheit.		Marks (at 15° C.) on Beaumé's hydrometer.	Or has a specific gravity of	Contains per cent of sulphate of lime.
103.	217.4	1.	12°.5	1.090	0.500
103.80	218.8	1.	12°	1.085	0.477
105.15	221.3	1.	11°	1.075	0.432
108.60	227.5	1.25	10°	1.070	0.395
111.00	231.8	1.25	9°	1.063	0.355
113.20	235.8	1.25	8°	1.056	0.310
115.80	240.4	1.50	7°	1.048	0.267
118.50	245.3	1.50	6°	1.041	0.226
121.20	250.2	1.50	5°	1.034	0.183
124.	255.2	2.	4°	1.027	0.140
127.90	262.2	2.	3°	1.020	0.097
130.	266.0	2.50	2°	1.013	0.060
133.30	271.9	2.50	1°	1.007	0.023

This table shows that when sea-water is boiled under a pressure of one atmosphere, or at a temperature of 103° C., it will become saturated with sulphate of lime, when, by evaporation, its density has been elevated to 12°.5 Beaumé, and it will then contain 0.5 per cent of the sulphate; at 1.25 atmospheres, or 108°.6 C., the water will be saturated with sulphate when it

* Cousté : Annales des Mines, v (1854), p. 80. The second and fifth columns have been added to Cousté's table.

marks 10° B., and will then contain 0.395 per cent of the sulphate. At a pressure of two atmospheres, that is, at a temperature of about 125° C., sea-water, in its natural state and without having undergone any concentration, is very near the point at which saturation occurs, for the density of sea-water is from 3° to 3°.5 B., and this, according to the table, would correspond to a temperature of about 125° C. Sulphate of lime becomes completely insoluble, either in fresh or sea-water, at temperatures between 140° C. and 150° C. (284°–302° F.).

Saturated and supersaturated solutions.—At any particular temperature a solvent can take up a definite amount of a substance soluble in it, and no more. The solution is said to be saturated when it contains as much of the dissolved substance as can be *taken up* at the given temperature. It is, however, often possible to prepare what are called *supersaturated solutions*, by making a saturated solution at some higher temperature and allowing the liquid to cool. Suppose, for example, that a saturated solution of nitrate of potassium was made at 60° using 100 c.c. of water; according to the diagram on page 4, at that temperature 100 grams of water would dissolve 110.33 grams of the salt. If, now, the solution were cooled to 20°, we should expect that there would then remain dissolved 31.70 grams, and that 78.63 grams would separate in the solid condition during the cooling; in this particular case, the expectation would be approximately realized; but, with many salts, if a saturated solution be cooled quietly without agitation, it happens that, when cold, the liquid still retains more of the salt than it could take up at the lower temperature. In fact, Storer says:* "It is often exceedingly difficult thus to obtain normally saturated solutions, even of our most common and easily crystallized salts, within the limits of time which can be conveniently allotted to a single experiment."

In the case of some particular salts the phenomenon of supersaturation is very marked. Thus, at a temperature of 33° C., water will dissolve about half its own weight of Glauber's salt (hydrated sulphate of sodium), and if the solution be protected from dust and allowed to cool quietly to the ordinary temperature, the whole of the compound remains in solution. If, now,

---

* Dictionary of Solubilities, Preface.

a small crystal of the same kind as the original salt be dropped into the solution, about three-fifths of the salt separates out in the crystalline form, and the whole mass becomes nearly solid.

Condition of mixed solutions.—Natural waters usually contain a variety of foreign substances, and it is worth while, at this point, to inquire into the condition of things which exist in a dilute solution containing at the same time several different salts. We will first take a simple case where chemical analysis shows the existence of, say a chloride and a sulphate, and of potassium and sodium. The question may be asked, whether the solution contains chloride of sodium and sulphate of potassium, or sulphate of sodium and chloride of potassium, or whether all four of these compounds exist at the same time. Now, while the latter is believed to be the true state of the case, chemical analysis is powerless to answer the question, and two solutions undistinguishable from each other could be prepared by taking each pair of salts indicated above in the right proportion.* If a number of soluble salts are mixed together in solution, the matter becomes more complicated, but in stating the results of analysis, certain conventional forms of statement are adopted. Thus we might mix together in dilute solution and in the right proportion, sulphate of sodium and chloride of calcium, but if the solution were analyzed, it would be reported as containing sulphate of calcium and chloride of sodium, for the reason that the sulphate of calcium is much less readily soluble in water than the other compounds, and if the solution in question were gradually concentrated by evaporation, the sulphate of calcium would separate in the solid form; if the evaporation were carried to dryness, the sulphate of calcium and chloride of sodium would remain, each crystallized by itself. For this reason chloride of calcium would never be represented as existing in the presence of sulphate of sodium, although, in a dilute solution, it is probable that a portion of the calcium would actually exist in the form of chloride. It should be said that much difference of opinion and practice exists with reference to the best way to represent the constituents of a mixed solution, and two chemists will often report

---

* We are not in absolute ignorance as to the laws which govern the partition of a base among different acids, or of an acid among different bases, or, indeed, of the acid and basic radicals among different salts. Our knowledge, however, is too limited to be applied practically to any considerable extent in such a case as that of a natural water.

very different statements of the analysis of the same solution, while the numerical results actually obtained are the same.

The following statement of the analysis of Croton water, by Professor Chandler, is an example of the form in which such reports are usually made :

SOLIDS CONTAINED IN ONE GALLON OF CROTON WATER.

	Summer, 1869. Grains.	May 11, 1872. Grains.
Chloride of Sodium..........................	0.402	0.284
Sulphate of Potash	0.179	0.205
Sulphate of Soda.............................	0.260	0.024
Sulphate of Lime.............................	0.158	0.024
Bicarbonate of Lime..........................	2.670	2.331
Bicarbonate of Magnesia......	1.913	1.338
Silica	0.621	0.222
Alumina and Oxide of Iron....................	a trace	0 058
Organic Matter...............................	0.670	0.874
Total................................	6.873	5.360

The following statement represents the actual results of analysis, from which the previous statement was made up according to the conventional plan usually adopted :

SOLIDS CONTAINED IN ONE GALLON OF CROTON WATER.

	Summer, 1869. Grains.	May 11, 1872. Grains.
Soda.................	0 326	0.157
Potash.......................................	0.097	0.109
Lime...	0.988	0.819
Magnesia.....................................	0.524	0.369
Chlorine.....................................	0.243	0.172
Sulphuric Acid...............................	0.322	0.124
Silica	0.621	0.222
Alumina and Oxide of Iron....................	a trace	0.058
Carbonic Acid (calculated)...................	2.604	2.074
Water in Bicarbonates (calculated)...........	0.532	0.421
Organic and Volatile Matter..................	0.670	0.874
	6.927	5.399
Less Oxygen equivalent to the Chlorine.........	0.054	0.039
Total...............................	6 873	5.360

Effect of the presence of one substance on the solubility of another substance.—When water has dissolved as much of a given substance as it can under the existing conditions, it is still able to take up more or less of a second substance. In general, the

presence of one substance in a solution will modify the action of
the liquid on another substance presented to it; thus, while
cyanide of silver is insoluble in water, it dissolves readily in an
aqueous solution of cyanide of potassium.   Again, although carbonate of lime dissolves only to a very slight extent in pure
water, it dissolves to a considerable extent in water containing
carbonic acid, and is a frequent constituent of natural waters.
When such waters are boiled, the carbonic acid escapes, and as
the water is no longer able to keep the carbonate of lime in solution, this compound separates out and is one of the substances
which cause trouble in steam boilers by forming an incrustation
or scale.   Undoubtedly, in such cases as those mentioned, chemical action takes place to a greater or less extent between the
substances dissolved.

  Various means of hastening solution.—The solution of a solid
substance is facilitated by any means which tends to bring continually fresh portions of the solvent into intimate contact with
the substance to be dissolved.   It is consequently of advantage
to reduce the solid to a fine powder, and to agitate the mixture.
Where there is no objection to heating the liquid, the solution is
facilitated by so doing.   Advantage may be taken of the fact,
that the solution has a greater specific gravity than the solvent,
by suspending the solid near the sur-
face of the liquid.   This may be
easily shown by putting crystals of
some colored salt, as bichromate of
potash or sulphate of copper, into a
cone of wire gauze, or into a funnel,
or into a tube over one end of which
a piece of cloth is tied, and suspending the apparatus in a vessel of water.
The solution, as it is formed, falls
toward the bottom of the vessel,
marking its path through the water

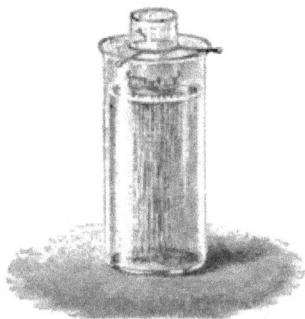

FIG. 2.

by colored threads, and this action continues until the solution is
saturated.

  In preparing brine or a solution of copperas—as a disinfectant,
for instance—much time may be saved by suspending the salt or
the copperas in a basket or coarse bag near the top of the tub or
barrel in which the solution is made, instead of putting the solid

at the bottom of the water and endeavoring to hasten solution
by stirring.

Effect of dissolved solids on various physical phenomena.—The
effect of dissolved solid substances is to increase the specific
gravity, and in the case of many substances tables have been
prepared from which the percentage of the substance dissolved
can be learned by observing the specific gravity of the solution.
Similar tables have also been prepared for solutions of gases and
liquids.

The presence of dissolved substances raises the boiling point
of the solution, and the stronger the solution, the higher the
boiling point. Thus, ordinary sea-water boils at about 101° C.
(213°.8 F.), while a saturated solution of acetate of potash does
not boil until the temperature reaches 169° C. (304°.2 F.).

The effect of dissolved solids is to lower the freezing point
and the temperature of maximum density. Thus, while pure
water is at its maximum density at 4° C. (39°.2 F.), and freezes
at 0° C. (32° F.), sea-water, according to Despretz, acquires its
maximum density at 3°.67 C. (38°.6 F.), and freezes at −1°.88 C.
(28°.6 F.).

Solution of Gases.

It is true of gases as of solids that they vary very much in
their deportment toward water, some being absorbed by it with
very great readiness, while others may be kept in contact with it
for a long time without suffering any considerable decrease of
bulk. It is generally true, however, of gases, that they dissolve
to a certain, even if to a slight, extent, and the amount is fixed
and definite under the same conditions of temperature and pressure. As a rule, increase of temperature decreases the solubility,
and by prolonged boiling, water may be freed from the gases
which it holds in solution.* The specific gravity of solutions of
gases is sometimes lower and sometimes higher than that of water.

The volume of a gas (expressed in cubic centimeters and
measured at 0° C., and under a pressure of 760 m.m. of mercury)
which one cubic centimeter of water will dissolve at a certain

---

* This is not invariably true. Thus, a strong solution of chlorhydric acid gas,
when heated, gives off the gas until the amount of acid in the remaining solution has
been reduced to 20.24 per cent by weight; the solution of this strength distills
unchanged at 110° C.

temperature, is called the coefficient of absorption at that temperature. The accompanying table gives the coefficient of absorption at various temperatures for oxygen, nitrogen, carbonic acid, and ammonia.[*]

TABLE II.—COEFFICIENT OF ABSORPTION OF VARIOUS GASES.

TEMPERATURE.	OXYGEN.	NITROGEN.	CARBONIC ACID.	AMMONIA.
0° C.	0.04114	0.02035	1.7967	1049.6
1	0.04007	0.01981	1.7207	1020.8
2	0.03907	0.01932	1.6481	993.3
3	0.03810	0.01884	1.5787	967.0
4	0.03717	0.01838	1.5126	941.9
5	0.03628	0.01794	1.4497	917.9
6	0.03544	0.01752	1.3901	895.0
7	0.03465	0.01713	1.3339	873.1
8	0.03389	0.01675	1.2809	852.1
9	0.03317	0.01640	1.2311	832.0
10	0.03250	0.01607	1.1847	812.8
11	0.03189	0.01577	1.1416	794.3
12	0.03133	0.01549	1.1018	776.3
13	0.03082	0.01523	1.0653	759.6
14	0.03034	0.01500	1.0321	743.1
15	0.02989	0.01478	1.0020	727.2
16	0.02949	0.01458	0.9753	711.8
17	0.02914	0.01441	0.9519	696.9
18	0.02884	0.01426	0.9318	682.3
19	0.02858	0.01413	0.9150	668.0
20	0.02838	0.01403	0.9014	654.0

From the table it is seen that the coefficient of carbonic acid is considerably, and that of ammonia enormously, greater than that of oxygen and nitrogen. In the case of gases like ammonia, hydrochloric acid, etc., we have no difficulty in believing that the great absorption is due to the fact that chemical combination takes place, and this is probably true also of carbonic acid, sulphuretted hydrogen, etc. It is a curious fact that, with hydrogen, the coefficient of absorption *in water* is the same at all temperatures from 0° to 20° C.

If the pressure be increased, a greater weight of the gas is dissolved at a given temperature, and the increase is, in fact, proportional to the increase of pressure, but since the increased pressure diminishes the volume of the gas in the same proportion, the same actual volume of gas is dissolved whatever the pressure. In the case of gases which are easily liquefied by pressure, or of those which are very soluble in water, this law does not hold good under all circumstances. Thus carbonic acid fol-

---

[*] Bunsen : Gasometrische Methoden, Braunschweig, 1877.

lows the law only when the pressure is small, and ammonia gas
only at high temperature.   The law is, in general, true also when
water is exposed to an atmosphere of mixed gases; that is, each
of the gases in the mixture is dissolved according to its own
coefficient of solubility; but in determining the actual *quantity*
of any one gas dissolved (*i.e.*, the volume at o° and 760 m.m.), it
must be remembered that the pressure exerted by the mixed
gases is made up of the partial pressures of the several gases in
the mixture.   Thus, whether water at o° C. be exposed to pure
oxygen with a pressure of 760 m.m., or to air at the pressure of
760 m.m., the same volume of oxygen will be dissolved in either
case, namely, as we see from the table, 0.04114 c.c. of oxygen in
each cubic centimeter of water; but in the one case we have
0.04114 c.c. of oxygen with a pressure of 760 m.m., whereas in
the other case we have 0.04114 c.c. of oxygen with a pressure of
one-fifth of 760 m.m., for in the air the oxygen forms only about
one-fifth part by volume.   It follows that the actual *quantity* of
gas (*i.e.*, the volume which it would have at o° and 760 m.m.) in
the first case is about five times as great as in the second.   It is
possible, knowing the composition of the mixture of dissolved
gases in any case, to calculate the composition of the atmosphere
to which the water was exposed, but this does not hold in the
case of a gas forming only a very small part of a mixture.
Owing to the fact that the coefficient of absorption for oxygen is
greater than that of nitrogen, water which has been exposed to
ordinary air contains these two gases in quite a different proportion from that in which they exist in the air, and this is one of
the proofs adduced to show that in the air the gases were simply
mixed together, and not chemically combined.   The relation is
as follows:

	Composition of Air by Volume.	Composition of " Dissolved Air " by Volume.*
Oxygen	20.96	34.91
Nitrogen	79.04	65.09
	100.00	100.00

Supersaturated solutions of gases.—As in the case of solids, it
is possible to prepare temporarily supersaturated solutions of
gases.   Thus, if ordinary "soda-water" be drawn from a siphon
or from a fountain, a quantity of gas escapes as soon as the

---

* Bunsen : Gasometrische Methoden, p. 224.

excess of pressure is removed. Afterward the gas escapes more slowly, until eventually the water contains no more carbonic acid gas than it would take up under the conditions to which it is now exposed. That we really are dealing with a supersaturated solution after the first rapid escape of gas, may be shown by dropping into the soda-water a teaspoonful of sugar, or some sand, or almost any powder; this causes immediate effervescence and escape of gas by furnishing free surfaces and sharp angles for the collection and liberation of the gas within the liquid.

Facilitating gaseous solution.—In preparing a saturated solution of a gas, the latter is generally allowed to simply bubble through the liquid to be saturated until the end is attained, the liquid being agitated or not, according to convenience. In the case of most gases, solution is facilitated by lowering the temperature, as, for instance, by surrounding the vessel in which the absorption takes place with cold water or ice. This is of especial use when the gas enters into chemical combination with the liquid, as is true of ammonia, hydrochloric acid, etc., when dissolved in water, because the heat of chemical action raises the temperature of the solution.

It is sometimes desirable to charge water with gas under increased pressure; thus water is charged under pressure with carbonic acid gas, to bear thenceforth the name of " soda-water;" sulphuretted hydrogen water, for use in chemical laboratories, is also prepared similarly.

Solubility of Liquids in Water.

Like solid substances, liquids differ among themselves as to their solubility in water, some liquids, as glycerine and common alcohol, mix with water in any and all proportions; others, like ether and amylic alcohol, dissolve to a limited and definite extent; others, like some oils and mercury, seem to be altogether insoluble, although by long contact with the water such insoluble liquids may undergo chemical change, and give up something to the water. It is more difficult than with solids to determine whether and to what extent an insoluble or difficultly soluble liquid dissolves in water, and to distinguish between solution and suspension, especially if the liquid is colorless and has nearly the same refractive index as water. In this case it is impossible to

obtain satisfactory indications with the eye, and complete separation of suspended particles is often impossible. The solution of
a difficultly soluble colorless liquid may sometimes be watched
by coloring the liquid with some substance which does not interfere with the action. Thus, if amylic alcohol be colored with a
little iodine, the process of solution may be followed more readily
than would otherwise be possible.

As in the case of solids and gases, we have the same grada-
tion from cases of marked chemical action, accompanied by dis-
play of heat and decrease of bulk, to cases where we seem to be
dealing with a simple mechanical mixture.

Distinction between Solution and Suspension.

There is a great deal of confusion, even among well-educated
people, as to the proper use of the terms *in solution* and *in suspension*, and in the same connection it may be said that a great deal
of confusion exists with reference to the distinction between
clear and *colorless*, terms which are by no means synonymous.
The accurate use of the terms can probably best be made plain
by illustrations. If, to take an example already made use of, we
put some common salt into a quantity of water, after a time the
salt disappears, the ultimate particles being distributed through
the water so that they are no longer distinguishable by the eye,
even aided by the most powerful microscope; the salt cannot be
removed by simple filtration; and, although the solution is somewhat less mobile than water, it is still transparent. This, as we
have seen, is a case of solution. Suppose that, instead of the
salt, we take a quantity of sulphate of copper (blue vitriol). The
phenomena will be similar, but the blue color of the compound
shows itself in the solution. The more concentrated the solution, the more will its transparency be diminished on account
of the depth of color; it is easy, however, by taking a thin layer
of the solution to satisfy one's self of the transparency of the
liquid and of the absence of suspended particles. Such a liquid,
although colored, is clear.

Suppose, now, we take some clay, shake it with water, and
then allow it to settle. The grosser particles will subside to the
bottom of the vessel, but the finer particles will remain in suspension. Very finely divided clay will refuse to settle for weeks,

and sometimes even for months. In such cases the liquid appears somewhat turbid and opaque; and, although the individual particles are too fine to be readily removed by ordinary filters and too small to be distinguished as particles by the eye, still the clay has not dissolved, and the very turbidity or opacity of the liquid shows the presence of solid particles, although they are extremely minute. Such an appearance is not to be described as "being colored," although finely divided clay and other material may be suspended in a liquid which does of itself possess a distinct color. One often meets with the expression, and that, too, in standard works, "the water is discolored by clay," when really it is a question of a colorless water carrying particles of clay in suspension. As we shall see further on, surface waters are often highly colored by vegetable extractive matter in solution, but the water may at the same time be perfectly clear and transparent. On the other hand, pond waters often appear decidedly green; but simple filtration gives a colorless water, and shows the green color to have been due to particles of green (vegetable) matter which were suspended in the liquid.

While for practical purposes there is no difficulty in distinguishing that which is really dissolved from that which is merely held suspended, and in applying the terms as already indicated, it is true that there are substances, generally considered insoluble, which admit of such minute subdivision that the finer particles will remain suspended in water for months, giving in some cases a faint opalescence to the liquid, but in other cases apparently only a color. Thus, by trituration with milk-sugar, metallic gold may be reduced to so fine a condition that it will diffuse through water, giving it a purple color, and it is hard to say that the gold does not exist in solution; after long standing, however, the metal separates out and settles to the bottom of the liquid, and this separation may be hastened by the addition of certain saline solutions.* The action of the saline solution is not fully understood, but it was noticed long ago that these minute particles showed under the microscope the so-called Brownian motion, and that the addition of small quantities of alum, glue, lime, carbonate of ammonia or other salts, caused this molecular motion

---

* Buchmann : Beobachtungen und Untersuchungen zum Nachweis der Löslichkeit von Metallen, etc. Leipzig, 1881, p. 54.

to cease, and the particles to flock together and settle out as minute, amorphous, curdy masses.* The same thing is illustrated on the large scale by the phenomena which take place when a river, like the Mississippi, loaded with silt, meets the waters of the ocean. Dr. Hunt † found that water taken near the mouth of the Mississippi contained about $\frac{1}{2000}$ of suspended matter, mainly clay, which required from ten to fourteen days to subside. He, however, observed that the addition of sea-water or of salt, sulphate of magnesia, alum, or sulphuric acid, rendered the water clear in from twelve to eighteen hours, owing to this same flocculation of the suspended matter.

---

* Naumann : Thermochemie, p. 33.
† Proc. Boston Soc. Nat. Hist., xvi, p. 301.

WATER SUPPLY.

CHAPTER I.

DRINKING WATER AND DISEASE.

WITH reference to their use for town and household supply, we shall roughly divide all natural waters into four classes, as follows:

1. Rain water;
2. Surface water, including streams and lakes;
3. Ground water, including shallow wells;
4. Deep-seated water, including deep wells, artesian wells, and springs.

Under each of these heads we shall study the advantages and disadvantages of the particular class of water, the liability of pollution, etc.; but first we will consider, in a general way, the connection which exists, or is supposed by some to exist, between drinking water and disease.

A water containing a considerable amount of dissolved substances—one which could properly be denominated a mineral water—would not be thought of for a public water supply, and would seldom be used as a regular beverage except for the sake of real or fancied medicinal effect; a small amount, however, of mineral matter is generally considered an advantage. The presence of the substances which ordinarily exist in solution in natural waters must not be regarded as necessary, because experience on ship-board has shown that distilled water, properly aerated, is perfectly wholesome. It appears that distilled water, soft surface water, and moderately hard* spring or well water are all wholesome, and may be drunk without inconvenience by persons accustomed to their use. It is, however, true that a person who

---

* A *hard* water is, generally speaking, one which contains compounds of lime or magnesia in solution. See pages 33 and 181.

2

is in the habit of drinking a soft water generally experiences
some derangement of the digestive organs on beginning to use
hard water, and *vice versa*. It is contended by some that the
human system needs salts of lime, etc., that these compounds are
furnished in an assimilable form in water, and that, consequently,
a somewhat hard water is more advantageous for town supply ;
statistics have been brought together to support this view by
comparing the death rate of various towns with the hardness of
the water supply, but the death rate depends upon too many
factors to be used as the chief argument in this connection. It
is, however, the result of general observation that a hard water
of which the hardness is due to salts of magnesia or to sulphate
of lime is not well suited for drinking, and is injurious to most
persons.

Waters, especially surface waters, containing much vegetable
matter are also, in some cases, unwholesome. The water of
marshes is sometimes the cause of diarrhœa and other diseases
of this character, and is supposed by some to cause malarial and
other fevers (see also page 100). The mere presence of vegetable
organic matter, however, is not sufficient to produce these effects,
because many waters which are quite deeply colored by vegetable
matter are proved by experience to be perfectly wholesome.*

While some waters are thus, in their natural condition,
unwholesome and may be the cause of sickness, the attention of
sanitarians and water experts is directed nowadays principally
to the effect of water which is polluted by the waste materials
from manufactories and dwellings, or by the sewage of towns
and cities ; and it is generally held, especially in England and the
United States, that water thus polluted may be, and frequently
is, the cause of certain specific diseases. Before discussing this
question directly, it is important to have a general idea of the
present prevailing view with reference to the so-called zymotic
diseases, and to understand what is meant by the " germ theory."

Many clear liquids containing organic matter of animal or
vegetable origin—such, for instance, as infusions of hay, infusion
of turnip, urine, etc., etc.,—if exposed to the air gradually become turbid or cloudy, or, perhaps, a film forms on the surface
of the liquid, or a deposit upon the walls of the vessel which con-

* See, however, a remark by Professor Mallet, page 26.

tains it. The cause of the turbidity is shown by the microscope to be the presence of countless minute organized bodies—some rod-like, others globular—which prove to be capable of self-propagation, and which are endowed with motion, at least under certain conditions. Similar organisms are found in the "dust" which floats in the air, and which may be collected by causing a current of air to impinge upon a surface moistened with glycerine ; they occur in rain water, particularly in that which falls in the beginning of a shower, in surface waters and elsewhere. They are found especially where there is decomposing organic matter, and perform an active part in promoting or producing the chemical changes which take place. In certain diseases of men and of the lower animals, organisms which, in their general character, are similar to those thus described have been found in the blood or in the substance of various organs, and their connection with the disease seems to be something more than a coincidence ; there seems, indeed, to be a causal connection.

The micro-organisms with which we are now concerned are referred to the vegetable kingdom ; they are regarded as related both to the *fungi* and to the *algæ*, and are designated scientifically as *schizomycetes* (Spaltpilze, Nägeli) ;* their study requires the highest powers of the microscope and the greatest skill in observation. The development of certain forms has been carefully studied, and it is known that they multiply not only by fission—as Nägeli's classification implies—but also by the formation of spores or permanent "germs." The "germ theory" of disease is that many diseases are due to the presence and propagation in the system of these minute organisms, which are popularly spoken of under the general name *bacteria*, under which term are included also organisms which, as far as known, are harmless. Some of the diseases which have, with more or less show of reason, been supposed to have their cause in such organisms are malarial (intermittent) fever, relapsing fever, typhus and typhoid, cholera, yellow fever, diphtheria, and tuberculosis.

---

* Nägeli : Die niederen Pilze in ihren Beziehungen zu den Infectionskrankheiten, Munich, 1877. Nägeli distinguishes three natural groups among the lower fungi : (1) the *mucorini*, Schimmelpilze, mould fungi ; (2) the *saccharomycetes*, Sprosspilze, budding fungi ; (3) the *schizomycetes*, Spaltpilze, fission fungi. The second class includes the organisms which produce the fermentation of wine and beer ; the third class includes the fungi of putrefaction, the so-called *bacteria*. The terms *microbes*, *microzymes*, as well as several others, are also used to include all these micro-organisms.

With reference to specific distinctions among the organisms themselves observers are not agreed. Some would very much restrict the number of true species, and refer the differences in appearance and action to differences in the attendant conditions ; others believe that there are many species, as distinct as those observed in higher organisms, and that each disease has its own

bacterium ; they believe that the observed differences are essential, and the inability to recognize, in all cases, satisfactory specific characters is due to the imperfection of the means of observation. For pur-

FIG. 3. a. *Microccccus prodigiosus ; b.* the same in the zoogloea stage ; *c. M. Urea.* 650 : 1.

poses of study, at any rate, the various observed forms may be classified in genera and species. Referring to a few terms of

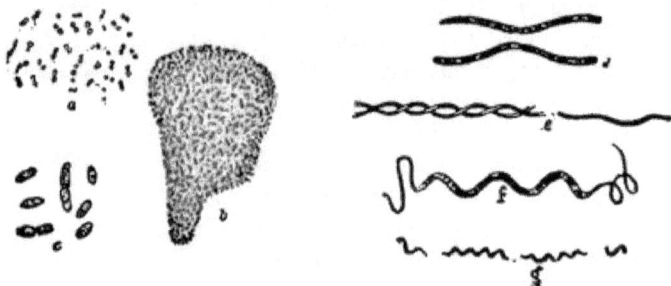

FIG 4. a. *Bacterium termo ; b.* Same in the zoogloea stage ; *c. Bacterium lineola ; d. Vibrio rugula ; e. V. serpens ; f. Spirillum volutans ; g. Sp. tenue.* 650 : 1.

somewhat common occurrence, the *micrococci* are globular or oval, the *bacilli* are rod-like, the *vibriones* (vibrios) are sinuous, and the *spirilla* are spiral. No attempt to represent these minute organisms by cuts can be very successful. Figures 3 and 4 may serve to give a rough idea of the general appearance of some of them.

The connection of the bacteria with disease has been most satisfactorily made out in the case of splenic fever (anthrax, charbon (Fr.), Milzbrand (Germ.), malignant pustule). In this disease the blood and various organs, especially the spleen, contain an organism known as *Bacillus anthracis*. Koch* cultivated

---

* Cohn's Beitrage zur Biologie der Pflanzen, ii. p. 277.

the organisms in appropriate fluids outside of the animal body, and observed the development and the formation of spores, and from these spores he reproduced the specific disease in living animals. He found that the organisms themselves, as observed in the blood, usually died in a few days, but that the spores retained their vitality for at least four years. The *Bacillus anthracis* in appearance is scarcely to be distinguished from the *Bacillus subtilis*, a harmless form which occurs in infusions of hay, and Dr. Buchner[*] has been able, as he claims, by a series of cultivations to transform one form into the other, and from the harmless *Bacillus subtilis* to obtain the *Bacillus anthracis*, and to prove its identity by producing the well-marked disease in animals. Naturally enough Buchner's conclusions are disputed, and, until his results are generally accepted by competent specialists, they cannot be looked upon by the world in general as showing more than a possibility.

Admitting the necessary presence of these minute organisms in the bodies of persons sick with certain diseases, organisms which, at least in certain stages of their development, can exist outside the human body and retain their vitality for a long time, the question arises how they can find their way into the systems of healthy persons to produce disease. The two most obvious of the possible carriers of disease are the air we breathe and the water we drink. We have no difficulty in supposing that emanations from sick persons, particulate or otherwise, may find their way into the air ; moreover, the dejections of the sick and the water in which their clothes or their persons have been washed may often reach wells or other sources of drinking water. Of these two media the former, *i. e.* the air, is *a priori* the most probable, partly because we take very much more air into our lungs than we take water into our stomachs, and also because the lungs afford a better chance for the organisms to enter the blood ; indeed, some maintain that any organisms entering the stomach are rendered harmless by the fluids therein, and that the drinking water is not to be considered at all as a means of conveying the germs of disease.

Of the diseases which are supposed to be caused by these micro-organisms—to be propagated by germs—those which have

---

been, with the greatest unanimity, ascribed to the use of impure drinking water are typhoid fever and cholera. With reference even to these diseases, however, there has been much discussion and controversy between the adherents and the opponents of the "drinking-water theory" since 1848, when Snow, Budd, and others in England ascribed the spread of the cholera then prevalent to the drinking of water fouled by the dejections of cholera patients. It would be unprofitable, in brief space, to attempt to review the numerous cases on record where the coincidences between impure water and cholera (and other diseases) have been so marked as to lead able and careful investigators to believe in the existence of cause and effect. The most able opponent of the theory is Professor Pettenkofer, of Munich, who holds that in these cases there is coincidence only, and that other circumstances, and notably the character of the ground and the condition of ground water, have been overlooked in the investigations. He and his sympathizers also bring forward many instances where the connection between a particular outbreak of a specific disease and the drinking water previously used by those attacked is not only not obvious, but absolutely out of the question.

Even the most earnest advocates of the drinking-water theory must admit that the theory is by no means *proved*, in the sense in which a mathematical proposition may be proved, and it certainly cannot be asserted that the drinking water is the only means by which the zymotic diseases may be propagated ; the coincidences, however, if coincidences they be, are most remarkable, and every year adds to their number. To choose a single example from the multitude which are accessible, we may take the case of an outbreak of typhoid fever in North Boston, Erie Co., N. Y., which occurred in the year 1843, consequently before the connection between typhoid and drinking water had become a theory. The community consisted of nine families (forty-three persons), and typhoid fever had never been known in the vicinity until in the year named a sick traveler took lodging at the tavern, and twenty-eight days thereafter died of what was pronounced by the physicians to be typhoid fever. The disease spread, twenty-eight persons in all were attacked, and only three families escaped. These three families were the only ones which did not use the well of the tavern, two of them on account of distance, and one on account of a feud between them and the inn-keeper. The latter family lived within four rods of the tavern. The physicians, at that time, ascribed the communication of the disease to a "contagium contained in the emanations from the body," but the people charged the family referred to *with poisoning the well*, so marked was the coincidence. Subsequently, Dr. Flint, in reviewing the case, regards it as "vastly probable, if not certain," that the disease was communicated by the drinking water, the source of which was so situated that it must, in all probability, have been contaminated by the dejections of the first patient.*

Many other instances might be cited where a number of families or persons using the same well or other source of water supply have become victims to the disease, which does not, at the time, appear elsewhere; there are many instances where the closing of the suspected source of supply has at once put a stop to the further spread of the disease; there are also instances where people have assembled in numbers on account of some celebration, and sickness has followed in the case of a large proportion of those who have used a certain water, while the others have not been affected; latterly there have been cases where sickness has broken out among families obtaining their milk from the same source, and investigation has shown that impure water was used in the dairy. The most weighty criticism urged against the acceptance of the theory which, in such cases as those mentioned, regards the water as the cause of disease, is that, in the investigations made, sufficient attention has not been paid to other features of the circumstances and surroundings which might, with equal likelihood, be factors in the production of disease. No doubt, in some instances this criticism is just; but if we rule out all cases where the observations are manifestly imperfect there still remain instances enough to make the connection between the water drank and the disease contracted extremely probable. As this is a matter which, in the present state of science, cannot be absolutely proved or disproved, the duty of those who have to advise or to decide in matters relating to water supply is perfectly clear; it is to err on the side of safety, to admit the hypothesis that specific diseases *may* be conveyed

---

* Austin Flint, M.D.   Reports and Papers Am. Public Health Assoc., i, pp. 164–172.

by the drinking water, and to guard all sources of domestic and
public supply from the possibility of contamination by the dejections of persons sick with zymotic diseases and by excremental
matter generally.

What has hitherto been said has had reference to the pollution of water by excremental matter from persons actually sick
with communicable diseases. Any pollution, however, by excremental matter should be guarded against, partly because at
some time the discharges of sick persons may accompany the
other excremental matter, and partly because there is evidence
that under certain circumstances the discharges of healthy persons and animal matter generally may give rise to disease. Under
what circumstances excremental matter becomes dangerous we
do not know. It is certain that it is often taken into the stomachs of men and animals, apparently without doing any harm.
Fish often gather about the mouths of sewers and seem to thrive ;
the Norwegians save up in summer the dung of the horses and
sheep to serve as food for the cattle in winter ; and in many
localities where wood is scarce, dried animal excrement is used
for fuel and in direct contact with the food to be cooked. Dr.
Emmerich, who does not believe in the " drinking-water theory,"
himself drank dilute sewage for a number of days in succession,
and persuaded several of his patients to do likewise, with no ill
effect : * moreover, the experience of every water-analyst shows
that there are many grossly polluted wells which have never been
known to produce disease. It is thus difficult to believe that in
ordinary excremental matter there is any specific poison ; but as
there seems to be abundance of circumstantial evidence to show
that disease does, at times, follow the use of water which has
received excremental pollution, we are forced to believe either
that the organic matter undergoes change, and in certain stages
of decomposition can produce sickness, or that it is accompanied
by something, not yet isolated, which is the real morbific principle, or, indeed, that its effect is to predispose to disease, which
fails to attack others not thus predisposed.

Next in importance to excremental matters is the refuse from
slaughter-houses, wool-pulling establishments, tanneries, etc.,—
animal refuse, in fact, from various sources. Here we are met

---

* Zeitschrift fur Biologie, xiv (1878), p. 591.

by the objection that much animal matter is consumed in a more or less decayed condition with apparent harmlessness, as for instance, ripe game or ripe cheese: but, to offset this, there are numerous cases on record where sickness has arisen from spoiled meat, especially in the form of sausages and potted meats. But, after all, as stated above, the evidence which connects disease with polluted water is purely circumstantial, and the amount of organic matter, even in waters classed as dangerous, is so small, that, as pointed out by Professor Mallet,* it furnishes "important evidence against any chemical theory of the production of disease from this source, any theory based on the simple assumption that some of the chemical products of the decomposition of organic matter are poisonous or noxious in their effect upon the human system." Instancing two particular waters, he says : " If *the whole* of the organic carbon and nitrogen found in such waters as Nos. 35 and 36, of the highly dangerous character of which there can scarcely be a doubt, existed as strychnine, it would be necessary to drink about a half a gallon of the water at once in order to swallow an average *medicinal* dose of the alkaloid. It is not easy to believe that the ptomaines, or any other chemical products of the putrefactive change as yet observed, can possess an intensity of toxic power so very much greater than that of the most energetic of recognized poisons. While numerous facts go to support the belief that, not to the effect of any chemical substances (such effect necessarily standing in definite relation to their quantity), but to the presence of living organisms, with their power of practically unlimited self-multiplication, we must in all probability look for an explanation of most, at any rate, of the mischief attributable to drinking water, it is of course possible that indirectly a large amount of organic matter in water may be more dangerous than a smaller quantity, as furnishing on a greater scale the suitable material and conditions for the development of noxious as well as harmless organisms."

Although there are many substances of vegetable origin which are violent poisons, such as the vegetable alkaloids, for example, it is generally held that refuse of vegetable origin is of much less importance as a source of pollution than that coming from animal sources. This is probably true, in general, but it is well known

---

* National Board of Health Bulletin, May 27, 1882.

that the vegetable refuse from certain manufacturing operations may be very offensive: such, for instance, is the refuse from starch factories, the water in which flax has been retted, etc. That such water would be unfit to drink, unless enormously diluted, one can hardly doubt. To quote again from Professor Mallet:

"If the theory be accepted, which has so much in its favor, attributing the production of disease by organic matter in drinking water not to any specifically poisonous *substance* or substances, but to the presence and action of living organisms, it seems quite conceivable that a water containing organic matter of any kind, including vegetable matter, may be harmless at one time, and harmful at another, when perhaps a different stage of fermentation or putrefactive change may have been entered upon, and special organisms may have made their appearance or entered upon a new phase of existence. Thus, there might possibly be safety in drinking a peaty water, or water filtered through beds of dead forest leaves, when fresh; danger when, after a certain amount of atmospheric exposure, bacterial organisms had become developed; and safety again, perhaps, after the growth of such organisms had fallen off, and more or less of the available organic matter had been consumed."

However views may differ as to the possible injury from this or that particular form of contamination, we are safe in accepting the two following principles as fundamental guides in the selection of a water for water supply:

1. A water suitable for domestic supply must be free from all substances which are *known* to produce an injurious effect on the human system, or which are suspected with good reason, or on good authority, to produce such an effect.

2. The water should be, as far as practicable, free from all substances and from all associations which offend the general æsthetic sense of the community, and thus affect the system through the imagination, even if there is good reason to suppose that it is in itself perfectly harmless.

The first of these principles needs no argument to justify it; with reference to the second, a word or two may be said. Dr. Emmerich, even, admits that not every one could drink dilute sewage as he did, because the mere idea of so doing, or the sight of a floating hair or other unattractive object, would no doubt with many persons produce disgust and nausea, and, if the water were forced down, it would most likely be thrown up again. While there is no doubt of this power of the imagination and its effect on the physical system, common sense must fix a limit to the application of this second principle, and some latitude must be allowed according to the circumstances of the particular case. Thus, if a lake is chosen as the most available source of supply, the fact that some persons bathe in its waters can hardly condemn it for use; and the fact that a limited amount of town drainage finds its way into a stream does not necessarily prevent its being used at some portion of its course, although a stream once seriously polluted should not be looked upon as an available source of supply. Again, most persons naturally object to water as muddy as that of many of our Western streams, in spite of the favorable testimony of those in the habit of using it, but by a short residence in St. Louis, for instance, most persons soon become accustomed to the turbidity. The turbidity is a real objection to the water, but, in the case of a water like that of the Missouri, a town would not be justified in postponing the introduction of the water because it was not able at the same time to adopt a scheme for its thorough filtration. In the same way, if the only objection to a river or pond water is a yellow or brownish-yellow color derived from vegetable, especially peaty matter, the water need not be condemned, although most persons would prefer a colorless water.

Undoubtedly, the best water for drinking is a moderately soft spring water, in which all possibility of contamination is out of the question. Unfortunately, however, it is comparatively seldom that such water is available in quantities sufficient for the supply of large towns. Many spring waters are so hard that, while not unsuited for drinking, they are unsuited for many manufacturing uses, for use in steam boilers, for washing and culinary purposes. It is a mistake to claim that the water which is absolutely best for drinking must be chosen, at any expense, as a town supply; when a soft surface water, free from appreciable pollution can be obtained, it entails a very serious and constant expense to reject it in favor of a hard water, which may, to be sure, be clearer to the eye and somewhat more pleasant to the taste. There are surface waters and there are surface-water supplies which are undoubtedly bad, but a good surface water, such as may be taken

directly from many streams or such as may be obtained from deep
lakes and from proper storage basins, is perfectly well suited for
domestic use or for town supply. There are some who maintain
an opinion contrary to that which has been expressed. The
Vienna Commission in 1864, rejected surface waters from among
the waters suitable for domestic use, on the ground of their variable temperature (see page 91) and their liability to pollution.
The German Public Health Association, at the Danzig meeting
in 1880, by a small majority and after a lively discussion, adopted
a resolution to the effect that spring water or properly protected
ground water were the only admissible sources of supply; but two
years later this dictum was modified so as to include filtered river
water as fulfilling the required conditions, and this conclusion is
sanctioned by practice and experience.

CHAPTER II.

IT is not the purpose of the present chapter to give in detail all the various methods employed in the analysis of water, or to serve as a guide to those wishing to make such analyses. Excellent manuals on this subject already exist. An attempt will be made, however, to explain what is the meaning of the various terms used in the reports of water analysis, and to indicate the significance to be attached to the figures given.

For this discussion we may classify the substances occurring in a natural water according to the following scheme:

1. Suspended matter......{ Inorganic.
{ Organic.... { Animal.
{ Vegetable.

2. Dissolved matter.......{ Gaseous.
{ Solid....... { Inorganic.
{ Organic.... { Animal.
{ Vegetable.

Suspended matter.—The determination of the amount of suspended matter is principally of value with reference to possible schemes of sedimentation or filtration. The operation is commonly conducted by passing a measured quantity of water through a paper filter which has previously been dried at 100° C. and then weighed; after the passage of the water, the filter with its contents is again dried at 100° and weighed for the second time. The difference between the two weights is the weight of the suspended matter. The filter with its contents is then transferred to a platinum crucible, and the crucible is heated until the filter has been burned up and the organic matter destroyed. The weight of what remains, minus the weight of the ash which a filter, such as was used, is known to leave, is the weight of the inorganic or mineral portion of the suspended matter. Another method, which is exact enough for most purposes, consists in evaporating a measured quantity of the water in its natural condition, and an equal quantity which has been filtered through paper. The residues in the two cases are weighed and the difference is approximately the weight of the matter which was in suspension.

It is quite as important to know the character of the suspended matter as to know its absolute amount. It is desirable to know whether it settles readily, and, if it contains much organic matter, whether this is mainly of animal or of vegetable origin. Some information as to the latter point may be obtained by observing the appearance and odor when it is strongly heated, but microscopical examination is of the greatest service in this connection.

In expressing in figures the results of the analysis, a considerable difference exists in the practice of different chemists as to the unit to be employed. The methods of expression in most common use are the following:

(1) In grains to the English (imperial) gallon, which measures 277 cubic inches and is equivalent to 10 lbs., or 70,000 grains, of pure water. This method is still quite common in England.

(2) In grains to the U. S. gallon, which measures 231 cubic inches and is equivalent to 58,372 + grains of pure water. This method is very common in the United States.

(3) On a decimal basis, as so many parts (by weight) in 1,000, 10,000, 100,000, or 1,000,000 parts of the water according to the amount of dissolved matter present. Thus, mineral waters are usually reported as containing so many parts in 1,000 or in 10,000 parts, while for potable waters parts in 100,000 or 1,000,000 are employed. The preference of the author is decidedly for " parts in 100,000," which is now generally used in France and Germany; also in the Reports of the Rivers Pollution Commission of Great Britain, and, in this country, in the reports of the National and of many State Boards of Health.

(4) As so many milligrams to the liter. This would be equivalent to so many parts in 1,000,000 if the water possessed the same density as pure water; that is, if a liter of the water actually weighed 1,000 grams. Practically, the error introduced by measuring instead of weighing the water taken for analysis, is, in the case of most potable waters, less than the error of analysis, thus:

If the specific gravity is	So many milligrams to the liter	Equal so many parts in 1,000,000.	Diff.
1.010	5.000	4.950	0.050
1.010	10.000	9.901	0.099
1.020	5.000	4.902	0.098
1.020*	10.000	9.804	0.196
1.040	5.000	4.808	0.192
1.040	10.000	9.615	0.385

* The specific gravity of sea water is about 1.029.

In the case of mineral waters, sea-water, etc., the difference is too great to be neglected; and, in such cases, it should always be distinctly stated whether the results are in milligrams to the liter, or in parts in 1,000,000 by weight.

Dissolved substances.—Gases.—Almost all gases dissolve in water to a greater or less extent. It is seldom, however, that a water which is proposed or used as a source of supply contains appreciable quantities of any gases other than those of the atmosphere—oxygen, nitrogen, and carbonic acid. These gases are present in very varying proportions. Oxygen is found in all waters which have been exposed to the air. The waters of artesian wells often contain none of this gas, but they absorb it at once on reaching the air; waters from highly polluted sources are also deficient in oxygen. Nitrogen occurs to a greater or less extent in all waters, and in some mineral or effervescent waters it forms the largest part of the dissolved gases. Carbonic acid is present in all potable waters; its presence is of important influence in determining the amount of carbonate of lime which a given water can contain, and the solvent effect of water on many minerals is due to the presence of carbonic acid.

It was formerly the general custom to make a complete quantitative analysis of the various gases present in a sample of water under examination. The analysis was made by boiling out the gases from a measured quantity of water and submitting the mixture obtained to the accurate but tedious methods of gas analysis. When, however, as often happened, the determinations were not made on the spot, but, on the contrary, on samples of water which had been standing for days or for weeks, they were nearly worthless, and are now rarely made except in the case of mineral waters. In fact, at the present time, it is seldom that the amount of any dissolved gas is determined, except oxygen; and for determining the amount of oxygen in a given water, a process was devised a few years ago by Schützenberger which admits of being performed with sufficient accuracy out of doors. A water which is polluted by decaying organic matter not only calls upon the air about it to furnish oxygen for the combustion of the decaying matter, but uses up in the process more or less, sometimes all, of the oxygen previously dissolved in the water. The amount of dissolved oxygen is thus considered by some to be an indication, in the inverse direction of course, of the

amount of impurity present. An example of the application of
this method may be found on page 61. The results thus obtained are of value, as in this case, in tracing the course of the
same polluted stream, but a knowledge of the absolute amount
of dissolved oxygen gives no means of judging of the purity of a
single sample of water; for, not only is the water of some artesian wells free from oxygen, as stated above, but the ground
water generally and the water of unpolluted springs and deep
wells is also deficient in oxygen.

In the case of all the gases, the amount present is indicated
as so many cubic inches to the gallon, or as so many cubic centimeters to the liter.

Total solids in solution.—The determination of the total
amount of dissolved matter is made by evaporating a measured
quantity of water to dryness in a weighed platinum dish, drying
at some definite temperature, and then weighing the dish with its
contents. The determination is, at the best, a rough one, and
the solid matter obtained by evaporation does not exactly represent what was originally in solution. In the evaporation some
substances pass off with the steam and are lost. Other substances are changed in character by the treatment. If the residue be
dried at the temperature of boiling water, which is that most commonly employed, some of the salts retain water of crystallization; at a somewhat higher temperature, even as low as 140° C.,
the organic substances begin to be decomposed and lose weight.
In spite of this, some chemists use a temperature as high as 180° C.
It is generally of no importance for sanitary purposes that the determination should be exact, for it is of no consequence whether
a water leaves 4 or 6 parts of "total solid residue," whether it
leaves 10 or 12 parts, but in the case of periodical examinations
of the same water the determinations should be made in the same
way at all times, in order that they may be compared with each
other.

It is seldom necessary for sanitary purposes to make a complete analysis of the water and to determine the amount of each
of the various compounds which make up the "total solids." A
few of the mineral constituents are almost always determined for
special reasons, and, in individual cases, others may be estimated,
but, as a rule, the indications of qualitative tests suffice. In a
water which has passed through metal pipes, or which receives

the flow from mines, or from manufacturing operations, poisonous metals should be looked for; lead and copper are the most
common, and less than one-tenth of a grain of lead to the gallon
has been known to do harm; arsenic is frequently found in running streams and sometimes in water which contains, or rather
which deposits, oxide of iron, but the amount is usually too small
to notice; arsenic has, however, been the cause of well-pollution
in the neighborhood of manufactories of aniline colors.

Chlorine.—Chlorine is almost always determined quantitatively.
It will be understood that this element never occurs free in natural waters, but always in combination as chloride of sodium or as
some other chloride. The amount is generally reported as so much
chlorine, although some analysts prefer to calculate the corresponding amount of chloride of sodium (common salt), and report
in this way. Although chlorides are present in all soils and natural waters, the quantity in the uncontaminated water of most
regions is very small. Where this is known to be the case, the
presence of any noticeable amount of chlorine (say much more
than 1 part in 100,000) indicates contamination from human
sources, as chloride of sodium is a constant constituent of sewage
and of animal refuse in general, and is not eliminated to any considerable extent either in passing through the soil or by the action
of vegetation. Chlorides remain as evidences of past contamination after all other evidences have ceased to exist, although
the amount present does not bear any constant proportion to the
amount of polluting substances which are or have been in the
water.

Hardness.—A determination of the " hardness " usually finds
a place in the examination of a water proposed as a source of
supply. The determination is made by taking advantage of one
of the properties which make hard water undesirable—namely, the
property of destroying soap. A solution of soap is prepared of
such a strength that a measured quantity of it is exactly destroyed
or neutralized by a known amount of some compound of lime.
The lime compound is previously dissolved in a certain amount,
say 100 cubic centimeters, of water, and the test is made by ascertaining how much of this same standard soap solution is destroyed
by 100 c.c. of this particular water. The hardness of another
portion of the water is determined after boiling for some time;
this is called "*permanent hardness,*" and is due to sulphates

3

and other soluble compounds of lime and magnesia. The total
hardness, less the permanent hardness, is the "*temporary hardness*,"
and is due to the bicarbonates of lime and magnesia, which are
decomposed by boiling. The hardness is generally expressed in
degrees, which have different significations in different countries.
In England, where the process originated, a degree of hardness
corresponds to a grain of carbonate of lime in one imperial gallon
of water; for example, a water of 5 degrees hardness means a
water, each gallon of which contains compounds of lime or magnesia or both equivalent in soap-destroying power to 5 grains of
carbonate of lime. In Germany the degrees of hardness indicate
the equivalent of so many parts of oxide of calcium (quicklime)
in 100,000 parts of water. In France the degrees mean so many
parts of carbonate of lime in 100,000 parts of water. In America,
in spite of the anomaly, many express the hardness in English
degrees, *i. e.*, in grains to the imperial gallon, while the other results are given in grains to the United States gallon. The
French system of parts in 100,000 is, however, to be preferred.

Combined nitrogen.—Nitrogen exists in potable waters under
a variety of forms of combination. Animal matter generally contains nitrogen, as do also many substances of vegetable origin:
this is usually spoken of as "organic nitrogen." Nitrogen also
exists in the form of ammonia and ammoniacal salts, and these
compounds are due almost entirely to the decomposition of nitrogenous vegetable and more especially animal matters. For this
reason, although in itself harmless, the ammonia is determined
quantitatively. The amount present, even in a polluted water, is
small, and when expressed in figures—as in the various tables on
following pages—seems insignificant, nevertheless, as a sign of organic pollution, its determination should not be omitted. Although
the amount of ammonia is so small—a water containing 0.1 part
by weight in 100,000 parts of the water being grossly polluted—
the figures are entitled to confidence because the method usually
employed is very delicate, and, by a process of distillation, the
ammonia in a large volume of water may be concentrated into a
small bulk. The "Nessler test," which is employed in estimating
ammonia, is capable of detecting 1 part by weight of ammonia in
20,000,000 parts of water.

A great diversity of opinion exists as to the value which attaches to a determination of the exact amount of nitrogen pres-

ent as nitrites and nitrates. The compounds themselves, in small amounts, are no doubt harmless, but it is also true that they result from the oxidation of nitrogenous organic matter. The nitrifying process is now believed to take place under the influence of minute organisms, and the process goes on in the various soils at very different rates according to the alkalinity of the soil, to the amount of moisture and to other conditions. Moreover, the nitrates once formed may again be reduced to ammoniacal compounds, or even to free nitrogen, so that the nitrates cannot be a quantitative indication of the amount of pollution.

In spite of this, Frankland lays great stress on the exact determination of nitrogen in this form, and has introduced into water reports the term "previous sewage contamination." The figures given, in any case, under this head are reached by determining the total amount of nitrogen which is present as ammonia, and also as nitrites and nitrates; after subtracting the small amount of nitrogen which rain water contains in these forms, there is calculated from the remainder how much of what is called "average London sewage" would be necessary to account for this amount of nitrogen. The composition of the so-called "average London sewage" is not, as might be supposed, deduced from a considerable number of examinations made at various times, but the average sewage is taken arbitrarily as containing 10 parts of combined nitrogen in 100,000 parts.

Mallet (in a report already cited) is "inclined to attach special and very great importance to a careful determination of the nitrites and nitrates in water to be used for drinking."

It is true that in consecutive examinations of the same water it is satisfactory to know exactly the amount of nitrates and the variation from time to time; but, in case of a single examination, it is generally sufficient to know whether there is much or little, or none. The test most commonly applied, although not the most delicate, is the sulphate of iron (ferrous sulphate) test. A small quantity of the water under examination is mixed in a glass tube with an equal volume of pure concentrated sulphuric acid. The mixture, which becomes very hot, is cooled to the temperature of the air, and there is then poured upon it a solution of sulphate of iron. If nitrates are present, a dark ring or layer forms between the two liquids. The amount of nitrates present may be inferred from the extent to which the water must be concentrated before it will give indications by this test, but the indications are strictly comparable only when the test is performed in precisely the same way and by the same person.

It should be understood that the argument drawn from the presence of nitrates is this: The nitrates indicate the previous existence of nitrogenous organic matter, which has been oxidized and converted into harmless compounds by natural agencies. If these same agencies could be relied on indefinitely it would be well, but no one can tell at what moment—owing to increase in the amount of the polluting substances, or to their gradual accumulation in the soil, or to other changed conditions—the natural agencies may prove inadequate to the task and allow incompletely oxidized and harmful substances to reach the source of supply.

Organic matter.—Of the polluting material which reaches water which may be used for drinking, the organic portion is felt to be that which directly or indirectly introduces the element of danger. Just how and from what particular substances the danger arises is unknown, and it is extremely doubtful whether the dangerous something will ever be an object of chemical determination, but in our present ignorance it is generally felt that it is desirable to obtain such indications as are possible of the amount and character of the organic matter present.

To a person unfamiliar with chemistry, it might seem to be no difficult task to determine exactly how much matter of animal and how much matter of vegetable origin is present in a given water. The truth is, however, that it is not only difficult but impossible, either to determine the total amount of organic matter or to decide upon its origin. As far as the total amount is concerned, the fact that it cannot be determined is a matter of no great consequence. Even if the chemist could say with certainty that a particular water contained exactly 1 or 2 or 5 parts of organic matter in 100,000, we should be far from having the data necessary to form an opinion as to the wholesomeness of the water, for it is evident to any one that a pound of sugar or of glycerine would have a very different importance from that of a pound of (dry) fæces, yet either is a pound of organic matter.

Formerly it was the general custom to subject the residue of evaporation ("total dissolved solids") to the action of a low red heat until all the carbonaceous matter was destroyed and to determine the loss of weight. Thus was obtained what is now generally tabulated as "loss on ignition," or "organic and volatile matter;" but the loss of weight is far from being entirely due to the destruction of organic matter. According to the degree of heat applied and the length of time during which it is continued, there is more or less loss due to the volatilization of alkaline chlorides. There is also loss from the decomposition and partial volatilization of several compounds; thus, the carbonates of lime and magnesia are more or less completely converted into oxides by expulsion of the carbonic acid, or in the presence of a sufficient quantity of silicic acid, into silicates. The nitrates are converted into carbonates, oxides, or silicates, chloride of magnesium is decomposed in the presence of hydrated compounds with escape of chlorhydric acid, and other changes take place which it is not necessary to particularize.

For these reasons, no two persons are likely to obtain the same result from the same water, and not much value is attached nowadays to the determination; it is sometimes of assistance in forming the final opinion in case of a doubtful water, but the way in which the residue acts when heated gives more information than a knowledge of the loss of weight.

Of the more modern methods in somewhat general use for reaching information about the organic matter in water, there are three which may be mentioned here, and which will be spoken of as the "permanganate" method, the "ammonia" process, and "Frankland's" method.* All of the processes possess a certain value, and all are widely open to criticism.

Permanganate of potash is a highly colored crystalline salt soluble in water, to which, even if the solution be very dilute, it communicates a marked pink color. This compound, which contains a considerable proportion of oxygen, possesses the property of oxidizing, with more or less readiness, most forms of organic matter, being itself destroyed in the process and losing the characteristic color. By successive additions of a perman-

* These various processes will be discussed only briefly in this place. They have recently been thoroughly investigated by Professor J. W. Mallet, under direction of the National Board of Health. The full report has not yet appeared, but a preliminary report was published as a Supplement (No. 19) to the National Board of Health Bulletin, May 27, 1882.

ganate solution of known strength until the color persists, it
is possible to determine how much permanganate is destroyed
by a known volume of a given water.   There are various ways
of applying the permanganate solution.   Some prefer to use the
reagent in alkaline, and others in acid solutions; some heat the
liquid to one temperature and some to another.*   The results
obtained are reported by stating how many parts, by weight, of
the crystallized permanganate are required for 100,000 parts by
weight of water; or how many parts, by weight, of oxygen (from
the permanganate) are used up in the process.   Some, indeed,
assume an arbitrary number, by which they multiply the amount
of permanganate employed, and call the result organic matter.
Where the expression "organic matter" occurs in German reports, the figures are probably obtained by multiplying the
amount of oxygen used up by 20,† but in American reports the
expression is quite likely to mean simply the "loss on ignition."
The results of the permanganate method cannot have an absolute
value, because different organic substances vary in the complete-
ness with which they are oxidized under the same conditions;
and, even if they were all completely oxidized under certain
attainable conditions, it would still be true that one gram of one
kind of organic matter would require a very different amount of
oxygen from that which would be required by one gram of some
other kind of organic matter.   Moreover, with the same water,
the results differ very much according to the method of employing the test, so that to be able to give a useful interpretation to
any particular results, it is necessary to know what method was
followed by the analyst.

The so-called ammonia method of water analysis was devised
by the English chemists Chapman, Wanklyn and Smith,‡ and
has been much used in England and in this country.   In this

* See Kubel's Anleitung zur Untersuchung von Wasser, bearbeitet von Dr. Ferd.
Tiemann, Braunschweig, 1874.   Also a paper by Dr. Tidy, Chemical News, xxxvii
(1878), p. 283.

† Or by multiplying the amount of permanganate consumed by 5.   This is according to Dr. Woods, but Dr. Letheby prefers to multiply the amount of permanganate
by 8.   Whatever number be used, it frequently happens that the "organic matter,"
as thus estimated, exceeds the weight of the "total dissolved solids."

‡ Water Analysis.   By J. A. Wanklyn and E. T. Chapman.   5th edition,
rewritten by J. A. Wanklyn, London, 1879.

method, advantage is taken of the fact that certain kinds of nitrogenous organic matter, when treated with a strongly alkaline solution of permanganate of potash, give off a definite portion or the whole of their nitrogen as ammonia; and the value of the method lies in the assumption that it is the nitrogenized organic matter which is to be regarded as the chief source of danger in polluted water. In working the ammonia method, the water under examination is put into a retort, made alkaline by means of carbonate of soda, and distilled as long as the water which condenses contains enough ammonia to be measured by Nessler's solution. Then a solution of caustic soda and permanganate of potash is added, and distillation is continued. Another portion of ammonia now comes off, owing to the action of the permanganate on the nitrogenous organic matter. The amount of ammonia thus obtained is determined, and is tabulated as "albuminoid ammonia," because albumin is one of the bodies which acts in this way.

It will thus be understood that the so-called "albuminoid ammonia" is not something which exists in the water ready formed ; moreover, because different amounts are obtained from the same weight of different nitrogenous substances, as well as on account of the fact already alluded to, that the oxidation of different substances by the permanganate of potash is more or less incomplete, the figures obtained have a relative rather than an absolute significance.

Although this method does not accomplish all that might be desired, the results, properly interpreted, are of great value, and the method has been of immense service in the cause of public health.

The third method, known as the "combustion" process, or Frankland's method, was devised by Frankland and Armstrong. and used by the Rivers Pollution Commission of Great Britain in the examination of the very large number of waters, the analyses of which appear in the various reports of the Commission. This method is by far the most elaborate of any that have been proposed : it consists in evaporating a given quantity of the water, under carefully regulated conditions, and in submitting the residue to a process of organic analysis, by which all the carbon is converted into carbonic acid and the nitrogen is liberated in the gaseous state. The mixture of nitrogen and carbonic

acid is then analyzed by processes of gas analysis. The results
are stated in so many parts of "organic carbon" and so much
" organic nitrogen," in 100,000 parts of the water, and sometimes
the sum of the two is spoken of as the amount of the " organic
elements." The character of the organic matter is inferred from
the relative proportion of carbon and nitrogen.

The process, as Frankland himself says, is " both troublesome
and tedious." The apparatus employed is frangible and somewhat costly, and the manipulative skill of a trained chemist is
required to carry out the work. It is moreover a process that
cannot be taken up off-hand, even by a trained chemist, but one
requiring tolerably constant practice. As Mallet says: " It is
better adapted to regular use in the examination of many
samples of water in a large public laboratory than to occasional
use by a private individual in now and then examining a single
water."

Although the combustion process is the most elaborate, and,
in some respects the most satisfactory that we have, even this,
"in its present form cannot be considered as 'determining' the
carbon and nitrogen of the organic matter in water in a sense to
justify the claim of 'absolute' value for its results which has
been denied to those of all other methods. It is but a method
of approximation, involving sundry errors, and in part a balance
of errors." *

Standards of purity.—Having followed this brief description
of the methods of analysis most frequently employed, a person,
who is not a chemist, may naturally ask for some directions in
order to interpret the figures reported by the analyst. Now, it
is true that it may be possible to fix certain numerical limits
and to reject without hesitation all waters exceeding these
limits ; but there always will be difficulty in deciding how near
to any limit a suspicious water may come and still be used with
a reasonable degree of safety. To condemn a water without
sufficient cause is, of course, undesirable, as the procuring a different supply may involve considerable expense.

Moreover, it cannot be insisted upon too strongly that different classes of water cannot be judged by the same standard, and

---

* For a full discussion of the sources of error, see Mallet's report, already alluded
to ; also, Amer. Chem. Journ., iv (1883).

the results of the analysis of waters belonging to different classes ought not to be put into the same table or otherwise arranged so as to invite comparison. If within the same geological area it is possible to analyze the water from a considerable number of un-polluted wells, a standard may be fixed for the well water of that region, and a surface water may be compared with other surface waters of the same or of a similarly situated region ; or a stream in one part of its course may be compared with its own unpolluted head waters. To fix, however, a definite standard which will apply to all waters and by which any one can judge of a given water from the numerical results of analysis is impracticable. Every doubtful water must be considered by itself with all the light that can be brought to bear upon it.

Bearing in mind what has just been said, we may note the in-terpretation which is given to the results of the several methods in common use for determining "organic matter," or, at least, for obtaining indications as to its amount and character. Wan-klyn's own interpretation of the results of the ammonia process is essentially as follows:

If a water yield no " albuminoid ammonia," it may be passed as organically pure, despite of much free ammonia and chlorides ; a water giving less than 0.005 part of "albuminoid ammonia" in 100,000 parts may be regarded as very pure. A water contain-ing 0.005 part of "albuminoid ammonia" together with a con-siderable quantity of free ammonia is suspicious, but in the absence of free ammonia, the "albuminoid ammonia" may be allowed to amount to something like 0.010 part ; above 0.010 should be regarded as very suspicious, and according to Wanklyn over 0.015 part should condemn the water.

The Rivers Pollution Commission, in interpreting the results of Frankland's process, make the following classification : "Sur-face water or river water which contains in 100,000 parts more than 0.2 part of organic carbon or 0.03 part of organic nitrogen is not desirable for domestic supply, and ought, whenever practi-cable, to be rejected. Spring and deep-well water ought not to contain in 100,000 parts more than 0.1 part of organic carbon or 0.03 part of organic nitrogen."

Dr. Frankland, while " deprecating a hard and fast division of water into classes," suggests a rough classification according to the amount of organic carbon present ; this classification is given in Table III, the figures indicating such a fraction of one part by weight of organic carbon in 100,000 parts by weight of the water.

Dr. Tidy, while admitting the impossibility of deciding of the quality of a water from an incomplete analysis suggests certain limits as a guide to the interpretation of the results obtained by the permanganate process, conducted, be it understood, according to a particular method. These also appear in Table III.

TABLE III.—CLASSIFICATION OF NATURAL WATERS.

Parts in 100,000.

CLASSIFICATION.	ORGANIC CARBON.— DR. FRANKLAND.		OXYGEN REQUIRED TO OXIDIZE ORGANIC MATTER.— DR. TIDY.
	Upland surface water.	Other waters.	
I Water of great organic purity .	0. –0.2	0. –0.1	0. –0 05
II Water of medium purity......	0.2–0.4	0.1–0.2	0.05–0.15
III Water of doubtful purity......	0.4–0.6	0.2–0.4	0.15–0.21
IV Impure water	0.6 +	0.4 +	0.21 +

Some of the limiting amounts which have been suggested by other chemists are given in Table IV :

TABLE IV.—STANDARDS OF PURITY.

Parts in 100,000.

	TOTAL SOLIDS.	ORGANIC MATTER.	NITRIC ACID (N_2O_5).	CHLORINE.	TOTAL HARDNESS.
Reichardt.............	50	2.	0.4	0.2–0.8	18
Kubel and Tiemann	50	5.	0.5–1.5	2–3	18–20
Wibel	50	5.	0.5–2.	3.5	18–20
Fischer...............	50	4.	2.7	3.5	17

Professor Mallet, in the report already alluded to, after recording the results of an examination into the various processes of analysis which have been briefly described, draws certain general conclusions as follows :

" 1. It is not possible to decide absolutely upon the wholesomeness or unwholesomeness of a drinking water by the mere use of any of the processes examined for the estimation of *organic matter*, or its constituents.

" 2. I would even go further, and say that, in judging the sanitary character of a water, not only must such processes be used in connection with the investigation of other evidence of a more general sort, as to the source and history of the water, but should even be deemed of secondary importance in weighing the reasons for accepting or rejecting a water not manifestly unfit for drinking on other grounds.

"3. There are no sound grounds on which to establish such general 'standards of purity' as have been proposed, looking to exact amounts of organic carbon or nitrogen, 'albuminoid ammonia,' oxygen of permanganate consumed, etc., as permissible or not. Distinctions drawn by the application of such standards are arbitrary, and may be misleading.

"4. Two entirely legitimate directions seem to be open for the useful examination by chemical means of the organic constituents of drinking water, namely, first, the detection of *very gross* pollution, such as the contamination of the water of a well by accidental bursting or crushing of soil-pipes, extensive leakage of drains, etc., and secondly, the periodical examination of a water supply, as of a great city, in order that, the normal or usual character of the water having been previously ascertained, any suspicious changes which from time to time may occur shall be promptly detected and their cause investigated.

"5. In connection with this latter application of water analysis, there seems to be no objection to the establishment of *local* 'standards of purity' for drinking water, based on sufficiently thorough examination of the water supply in its usual condition."

These conclusions are given, as they coincide almost exactly with what the author has frequently had occasion to assert, and has for years tried to teach. "In the majority of cases, chemical examination alone cannot be relied upon as giving conclusive evidence as to the suitability of a water for drinking. Of course, if a water is hard, the chemist can say, without hesitation, that the water is unsuited for supply on account of its probable effect on steam boilers, and because it will be uneconomical for use in washing. If the water contains arsenic or lead or other poisonous metal, the chemist can discover it. If the water is grossly polluted, or is of exceptional purity, chemical examination can determine these facts; but, in a vast majority of cases, while chemistry may teach something and aid in the decision, it cannot teach everything, and it cannot *decide*. Now, it would be very convenient, if it were possible, to take each item which is made

the object of analytical determination, and say that a good water
may contain so much, and if a water contains more, it is not
good. This is impossible: a certain amount of the same substance might in one case be a sign of fearful contamination, while
in another it might indicate only a normal constituent of the
water.

"In view of the impossibility of saying exactly what is and
what is not harmful, any considerable departure from the normal
character of the water in a given locality should be regarded with
suspicion. It is true that various students of the matter of water
supply have formulated 'standards' which a water may not
overpass. They are, however, only of relative value." *

It should not be inferred that the chemical analysis is value-
less because it cannot furnish data for absolute decision, but it is
a great mistake to suppose that the proper way to consult a
chemist is to send a sample of water in a sealed vessel with no
hint as to its source. On the contrary, the chemist should know
as much as possible as to the history and source of the water, and
if possible should take the samples himself—that is if he is to express an opinion as to the suitableness of the water for drinking.
Nor is it sufficient that some other competent person should
possess the knowledge of the locality, etc., and endeavor to interpret the figures furnished by the chemist. There are many
things which guide the chemist that he cannot put into numerical results or even on to paper at all. Many observations are
made in the course of an analysis by an experienced person, of
which he is himself hardly conscious, but which aid in making up
the final opinion. Fox† very truly says:

"It is a golden rule in water analysis never to give an opinion
unless the analyst knows (1) the nature of the source of a water—
whether it comes from a spring or well or river or rain reservoir,
etc.; (2) the depth of the well, if it is withdrawn from one; (3)
the geology of the district from which it is derived, together with
the character of the soil and subsoil; (4) the distance from the
source of the water of the nearest filth or drain."

At the present time, chemical examination, in connection
with a thorough knowledge of a proposed source of supply, must

* Buck's Hygiene, Vol. i, p. 303.
† Sanitary Examination of Water, Air and Food. London, 1878.

be the main guide in the selection or rejection of a water; but there is reason to hope that eventually the decision may be thrown largely upon the biologist. Investigations have been made from a biological stand-point in two directions: (1) by an examination of the organisms in the water itself or which develop in it when the water is allowed to stand; (2) by injecting the concentrated water, or a solution of the residue of evaporation, under the skin of rabbits or other animals, and observing the effect on the temperature, etc., of the animals experimented upon.

With reference to the first method, it may be said that a microscopical examination of the suspended and sedimentary matter should always accompany the chemical examination, and there is no difficulty in recognizing grains of starch, fibers of cotton, silk, wool, etc., and many other sorts of animal and vegetable debris if present; of course, substances like those mentioned are evidence of more or less contamination. With regard to living organisms, we do not know as much as we have a right to hope to know about their connection with the wholesomeness of a water. It may be said, in a general way, that bacteria occurring in considerable numbers are a sign of impure water, as are also certain infusoria, such as paramecium, vorticella, monas, etc. The occurrence of leptothrix, crenothrix, etc., are also suspicious signs, but the diatoms and the green algæ, as a rule, do not indicate impurity, and are, generally speaking, harmless unless sufficient numbers are present to affect the water by their death and decay. (See also Chapter IV.—Surface water as a source of supply.)

The second method of biological investigation was proposed by Emmerich,* who says: "If the water under examination, or the aqueous extract (of the residue), to the bulk of 40–80 c.c. be injected subcutaneously into a full-grown rabbit, and fail to produce a continued elevation of temperature of more than $1°$ C., followed by death, then the water contains no putrid substances dangerous to health, or contains them in so small an amount that they are not worth considering." He further suggests, that the amount of such dangerous substances may be estimated from the amount of water which must be evaporated in order to obtain an extract which will produce in animals the effects which he describes.

---

* Zeitschrift für Biologie, xiv (1878), 563–603.

Something has been done in this same direction by Dr. George
M. Sternberg, U. S. A., * in connection with his investigation of
malarial fever, and also by Prof. H. Newell Martin, of the Johns
Hopkins University, in connection with Prof. Mallet's investigation into the different methods for the analysis of drinking
waters. Whatever may develop in the future from this method
of research, it is certain that it has not yet become a method on
which we can rely, and that Emmerich's statement is altogether
too sweeping.

In this connection should also be mentioned the proposal by
Koch † to examine the water by means of culture experiments
in gelatine with subsequent microscopic examination; but this
method, like the preceding, is at present simply developing. A
somewhat similar method of experimenting has, for a longer time,
been occasionally employed. It consists in carefully collecting
some of the water in flasks that have previously been sterilized
by heat and introducing a small quantity into each of several
test-tubes containing some freshly boiled Pasteur's solution, so-
called. This solution is particularly favorable to the growth of
" bacteria," if any such or their germs are in the water. The
tubes are plugged with cotton-wool, and an attempt is made to
estimate the amount of impurity in the water from the degree of
turbidity produced in a given time. None of these methods have
yet reached the stage of practical utility, and it must be left entirely with the specialists to interpret the results of their own
observations.

Popular tests.—The writer has little sympathy with popular
tests. It is true that the observations on odor and taste and
color may be made by a person who is not a chemist ; there are
also certain qualitative tests that any intelligent person can learn
to make satisfactorily, and which would serve as indications to
the chemist. It is, in general, true of popular tests, that they
are apt to lead either to an unjustified sense of security or to an
unnecessary feeling of alarm. The following test for sewage
contamination, proposed by Heisch, and recommended by others,
has some value :

Put some of the water—say half a pint—into a clean, colorless,

---

* Supp. No. 14, Bulletin National Board of Health, July 23, 1881.
† Mittheilungen aus dem kaiserlichen Gesundheitsamte. I Band. Berlin, 1881,
page 36. See also a paper by Angus Smith, in The Sanitary Record, February, 1882.

glass-stoppered bottle, add a few grains of white sugar, shake until the sugar has dissolved, and leave the bottle freely exposed to the light in a warm room for a week or ten days. If the water becomes turbid, it is open to suspicion of sewage contamination ; if it remains clear it is probably safe.

Collection of samples.—In connection with the chemical examination of water, the importance of taking due care in the collection of samples may be alluded to. The best vessel for collecting water for analysis is a glass-stoppered bottle ; a clean demijohn which has never been used for any other purpose and which is stopped with a new and clean cork answers perfectly well and is often more convenient. Tin cans or stoneware jugs are not suitable.

Considerable care is necessary in order to get a fair sample of the water. The demijohn should be rinsed several times thoroughly with the water to be collected and finally filled not quite to the mouth. The cork should be washed with the same water and the demijohn stoppered tightly. The stopper should be tied over with a piece of cloth or "bandage gum," and the string sealed with sealing wax, that the water may not be tampered with in transit.

If the water is taken from a pump or from a faucet, enough water should be pumped or allowed to run to waste to thoroughly clear the pipes. In taking water from a pond or river it will generally be most convenient to use a clean crockery pitcher, which may be filled by plunging it beneath the surface (so as to avoid any scum or floating material) and then emptied into the demijohn; or a new and clean tin dipper may be employed. If a glass bottle is used, it may be plunged directly into the water and thus filled. In taking water from a river, the middle of the stream should be chosen if only one sample is taken.

CHAPTER III.

THE collection of the rain directly as a source of public supply, in our latitude, would be undertaken only under very exceptional circumstances. In many localities, however, where there is no sufficient public supply and where wells are out of the question, the collection of rain water by the individual householder becomes a necessity; also in cases where the public supply is hard and unfit for washing. A house covering an area of 40 by 20 feet, or 800 square feet, would receive upon its roof, with a rainfall of 42 inches, 2,800 cubic feet of water in the course of the year. If three-quarters of this could be collected, it would furnish a supply of something over 40 gallons per day, on the average.

The rain which falls, even in the open country, is far from being pure in the chemical sense, as it washes from the air both gaseous and solid substances. The Rivers Pollution Commission of Great Britain obtained the following average results from the examination of 73 samples of rain water, all but two of which were collected at the experimental farm of Messrs. Lawes and Gilbert, Rothamsted, England:

Total dissolved solids	3.95 parts in 100,000.
Organic carbon	0.099
Organic nitrogen	0.022
Ammonia	0.050
Nitrogen as nitrites and nitrates	0.007
Total combined nitrogen	0.071
Chlorine	0.63

In manufacturing localities, the air, and consequently the rain, may contain much impurity; and, in any event, when the rain is collected near habitations the impurity is considerable. The excrement of birds, the dead bodies of insects, leaves from the trees, and various sorts of dust and dirt lodge on the roofs and are washed off, mainly by the first portions of the rain.

Devices, some of them automatic, have been invented, by which the first portions of the rain are allowed to go to waste, but they have not come into general use. Besides the sources of impurity to which rain water is naturally and unavoidably liable, there are accidental sources of contamination: thus, instances have been known where servants have emptied the house slops from the upper stories on to the roof, thence to find their way into the cisterns. It is to be hoped that such instances as this are extremely rare.

The proper storage of rain water is as important as its collection. For the storage of water in small quantity there is nothing better, from a sanitary point of view, than slate tanks; iron tanks protected from rusting by a coating of coal-tar paint are also unobjectionable. Tanks situated at the top of the house are sometimes in direct communication with the drains by means of the overflow pipes, and in some cases it has been thought that the water has been rendered impure and injurious to health by gases from the soil-pipes. Any mode of construction which admits the possibility of such communication is faulty. Rain water is generally stored in underground cisterns built of brick and cement, and acquires a slight hardness by dissolving lime from the cement, especially when the cistern is new. The overflows from such cisterns should be constructed so as to preclude all possibility of contamination from the liquids or gases of drains or sewers. In some localities wood is used for the construction of the rain-water tanks; thus in New Orleans, according to Dr. Smart,* the cisterns are constructed of cypress wood, and vary in capacity from 500 to 60,000 gallons. "The usual capacity of the dwelling-house cistern is about two thousand gallons. They are raised a few feet from the ground, and their contents are protected by a lid or cover. Some are placed under the shade of a balcony; a few have a special roof over them; but the majority have only such protection from the rays of the sun as is afforded by their position against the house wall. Many, especially in the older parts of the city, are situated in unventilated inclosures which are rank with the emanations from unclean privies."

---

* Report on the Water Supply of New Orleans and Mobile. Bull. National Board of Health, April 17, 1880.

4

On account of the sediment which accumulates in the cisterns in which rain water is stored, it is desirable that such cisterns should be thoroughly cleansed from time to time, and that the water should be filtered before being used for drinking or for culinary purposes. The matter of filtration will be discussed in a subsequent chapter (page 151). Dr. Smart examined a number of cisterns in New Orleans which had not been cleaned in many years, and found that the rate of deposit was, on the average, about an inch a year. After a few days' repose, the sediment carried in by the rain has settled to the bottom and the water has become clear, " but every succeeding rainfall not only increases the quantity of this sediment, but, by its inflow, stirs up that which has already accumulated, rendering the water impure until sedimentation is again accomplished. As time passes the sediment increases, and the water becomes unfit for use after each rainfall. These conditions are aggravated in the dry season, when the water is low in the cistern and the quantity of sediment is relatively much increased."

Underground cisterns, being out of sight and consequently too often out of mind, are not only liable to be neglected and allowed to go uncleaned for a long time, but are also liable to become leaky and thus to allow of the contamination of the water by soakage from the soil. Dr. Smart, in his investigation of the water supply of Memphis, examined a considerable number of the 4,000 cisterns said to be in use. He found—

Undoubtedly sound	163
Probably sound	82
Probably siping	94
Undoubtedly leaky	190
Total number examined	529

Examination of Cistern Water.

It is often very difficult to decide, by chemical examination, whether a cistern water is to be regarded as fit to drink or not. Gross pollution can be easily detected, but, as the presence of more or less organic matter is a necessary consequence of the mode of collecting the water, it is impossible to say just how much is permissible, and where the line should be drawn. The most valuable indications are afforded by the chlorine, which

should be present only in trifling quantity, as a rule, not over
0.5 part in 100,000, except near the sea. The total solids should
not much exceed 4 or 5 parts in 100,000, but a larger amount is
sometimes due simply to the solvent action of the water on the
cement lining of the cistern. Dr. Smart considers cistern waters
containing from 0.010 to 0.020 part of albuminoid ammonia in
100,000 as usable, and regards those containing over 0.020 part as
dangerous, but as much as 0.010 ought to awaken suspicion and
give rise to inquiry. The following table contains the results of
the examination of a number of cistern waters in various localities.

TABLE V.—EXAMINATION OF CISTERN WATERS.

[Results expressed in Parts in 100,000.]

LOCALITY	TOTAL SOLIDS.	AMMONIA.	"ALBUMINOID AMMONIA."	ORGANIC CARBON.	ORGANIC NITROGEN.	CHLORINE.	AUTHORITY.
Oakham, Eng.....	11.70	0.005	....	0.331	0.090	1.10	Riv. Poll. Com. †
Epsom, Eng......	8.10	0.009	....	0.167	0.021	0.90	" " "
Goring, Eng......	9.42	0.032	....	0.215	0.061	0.80	" " "
Podehole, Eng....	5.28	0.	....	0.142	0.029	0.90	" " "
Sheffield Barracks..	12.00	0.130	....	0.154	0.053	1.60	" " "
Boston, Mass.....	5.28	0.013	0.008	....	....	0.32	W. R. Nichols ‡
Same, filtered *...	6.56	0.012	0 007	....	....	0.36	" "
Another	3.24	0.005	0.011	....	....	0.10	" "
Same, filtered *...	4.80	0.024	0.016	....	....	0.12	" "
Another..........	3.48	0.021	0.007	....	....	0.69	" "
Same, filtered *....	5.20	0.007	0.007	....	....	0.70	" "
Wilmington, N. C.	5.05	0.002	0.015	....	...	0.70	C. W. Dabney §
Another..........	6.90	0.016	0.008	....	....	0.52	" "
Another..........	3 60	0.005	0.008	....	....	0.52	" "
Cincinnati, O......	2.68	0.004	0.123	....	....	0.55	C. R. Stuntz ∥
Another..........	4.72	0 275	0.055	....	....	2.76	" "
Another..........	4.48	0.027	0.118	....	....	1.97	" "
Another..........	7.96	0.004	0.016	....	....	trace	" "
Another..........	4.10	0.020	0.360	....	....	trace	" "

The table might be extended indefinitely, but the results have
little real significance except in connection with a minute knowledge of the history of the various samples.

While rain water, on account of its softness, is peculiarly

---

* These cisterns were provided with a brick filtering-wall.
† Sixth Report, p. 29.
‡ Filtration of Potable Water, p. 83.
§ Report North Carolina Agricultural Experiment Station, 1881, p. 158.
∥ Report of Water Department, Cincinnati, 1880, p. 80.

adapted to use in washing and in cooking, it is also wholesome as a beverage if collected so as to be reasonably pure. There has, however, long been an opinion that snow water is unwholesome. Dr. Charles Brewer, U. S. A., says that " mountaineers (in the West), to whose long observation and experience in the wilds some attention is due, attribute the origin of the so-called mountain fever to the melting of snows and the drinking of snow water." Dr. Smart * quotes facts to show that this suspicion is well grounded, and says that " snow water, therefore, pure as it seems, must not be accepted as innocent until its freedom from organic ammonia in deleterious or suspicious quantity has been proved." This applies especially to snow melting and flowing in the mountain streams. As collected with the rain and stored in cisterns it is wholesome, as far as we know. (Compare p. 100).

NATURAL AND ARTIFICIAL ICE.

As the rain is water which has been more or less completely purified by a natural process of distillation and condensation, so ice is water which has been more or less completely purified by another natural process—that of crystallization. It is, therefore, not inappropriate to consider ice in this connection.

The great extent to which ice is used in many parts of the United States makes its purity a matter of very considerable importance. The surface water supplies, even of Northern cities, become heated in summer so that, to cool the water, at least half its own weight of ice is needed, and very much more than this is often used in practice.

When ice forms in or on a body of water, the bulk of which remains unfrozen, it is generally supposed that foreign substances are excluded and that the ice itself is essentially pure. It is true that foreign, especially saline, substances are excluded to a large extent, but the ice always retains more or less, and, if the water contains organic impurities, the ice will contain them also. In fact, a pond or river which is not fit for a water supply on account of present evident contamination should not be used as a source of ice supply. It is also, unfortunately, the case that ice is often cut in winter on shallow ponds which for a consider-

---

* Buck's Hygiene, ii, p. 133.

able portion of the year have no existence or exist merely as stagnant pools. That such ice should be wholesome, ought not to be expected, and there are well authenticated cases on record where sickness has arisen from the use of impure ice. Such a case of well-marked character occurred in 1875 at Rye Beach, N. H.* The ice had been cut on a brackish stagnant pond into which a small brook brought a quantity of saw-dust from several saw-mills. Here, the trouble was ascribed to the presence of decomposing organic matter. That, in some cases, the germs (if they be germs) of specific diseases might retain their vitality even if frozen into the ice, we can but regard as possible from what we know of the endurance of the spores of the lower algæ ; at any rate, ice should not be cut on contaminated waters.

It is unfortunately true that when public attention is called to a possible, but hitherto little noticed cause of disease, exaggerated statements are sure to be disseminated through the public prints and otherwise—statements which have a basis of truth, but which are so presented as, oftentimes, to awaken unnecessary anxiety and alarm. The statement—" The old idea that water purifies itself by freezing is now pretty generally abandoned "—is true, if it means that water does not thus purify itself completely ; it is untrue as far as it naturally leads to the inference that water, in freezing, does not purify itself at all. Further, the author believes that the following statements (in which the italics are his), even if hereafter proved true, are certainly premature, and have not been proved by experiments hitherto published. " The even more dangerous organic impurities resulting from human and other animal waste are retained in ice unchanged as regards both quality and quantity, *the latter indeed being likely to be increased.*" " The germs of infectious disease . . . are retained in ice unaffected, and *from their comparative lightness are so concentrated therein as to number that they exist in even greater quantity than in the same amount of water, under similar circumstances, at other seasons of the year.*" †

Large quantities of artificial ice are now made in the United States, and in a number of Southern cities the artificial product

---

* See a paper by A. H. Nichols, M. D., in the Seventh Report of the Mass. State Board of Health, 1876, p. 465.

† The Dangers of Impure Ice in *The Sanitarian* for May, 1882. See also a paper on Impure Ice, in the Fifth Annual Report of the Connecticut State Board of Health, 1883.

has driven the natural ice from the market. With some of the machines, distilled water alone is frozen ; with others, ordinary well or other water. Ice machines, on a small scale, are used also in hotels for freezing carafes, etc. Particular care should be used with reference to the water employed in making artificial ice, because the water is frozen solid, and whatever is dissolved or suspended in the water must remain in the ice. In one machine, however (Beath's patent), the ice is formed by causing water to flow over pipes through which the freezing agent flows. Only a part of the water used is actually frozen as it flows over the pipes or the continually increasing thickness of ice, and the bulk of the impurities, dissolved or suspended, flows away.

Chemical Examination of Ice.

The standard of purity for ice should be placed very high. Ice should contain very little dissolved matter, next to no chlorine, and the "albuminoid ammonia" should not exceed 0.005 part in 100,000. Great care must be exercised in preparing the sample for analysis, because the ice in melting attracts organic impurities from the air.

In fact, one method which has been proposed for examining the air for organic matter, consists in employing a glass funnel drawn to a point and filled with fragments of ice.* The moisture in the air condenses as dew upon the outside of the funnel,

FIG. 5.

trickles down into the vessel below, and the water thus collected is examined for organic matter in various ways. For this reason, also, the fact that the drip from refrigerators often becomes offensive when allowed to stand in a warm room, does not show necessarily that the ice used was impure.

In melting ice for analysis, a fair specimen cake should be selected and broken into fragments in a clean place. The fragments may then be placed in a wide-mouthed bottle covered with a plate of glass, and, when enough of the ice has melted to have washed itself,

* Smee : Social Science Transactions, 1875, p. 486. The figure is from Fox's Sanitary Examination of Water, etc.

this portion of water should be poured away, and the remainder, after melting, be subjected to analysis. Or the fragments may be placed in a large funnel covered with a plate of glass until 5 or 10 per cent has melted, and the remainder be then transferred to the wide-mouthed bottle without touching the ice with the hands. Since even the best of ice is liable to have bits of organic substances frozen into it here and there, the "albuminoid ammonia" should be determined also in the water which has been filtered through paper. It must also be remembered that the ice which is sold for family use often is partly "snow ice," and that the snow, in falling, always brings down ammonia from the atmosphere. Table VI contains the results of a number of chemical examinations of ice from various sources.

TABLE VI.—EXAMINATION OF (MELTED) ICE.

[Results expressed in Parts in 100,000.]

DESCRIPTION.	TOTAL SOLIDS.	AMMONIA.	"ALBUMINOID AMMONIA."	CHLORINE.	AUTHORITY.
Rye Beach, N. H. Supposed cause of sickness.	13.52	0.0208	0.0704	....	W. R. Nichols.
Same, filtered through paper	9.72	0.0213	0.0165	3.2	"
Boston Ice Company, 1875....................	0.76	0.0045	....	trace	"
Fresh Pond, near Boston, 1878...............	5.00	0.0060	0.0075	...	S. P. Sharples.
Spy Pond, " "	5.00	0.0064	0.0064	....	"
Little Spy Pond, near Boston, 1878	2.50	0.0060	0.0110	....	"
Horn Pond, " " 1876*......	9.2	0.0026	0.0440	0.4	F. S. Wood.
Hammond's Pond, " " 1877...............	2.4	0.0066	0.0190	...	"
Jamaica Pond Ice Co., 1877................	0.8	0.0180	0.0160	0.3	"
Another sample of same	1.2	0.0260	0.0160	0.3	"
Pittsfield, Mass., 1876	1.51	0.0072	0.0061	...	W. R. Nichols.
Same, filtered through paper.................	0.44	0.0077	0.0013	0.02	"

* The large amount of impurity in this case was probably due to some local and accidental cause : this ice was thought to cause sickness.

CHAPTER IV.

SURFACE WATERS AS SOURCES OF SUPPLY.

THE character of the water which flows in the streams and is stored in the lakes and ponds of any region depends largely upon the geological character of the country. Where impervious rocky strata predominate, the water flows off from the surface readily, and the streams carry water free from any very considerable amount of dissolved substances: where the water soaks quickly into the ground and the streams and lakes are fed by springs, or, at least, by water which has passed for some distance underground, the amount of dissolved matter becomes more considerable. As a rule, the surface waters contain less dissolved matter and are softer than the well waters (ground water) of the same region; on the other hand, they generally contain more organic matter of animal and vegetable origin, they are often colored, they are liable to be turbid or to become so at time of flood, and are, in several respects, more subject to variation than the ground water.

While much that might be said with reference to surface waters will apply both to running streams and to ponded waters, it will be convenient to divide the subject, discussing first the matters of turbidity and pollution, which are peculiarly felt in the case of rivers, and subsequently discussing the difficulties arising from variable temperature and from animal and vegetable growths, which are felt peculiarly in the case of ponded waters.

Turbidity of Streams.

. It is hardly necessary to dwell upon the fact that rivers are frequently objectionable as sources of supply, on account of the large amount of suspended matter, mainly clay, which many of them carry invariably and others at time of flood. Something will be said of this matter in connection with sedimentation in Chapter VIII: at present, it will suffice to call attention to Table VII (made up from statements in Geikie's Text-book of Geology) which shows the amount of suspended matter in various rivers, and also shows that the amount varies very much in the same stream under different circumstances.

TABLE VII.—AMOUNT OF SUSPENDED MATTER IN VARIOUS RIVERS.

River.	Date.	Locality and Condition.	Suspended Matter Expressed in Parts in 100,000		Parts of Water for 1 Part of Sediment.		Authority.
			by weight.	by volume.	by w'g't.	by vol.	
Rhone	1844.	Lyons	5.88	....	17,000	....	....
Rhone	...	Arles, low water	14.29	....	7,000	....	....
	....	" flood	434.78	....	230	....	....
	....	" maximum	2,222.22	....	45	....	....
	....	" mean	50.00	....	2,000	....	....
Rhine	...	Strasburg, July and Aug	2.00	....	50,000	....	Daubrée.
	...	Bonn		6.25	....	16,00	Horner.
	...	Bonn	20.50	....	4,878	...	Bischof.
	...	Bonn, after dry weather	1.73	....	57,800	....	
	...	Uerdingen, after sudden floods	78.00	....	1,282	....	Stiefensand.
	...	In Holland	....	1,000.00	....	100	Hartsoeker.
Maas	Dec. 1849	Maximum	47.61	....	2,100	....	Chandellon.
	....	Minimum	1.40	....	71,420	...	"
	....	Mean	10.03	....	10,000	....	"
Danube	1862-1871	Mean	32.68	17.20	3,060	5,814	Hartley.
Vistula	....	Maximum	....	2,083.00	....	48	Spittell.
Po	....		....	333.00	....	300	Lombardini.
Durance	.. .	In flood	2,083.33	....	48	....	Payen.
	....	Mean	100.00	....	1,000	...	
Ganges	....	In flood	233.95	116.82	4-8	856	Everest.
	....	Yearly mean	196.08	97.94	510	1,021	
Irrawaddy	....	In flood	58.82	...	1,700	....	Login.
	....	Low water	17.47	...	5,725	....	
Mississippi	....	Mean	66.66	34.48	1,500	2,900	Humphreys and Abbot.

The Pollution of Streams.

Owing to facilities for transportation, to available water-power, and also to the opportunities furnished for the discharge of waste material, running streams naturally attract to their banks manufactories and towns, and, in turn, become polluted by their refuse.

In a thickly settled manufacturing country like England, where, moreover, the streams are comparatively small, the pollution may become very serious. In Great Britain the matter has been the subject of thorough investigation by two Royal Commissions, appointed respectively in 1865 and 1868, "to inquire into the best means of preventing the pollution of rivers."

The statement of the Commissioners with reference to the Aire and Calder, although it has been frequently quoted, has not lost in emphasis:

" The rivers Aire and Calder and their tributaries are abused by passing into them hundreds of thousands of tons per annum of ashes, slag and cinders from steam-boilers, furnaces, iron-works and domestic fires; by their being made the receptacle, to a vast extent, of broken pottery and worn-out utensils of metal, refuse brick from brick-yards and old buildings, earth, stone and clay from quarries and excavations, road-scrapings, street-sweepings, etc.; by spent dye-woods and other solids used in the treatment of worsteds and woollens; by hundreds of car-casses of animals, as dogs, cats, pigs, etc., which are allowed to float on the surface of the streams or putrefy on their banks; and by the flowing in, to the amount of very many millions of gallons per day, of water poisoned, corrupted, and clogged by refuse from mines, chemical works, dyeing, scouring and fulling worsted and woollen stuffs, skin-cleaning and tanning, slaughter-house garbage, and the sewage of towns and houses."

" Bradford is an ancient town situated on a 'beck' about four miles south of the river Aire, into which the water of this beck falls. It is the center of the worsted district." The Commis-sioners allude to the increase of population and to the increased pollution from dye-works, from soap-suds, and from refuse of various kinds produced in manufactures. " The whole of the sewage of Bradford, and of the populous district above the town, flows into the beck, producing an indescribable state of pollu-tion. It has become a Yorkshire proverb of comparison for any foul stream, to say of it that it is as polluted as Bradford Beck. At the time of our inquiry Bradford Beck was the source of supply of the Bradford Canal, the fluid of which became so cor-rupt in summer that large volumes of inflammable gases were given off, and, although it has usually been considered an impos-sible feat ' to set the River Thames on fire,' it was found practi-cable to set the Bradford Canal on fire, as this at times formed part of the amusement of boys in the neighborhood. They struck a match placed on the end of a stick, reached over, and set the canal on fire, the flames rising six feet high and running along the surface of the water for many yards like a will-o'-the wisp; canal boats have been so enveloped in flame as to frighten persons on board."

The river Irwell, near its source, " is of excellent quality for all domestic purposes." It flows, however, through the midst of a manufacturing district, and finally passes through Manchester before it empties into the Mersey. At Manchester the sluggishly flowing stream is black as ink, and it is there joined by the Irk and Medlock, streams not less polluted than itself.

Of the Clyde, the following are bits of evidence :

"At one time the Clyde was comparatively pure and limpid—salmon fishing within the precincts of the harbor being very productive. Now, through Glasgow downwards, but diminishing below the mouth of the Cart, it is very foul and turbid ; in short a gigantic open sewer, noxious gases being continually evolved, which, during summer, are so overpowering as to force the bulk of the passenger traffic from the river to the rail."

"The harbor is more like a gigantic cesspool than a harbor in the proper acceptation of the term."

"In summer time there is a perfect commotion with air and gas bubbles over the whole surface of the water, and it is so bad that we cannot use it for the boilers of the little steam ferry-boats that ply across the river."

While the rivers of Great Britain are probably polluted generally to a greater extent than those of most other countries, the trouble is by no means peculiar. In France the condition of the Seine below Paris has led to the appointment of several departmental and municipal commissions, and to the proposal of extensive and costly plans for disposing of the sewage of the city. Other rivers of France, as, for instance, the Vesle, at Rheims, have become the receptacles of town and manufacturing refuse so as to call imperatively for restrictive action. In Germany the increasing pollution of the sluggish Spree by the sewage of Berlin was one of the moving causes which has led to an entire change of the system of sewerage, and to the attempt at purification and utilization of the entire sewage of the city on sewage farms.

In this country, many of our streams carry such a volume of water that the refuse of the largest cities is soon lost; but some of the smaller rivers, for a portion of their course at any rate, are rendered unfit for domestic use. The Blackstone River, in Massachusetts, receives the sewage of Worcester and causes complaint from the towns and manufactories on its banks. The Schuylkill and Passaic rivers are no longer fit for water supply where water-works now exist. The Chicago River was an exceedingly foul stream—if stream it could be called—until it was diverted into the Illinois River; and other examples might be cited. The contamination of the water of the Great Lakes, in the neighborhood of cities like Cleveland, Chicago and Milwaukee, is a very serious matter. There is a limit to the distance to which tunnels can be carried into the open lake, and the problem of disposing of the sewage of the cities, otherwise than by discharging it into the lake, is one which will soon compel solution.

It is not our purpose to enter into details as to the nature and amount of the polluting materials which are discharged by various manufacturing industries, nor to discuss how far the individual substances are injurious to plants or to fish, or how far they render the water unfit for drinking and for other domestic purposes.* We may admit that certain substances are injurious, even in small amount; but, while this is true, it is also true that much manufacturing refuse is of such a character as to be, except in excessive quantities, of no appreciable influence on the human system. Thus, the addition to a water of most of the ordinary salts of lime, soda, potash, etc., would not produce any deleterious effect, although the addition of lime compounds would increase the hardness and render the water less desirable for washing. Again, in the case of many waste liquors of offensive appearance, the actual amount of matter which is really injurious or of suspicious character is comparatively small. Thus, in the case of some of the organic dyestuffs, the weak, spent dye-liquors, although they communicate a very foul appearance to the water for some distance, yet contain a comparatively small amount of solid matter, and, if discharged into a stream of considerable size, are soon disseminated through it, and diluted to a very great extent.

Very different, however, in character and importance, from much of the refuse of manufacturing establishments, is, as we have seen, the sewage proper—that is, the excremental matters from factories and towns—and the refuse from particular operations, such as tanning, slaughtering, rendering, wool-pulling, etc.

---

* These matters are very fully discussed in the reports of the Rivers Pollution Commissions of Great Britain. A brief statement with reference to the chemicals and other materials used in various manufacturing operations and with reference to the liquid refuse discharged from them, is given in the Report of the Mass. State Board of Health, 1876: Special Report on the Pollution of Rivers by J. P. Kirkwood, C.E.

With our present information, too much stress cannot be laid upon the importance of preventing the discharge of such refuse, and of sewage in its more restricted sense, into any stream or pond used, or likely to be used, as a source of water supply.

The importance of this matter is underrated for two reasons: first, because of a belief that an impure and polluted water rapidly purifies itself by natural means; and, second, because of the feeling that a water to be prejudicial to health must be polluted to such an extent that the animal matter may be recognized by chemical tests.

That a polluted water in its flow does become purer, no one can doubt who has followed the course of a polluted stream; chemical analysis proves the same thing. There is, however, much difference of opinion as to the method by which the purification takes place, and also as to the extent to which we may suppose that the disease-producing something is eliminated.

TABLE VIII.—The Seine above and below Paris. [*]

Kilometers.	Locality.	Organic Nitrogen. Grams per cubic meter.	Total Combined Nitrogen. Grams per cubic meter.	Dissolved Oxygen. Cubic centimeters per liter.
	Corbeil (above Paris)............	..	..	9.32
0	Pont de la Tournelle, Paris........	..	..	8.05
8	Auteuil (below the city but above the outlets of the main sewers)...	..	..	5.99
	Pont d'Asnières (above main sewer)	0.85	1.9	5.34
31	Epinay (below all sewers)........	1.26	3.0	1.05
78	Pont de Poissy..................	0.45	2.2	6.12
93	Pont de Meulan.................	0.40	..	8.17
109	Mantes	..	1.4	8.96
150	Vernon	..	..	10.40
242	Rouen.........................	..	..	10.42

Table VIII contains the results of partial examinations of the Seine above and below Paris. At Epinay, below all the sewers, the river is at its worst as regards the amount of nitrogen in the form of ammoniacal salts and organic compounds, and the dissolved oxygen is reduced to a minimum. After flowing some 75 or 100 kilometers, the river regains its purity as far as appearance and chemical tests can indicate.

* Assainissement de la Seine, etc., deuxième partie, II Annexes, p. 8; also Rapport de MM. Schloesing et A. Durand-Claye. Congrès international d'hygiène, Paris, 1878, p. 314.

TABLE IX.—SELF-PURIFICATION OF STREAMS.

[Results expressed in Parts in 100,000.]

MILES.	LOCALITY.	TOTAL SOLIDS.	AMMONIA.	"ALBUMINOID AMMONIA."	CHLO- RINE.
	Blackstone River, 1875.				
	North Pond, above pollution...........	4.20	0.0107	0.0213	0.18
	City Reservoir, gate-house	3.76	0.0072	0.0235	0.12
0	Mill Brook, below sewers...............	23.44	0.9600	0.1109	3.80
5	Blackstone River, at sash factory........	8.04	0.0092	0.0307	0.92
25	Blackstone River, at Blackstone.........	4.80	0.0099	0.0139	0.36
	Merrimack River, 1873.				
0	Mean of 11 examinations above Lowell...	4.10	0.0047	0.0114	0.14
11¼	Mean of 12 examinations above Lawrence.	4.10	0.0044	0.0110	0.20
13½	Mean of 11 examinations below Lawrence	4.43	0.0031	0.0127	0.18
	Merrimack River, 1879.*				
0	Mean of 2 examinations above Lowell....	5.50	0.0021	0.0132	0.40
11½	Mean of 4 examinations above Lawrence .	7.56	0.0018	0.0131	0.44

Table IX contains results which are less striking but which point in the same direction. The Blackstone Valley is the seat of considerable manufacturing industries, there being on the stream and its tributaries 44 woolen mills, 27 cotton mills, 12 iron works, 1 tannery and 1 slaughter house. Some of the mills cause local pollution, but the chief source of contamination is the sewage of the City of Worcester—some 2,000,000 gallons in 24 hours—which flows into Mill Brook and thence into the river.

"The water of Mill Brook, after it has received the sewage of Worcester, is shown to be very impure in this table, and on the Blackstone River, at the sash factory, about five miles lower down, it still gives unmistakable signs of the influence of this pollution; but at Blackstone, twenty-five miles below Mill Brook, the dilution produced by numerous small streams delivering into the main river between these points has all but obliterated the evidence of impurity, so far as analysis can expose it, the only marked difference here in the table between the water at Blackstone and the head water of the river, being in the amount of chlorine, the increase, however, of this evidence of impurity not being so great as to condemn the water (by this test) for domestic or any other use. It is to be noted, however, that the river at this time was not at its very low dry-weather stage,

* E. S. Wood, M.D.

which usually occurs in October or November, when it occurs at all. In extreme low water, the river would give greater tokens of impurity." *

Of the Merrimack River it may be said that, in 1873, when some of the examinations were made, Lowell had a population of about 41,000 and Lawrence of about 30,000; further, at Lowell there are some 75 mill buildings, in which about 16,000 operatives are employed. About 10,000 horse power is derived from the river, and, in addition, steam power is used to the extent of 6,000 horse power. The Merrimack Manufacturing Company alone consumes, among other things, 7,500 gallons of oil per annum, 225,000 pounds of starch, 1,100 barrels of flour, 2,500,000 pounds of madder, 50,000 of copperas, 170,000 of alum, 200,000 of sumac, 1,120,000 of sulphuric acid, 300,000 of bark, 350,000 of soda-ash, and 40,000 of soap.†

At Lawrence there are some 25 mills (buildings), employing 9,000 operatives. The manufacturing industry is less at Lawrence than at Lowell, but it is still very considerable. The Pacific Mills, which is the largest corporation, use some 800,000 pounds of starch, 540 barrels of flour, 8,300 gallons of oil, etc.‡

The questions naturally arise, to what causes are we to ascribe the disappearance of the large amount of polluting material in the Seine, and in the Blackstone, and why, in the case of the Merrimack River, are we not able to trace a greater effect as produced by the large manufacturing cities of Lowell and Lawrence.

In studying the self-purifying power of streams, let us first take an instance of a substance whose course we can trace more easily than that of animal refuse, with which we are, of course, more concerned. The following account from the First Annual Report of the Mass. State Board of Health, Lunacy and Charity (1880), will furnish the illustration :

"On the night of June 2, 1879, a fire occurred in a chemical works situated on a brook whose waters eventually find their way into Mystic Pond, from which a portion of the city of Boston, Mass., obtains its supply of water. As a result of the destruc-

* Seventh Annual Report of Mass. State Board of Health, 1876, p. 84.

† These figures are taken from the " Statistics of Lowell Manufactures, January, 1873," published by Stone & Huse, Lowell.

‡ " Statistics of Lawrence Manufactures, January, 1872." Published by Geo. S. Merrill & Co., Lawrence.

tion by fire of the sulphuric acid chambers, a considerable quantity of sulphuric acid, estimated at fifty tons of oil of vitriol, together with salt cake and other chemicals, was washed directly into the brook, or flowed upon the adjoining meadow-land, from which it would slowly find its way to the stream. Large numbers of fish, driven before the acid water, or actually killed by it, passed into the mill-ponds below and through the wheels of the mills. Anxiety was felt lest the acid should reach Mystic Pond itself; and, five days after the fire, specimens of the water were collected for analysis. As far as Mystic Pond itself was concerned, the fears proved groundless; but in the brook and in some of the upper ponds there was an abnormal amount of dissolved matter and especially of sulphates. The most interesting point, however, was with reference to the *acidity* of the water. As a rule, our surface waters in Massachusetts are naturally slightly alkaline, and, when the water is evaporated to dryness, the residue effervesces, at least slightly, when treated with acid.* It was found that even five days after the fire the water of the brook itself and of the nearest ponds was distinctly acid. The amount of acid was estimated by means of a dilute solution of baryta, using rosolic acid as an indicator.

"The acidity was found to be as follows, the results being expressed by stating how many parts by weight of sulphuric acid

No.	Date.	Locality.	Acidity. Parts of Acid in 100,000 of Water.	Parts of Water for one Acid.
	1879.			
I	June 7, A.M.	From brook just below works ...	1.74	57.500
IV	June 7, A.M.	Lower end of Richardson's Pond, about 1¼ miles below works...	0.74	135,000
V	June 7, A.M.	Frye & Thompson's Pond, about 3 miles below works...	0.37	270,000
II	June 7, P.M.	From brook midway between Chemical Works and Richardson's Pond, about ¼ mile below works.....	0.18	555,500
VI	June 7, P.M.	From canal at Montvale, about 3¼ miles below works.....	0.37	270,000
III	June 8, P.M.	Upper end of Richardson's Pond, ¼ mile below II..	0.15	666,600

(H_2SO_4), or its equivalent, were present in 100,000 parts by weight of the water; and also by stating, in round numbers, with how

* Whether the alkalinity is to be regarded as due in part to the presence of alkaline carbonates, or as solely due to the presence of dissolved carbonate of calcium, is uncertain, as there are no analyses which are sufficiently particular to determine.

many parts of water by weight one part of sulphuric acid was diluted.

"From the point numbered VI, that is from the canal at Montvale, samples were taken at intervals until the water returned to its alkaline reaction. The results of the examination were as follows:

DATE.	LOCALITY.	Total Solid Matter dried at 100° C.	Acidity in equivalent of H_2SO_4.	Total Sulphuric Acid free and combined, reckoned as SO_3.	REMARKS.
1879 June 6	Canal at Montvale Avenue, Montvale	11.6	0.22	4.7	
June 7		13.9	0.37	....	
June 9		12.8	0.26	....	The residue of evaporation did not effervesce with acid.
June 10		11.6	0.22	....	
June 13		9.4	0.16	....	
June 15		10.1	Slightly alkaline.	....	
June 19		9.4	0.16	1.2	Residue did not effervesce.
June 30		7.7	Slightly alkaline.	....	Residue did effervesce with acid.
July 8		8.4	Slightly alkaline.	....	

"While the water was acid, the residue of evaporation did not effervesce with acid, showing that a part, at any rate, of the sulphuric acid was neutralized by the carbonates in the water. It may also be noted, that some fragments of marble were put into some of the water No. IV, which had an acidity of 0.74; after standing for fifteen hours the acidity had decreased to 0.11, and after standing for two and a half days the reaction was neutral or faintly alkaline."

Mystic Pond is about eight miles below the works: samples were taken from the upper end of the pond for several days, but no acid reaction was at any time perceptible.

Thus, in the disappearance of the sulphuric acid, we have two actions concerned: first, the chemical action by which it was converted probably into sulphate of lime, and then the action of dilution, by which all traces of it were apparently lost. With many inorganic substances we may predict what will happen when they come into a stream, and the same thing is true

5

of certain particular organic substances whose changes have been studied under various conditions; but of the heterogeneous mixture which we speak of collectively as "sewage," it would be difficult to declare *a priori* what changes would take place and what products would be formed. There are, however, three principal ways in which a natural water frees itself from organic pollution: (1) by oxidation and other chemical changes; (2) by deposition; (3) by dilution.

Oxidation.—The disappearance of organic refuse is, no doubt, to a certain extent, due to chemical changes, by which the organic matter is oxidized and converted into simpler compounds; under favorable circumstances the destruction may be complete, the nitrogen appearing in ammoniacal compounds and nitrates, or escaping in the free state, and the carbon appearing as carbonic acid. That chemical action takes place is made evident enough, when the pollution is considerable, by the escape of sulphuretted hydrogen, marsh gas, and other gaseous products of decomposition, as in the case of the Bradford Beck—alluded to on page 58. Of the Seine, it was said in 1874 that, for the greater part of the year, especially in warm weather, bubbles of gas—sometimes a meter or a meter and a half in diameter—were continually rising to the surface of the water, and the passage of a boat caused a great ebullition, and left a mass of foam persisting for some minutes. The chemical change is also marked by the partial or total disappearance of dissolved oxygen, as instanced in Table VIII.

Attempts have been made to reach, by laboratory experiments, some idea of the amount of oxidation which may take place in a running stream polluted by sewage. The Rivers Pollution Commission mixed urine with water in the proportion of one gallon of urine to 3,077 gallons of water. The mixture was agitated from time to time, and samples taken for analysis. The results (expressed in parts in 100,000) were as follows:

	Organic Carbon.	Organic Nitrogen.
Immediately after mixture, Feb. 17, 1874	0.282	0.243
" 18,	0.298	0.251
" 19,	0.244	0.255
" 24,	0.225	0.253
" 25,	0.214	0.259
" 28,	0.214	0.276

In other experiments, a stream of impure water was allowed to flow from one vessel to another, freely exposed to the air. As a general result, the commissioners concluded that the purification due to actual oxidation had been much overrated, and that there was no river in the United Kingdom long enough, if once seriously polluted, to purify itself in this way.

Certain chemical changes, other than those already alluded to, will be mentioned in the next paragraph: we may here allude to the fact that in the destruction of organic matter a certain part is, no doubt, played by the fish and other animal inhabitants of the water, and many of the changes which seem to be purely chemical appear to be brought about wholly or in part by some of the lower algæ or by those minute organisms which are frequently spoken of together as "bacteria." Thus we know there are certain algæ which reduce the sulphates to sulphides, and the formation of nitrates in the soil and in water is ascribed also to micro-organisms.

Deposition.—Much waste material thrown into rivers is made up wholly or in part of substances insoluble in water. A portion, and a very considerable portion, even in a running stream, is deposited upon the bottom or stranded upon the banks. This deposition can often be very plainly observed in the immediate neighborhood of the points of discharge. It is not, however, suspended matters only that are removed by deposition. In the first place, many substances which seem to be perfectly dissolved are dragged out of solution and carried down by almost any finely divided substance. This is especially true of organic coloring matters and of the nitrogenous matter which gives rise to the "albuminoid ammonia" revealed by analysis; it is true, but to a very limited degree, of some mineral salts. In the second place, chemical changes take place in the stream, especially when refuse liquids from different sources meet and mix, which result in the formation of new and insoluble substances, and these when formed settle out, dragging other substances with them as just indicated. The improvement in the condition of polluted streams which appeals to the eye is largely due to deposition.

The deposits, once formed, continue to undergo chemical change; they shift their position with changing currents, and in time of flood may be washed up and, mingling with earthy

material held in suspension, be swept on to the sea or deposited
in some new position, either lower down on the stream or on
the surface of overflowed territory.   Often, however, the character
of the bed of the stream becomes permanently altered unless
means are taken by dredging or otherwise to remove the accumulations as they increase.

Dilution.—Probably the most important reason of the apparent disappearance of sewage and other waste material, is the fact
that the amount of solid matter is so small compared with the
volume of water into which it is thrown, that it is disseminated
through the mass, and thus lost to observation, and, in many
cases, to chemical tests.

A river in its flow loses water by evaporation, by being diverted for manufacturing and other purposes, and in some places,
through crevices in a rocky bed or by a slower process of percolation if the bed be gravelly.   On the other hand, the stream
receives water from tributaries more or less pure than itself,
and its volume is further increased by the entrance of ground
water or by actual springs rising in its bed.   On this account we
cannot calculate the extent to which dilution will take place with
any great accuracy, but that the *apparent* disappearance of much
of the foreign matter which finds its way into the stream is
really owing to dilution is evident when we undertake to trace
the course of some substance not liable to undergo any changes
which will result in its actual disappearance.   The chlorine,
which exists in the form of chloride of sodium (common salt)
and other chlorides, furnishes us with what we need.

All natural waters contain a small proportion of chlorine, very
small in inland waters, slightly increased in waters near the sea.
Chlorine is a universal accompaniment of sewage, generally in
the form of chloride of sodium (common salt), and occurs also in
most manufacturing refuse.   All the chlorine used in the process
of bleaching is eventually washed away, and that contained in
the various compounds of this element which are used in dye-
houses and print-works finds its way in the end into the drains
of the establishments.   On this account, although harmless in
the combinations in which it finally exists, its presence indicates
the presence, now or formerly, of refuse material.   Of course, in
regions containing salt-springs and salt-deposits, these statements
would require modification.   It is to be remarked further, that

while there do exist compounds of chlorine which are insoluble in water, and other compounds which are gaseous, and while it is true that chlorides are absorbed to a limited extent by earth filters and by growing plants, for all practical purposes we may say that the chlorides once dissolved in the water are not removed either as insoluble or gaseous compounds.

If, now, we take the case of the Blackstone River as instanced in Table IX, page 62, we shall see that the 3.80 parts of chlorine in Mill Brook have become 0.92 part five miles below, after the brook has been merged in the river, and twenty miles further still the river water contains only 0.36 part. Believing, as we do, that this decrease of the chlorine is due almost entirely to dilution, we must believe also that the decrease in the amount of the organic matter is largely due to the same cause. Owing to the fact that the organic matter is much more liable to conversion into insoluble and volatile compounds, no one would deny that an appreciable amount of organic matter is chemically changed and actually destroyed, but emphasis should be laid upon what we believe to be a fact—namely, *that the apparent self-purification of running streams is largely due to dilution, and the fact that a river seems to have purified itself at a certain distance below a point where it was certainly polluted, is no guaranty that the water is fit for domestic use.*

Referring again to Table IX, it would appear that no effect is produced upon the waters of the Merrimack by the cities of Lowell and Lawrence, which throw into the stream the greater part of their sewage and the waste from all the mills. Is the organic matter of all this refuse destroyed by oxidation or other chemical change? ·Certainly not! Let us take simply the results of examination above and below Lawrence. Between these two points the river receives the refuse from nearly all the manufacturing establishments, a large proportion of the excreta of the factory operatives, and a portion of the sewage of Lawrence. Moreover, the lower station is so short a distance below the city, that no chemist, probably, would believe that any considerable destruction of organic matter could take place in the rapid flow for so short a distance, and if, upon chemical grounds, the evidence was not sufficient, the floating soap-suds, with still unbroken bubbles, and other materials borne down upon the current show the same thing. Now, in spite of this addition, which must be considerable, there is only a slight increase in the total dissolved solids, and in the albuminoid matters, while the chlorine is practically the same or slightly decreased. We know, positively, that chlorine compounds, in large quantity, are thrown into the river at Lawrence, and yet, just below the city, the proportion is not increased. Although absolutely large, the amount is too small compared with the great volume of water to produce an appreciable increase. From these considerations with reference to the chlorine, it is evident that, in the case of the soluble *organic matter* it is not necessary to suppose any destruction or decomposition ; the apparent decrease or lack of increase may be explained, as in the case of chlorine, by the fact of dilution, and where the distance between the two points of examination is so short as in the instance now under discussion (above and below Lawrence), this is no doubt the main cause concerned.

It may be well, in this connection, to say that it is often difficult to prove satisfactorily the actual pollution of a stream until by the accidental or unusual discharge of some peculiarly offensive or characteristic substance the matter is placed beyond doubt. Carbolic acid has sometimes served this purpose ; thus, a few years ago, the taste and odor of carbolic acid were so strong in the water supplied to Newark, Jersey City and Hoboken, that the water could not be used for domestic purposes. These cities take their water from the Passaic River at a point where the stream is always polluted, but at this time particular attention was called to the polluted condition of the water supply by the washing of a quantity of carbolized paper at a mill on one of the tributaries of the stream.* The following circumstance is related with reference to the water supply of Cincinnati, Ohio.†

" The eddy of the Deer Creek Canal caused much pollution, which was brought to the attention of the consumers in a marked manner in 1867 by the burning of a large distillery on the canal. The whiskey found its way into the canal, thence into the river, and thence to the consumers."

Much depends, of course, upon the size of the stream into which the refuse is thrown. Thus, while into the Merrimack at

---

* Leeds : Journ. Amer. Chem. Soc., iii.
† Engineering News, 1881, p. 162.

Lowell, even during the summer, it would be necessary to throw more than one hundred tons of solid matter daily in order to increase the amount in the water by one grain to the gallon,* another and smaller stream might be hopelessly fouled by a single factory.

Ullik has made some interesting calculations with reference to the Elbe, in Bohemia, and shows that the entire product of the well-known sulphuric acid works at Aussig, if allowed to flow into the river, would increase the amount of sulphates by only one twenty-fourth, and that the mineral matter in the sewage from all of the 5,000,000 inhabitants of Bohemia would increase the mineral matter in the stream by only one twentieth.†

A question which we should be glad to have answered is this: To what extent must a polluted liquid be diluted in order to be safely used for domestic purposes? The answer, however, none can give. We do know this: it has been shown by actual experiment that the spores of some of the lower orders of vegetable organisms are very difficult to deprive of vitality; they may be frozen or heated to the boiling temperature, or they may be kept in a dry condition for years, and then, if placed in a favorable medium, become active and produce their kind. Admitting the presence of disease germs in a liquid, the liquid may be diluted until the chance of taking even a single germ into the system is so small that it may be disregarded; and yet, if the prevailing theory be true, a single germ, if taken, *might* produce disastrous results. It is easy to push the demands for purity to an absurd extent; all reasonable precautions should be taken to insure purity, but there is a point beyond which it is foolish to attempt to go. In the present state of our knowledge we should, however, err on the side of safety, and the mere fact that chemical analysis fails to detect impurity should not be accepted as a guaranty that a water is fit to drink.

Prevention of Pollution.

The pollution of streams can be prevented only by legal enactments. Cities and towns claim the right to discharge their

---

* Fifth Annual Report of the Mass. State Board of Health.
† Abh. d. math. wissenschf. Classe d. k. böhm. Ges., x.

sewage into a water-course on which they may be situated, and unless a nuisance is thereby created within their own boundaries, they are not likely, of their own motion, to do anything toward a different disposal of the sewage, as all other methods involve additional expense. Riparian owners, especially when they have located manufactories for the sake of the conveniences which the stream affords, will not, as a rule, adopt any method for disposing of their sewage or manufacturing refuse which involves expense, unless compelled to do so. Even where waste material may be utilized, so that the expense is met by a corresponding return, the *vis inertiæ* is so great that legal pressure is generally necessary to secure the adoption of plans which, in the end, may prove as advantageous to the manufacturer as to his previously injured neighbor.

The following is a very brief summary of the legal restrictions which exist in several European States:*

" In Prussia, though there are no special regulations for the inspection of factories in order to prevent the pollution of running waters, there are very simple means of interference in every separate case of pollution by manufacturing refuse. Thus, by the statute of July 1, 1861, most of the processes which are likely to pollute water require a special police license ; and by a statute passed as far back as 1843, no water applied to dyeing, tanning, fulling, or other similar purposes, is to be suffered to enter a river, if thereby the means of procuring clean water be endangered to the neighborhood ; and by a regulation dating from October 28, 1846, the owners of such works as impregnate the water used in any manufactory, with materials hurtful to meadow land, must, in accordance with the judgment and direction of the police authorities, precipitate their materials in subsidence ponds, or otherwise, under penalty of fine.

" In Belgium there are various local regulations, having the force of law, which impose a penalty upon those who pollute rivers, either by throwing in solid materials, which may impede the course of the stream, or by allowing liquid matter, which may foul or corrupt the water, to flow into it. Manufactories which produce such refuse are bound to construct reservoirs sufficiently large to contain a day's supply of this refuse, in order that suf-

* Rivers Pollution Commission. First Report 1870, p. 42.

ficient settlement may take place, and the supernatant liquid only
is allowed to be run off."

In France, several royal ordinances and decrees of the Council (1669, 1672, 1773, 1777, 1783), forbid the pollution of streams.
All of these ordinances and decrees, which still have the force of
law, prohibit, under penalty, casting into the Seine or into other
water-courses, "*aucunes ordures, immondices, gravois, pailles et
fumiers.*" The laws of December 22, 1789, and August 16–24,
1790, grant to departmental and municipal authorities power to
preserve the purity of streams, and to interpose if the waters
become a source of ill-health. A ministerial decision, dated July
24, 1875, reaffirms, in principle, the decrees of 1773 and 1777.*

That the laws, even of well-policed countries like Germany
and France, do not succeed in wholly accomplishing the object
desired, is evident from the present condition of certain streams,
notably of the Seine and Spree. In England, there were formerly
laws similar to those existing in France ; but the enormous development of the manufacturing industry in that country, and
the national sensitiveness as to the liberty of the subject, served,
in course of time, to render them all dead letters.

The Public Health Act, of 1848,† gave local authorities power
to build sewers and discharge them into streams wherever they
saw fit. Then began, on a large scale, the pollution of the rivers
of the country which has since become so great an evil. By the
Nuisances Removal Act, 1855, provision was first made for en-
joining individuals, towns and corporations against the pollution
of streams. To provide for the full carrying out of the requirements of the act, Section IX contains a clause that the local
authorities *shall* appoint or employ a sanitary inspector or in-
spectors. In 1858, local authorities were rendered liable to
injunction for polluting streams.

In the Sewage Utilization Act of 1865, we find this clause ;
"Nothing contained in this act or any other acts referred to
therein (*i. e.,* all the sanitary acts previously passed), shall authorize any sewer authority to make a sewer so as to drain direct into
any stream or water-course." By the same acts the powers of
sewer authorities were extended as to the pollution of streams.

* Schlœsing et Durand-Claye. Rapport.
† This sketch of English legislation is condensed from the Seventh Annual
Report of the Mass. State Board of Health.

Seventeen years had sufficed to reverse entirely the laws on the subject. In 1848, towns were urged to empty sewage freely into the most convenient water-courses.

The first Rivers Pollution Commission was appointed in 1865 ; the second was appointed in 1868, and their last report (the sixth), was printed in 1874. Largely as a result of the careful and comprehensive investigations of these commissions, and especially of the second one, there was passed, in 1876, a Rivers Pollution Prevention Act,* which was certainly a great step in advance, although the act is not satisfactory to sanitarians in all respects. The provisions of the act are, briefly, as follows : †

I. Prohibition as to casting solid matter (ashes, dead animals, etc.) into water-courses.

II. Prohibition as to casting sewage proper into water-courses. In case, however, of sewage discharged by channels in use or process of construction at the date of passage of the act, it will be sufficient to show that the best practicable and available means are used to render harmless the sewage so discharged, and the Local Government Board may allow to sanitary authorities time, in order to adopt such means.

III. (1) Prohibition as to casting poisonous, noxious, or polluting refuse from manufactories into water-courses, with the same provision as above with regard to channels already in use or in process of construction. Proceedings against manufactories can be taken only by consent of the Local Government Board, who must be satisfied that means for rendering the manufacturing refuse harmless are reasonably practicable and available, under all the circumstances of the case, and that no material injury will be inflicted upon the interests of the manufacturers.

(2) Restrictions as to solid matter from mines.

The following definition was formulated by the Rivers Pollution Commission (1868) of liquids which should be deemed polluting and inadmissible into any stream, but they have not been established by legal enactment.

(a) Any liquid which has not been subjected to perfect rest in subsidence ponds of sufficient size for a period of at least six hours, or which having been so subjected to subsidence, contains

---

* The text of this act may be found in the Eighth Annual Report of the Mass. State Board of Health, p. 73.

† Quoted from Ninth Annual Report of the Mass. State Board of Health.

in suspension more than one part by weight of dry organic matter in 100,000 parts by weight of the liquid, or which, not having been so subjected to subsidence, contains in suspension more than three parts by weight of dry mineral matter, or one part by weight of dry organic matter in 100,000 parts by weight of the liquid.

(*b*) Any liquid containing, in solution, more than two parts by weight of organic carbon or 0.3 part by weight of organic nitrogen in 100,000 parts by weight.

(*c*) Any liquid which shall exhibit by daylight a distinct color when a stratum of it one inch deep is placed in a white porcelain or earthenware vessel.

(*d*) Any liquid which contains in solution, in 100,000 parts by weight, more than two parts by weight of any metal except calcium, magnesium, potassium, and sodium.

(*e*) Any liquid which in 100,000 parts by weight contains, whether in solution or suspension, in chemical combination or otherwise, more than 0.05 part by weight of metallic arsenic.

(*f*) Any liquid which, after acidification with sulphuric acid, contains, in 100,000 parts by weight, more than one part by weight of free chlorine.

(*g*) Any liquid which contains, in 100,000 parts by weight, more than one part by weight of sulphur, in the condition either of sulphuretted hydrogen or of a soluble sulphuret.

(*h*) Any liquid possessing an acidity greater than that which is produced by adding two parts by weight of real muriatic acid to 1,000 parts by weight of distilled water.

(*i*) Any liquid possessing an alkalinity greater than that which is produced by adding one part by weight of dry caustic soda to 1,000 parts by weight of distilled water.

(*k*) Any liquid exhibiting a film of petroleum or hydrocarbon oil upon its surface, or containing in suspension, in 100,000 parts, more than 0.05 part of such oil.

To these standards was attached the proviso, that " no effluent water shall be deemed polluting if it be not more contaminated with any of the above-named polluting ingredients than the stream or river into which it is discharged."

In this country comparatively little has been done in the way of legislation from a sanitary point of view, as the polluted streams are still few in number, and the necessity for legislation has not become pressing. In some States there are general laws against the obstruction and pollution of water-courses, or special provision for securing, to a certain extent, the purity of streams or other waters actually used as sources of supply.

In the District of Columbia there is a law of the United States (1859), which provides penalty for committing any act by reason of which the supply of water to the cities of Washington and Georgetown becomes impure, filthy, or unfit for use. In Iowa, by an act of 1864, it is punishable by fine or imprisonment to throw any dead animal into any river, well, spring, cistern, reservoir, stream, or pond. In Michigan, an act of 1865 prohibits the putting of offal, etc., into waters where fish are taken. In Nebraska, by act of 1873, there are penalties for putting carcasses or other filthy substances into well, spring, brook, or any running water of which use is made for domestic purposes; the corrupting of any water-course is declared to be a nuisance.

In Tennessee, by act of 1866-7, rendering water unwholesome is declared a nuisance. In Vermont, by act of 1852, a penalty was enacted against any one putting any dead animal or animal substance into rivers, ponds, springs, etc. In Wisconsin there are laws providing against the erection of slaughterhouses on the banks of any river, stream or creek, or throwing any carcass or offal therefrom in or upon the bank of any such river, etc. In Texas, by act of 1860, polluting or obstructing any water-course, lake, pond, marsh, or common sewer, or continuing such obstruction or pollution, so as to render the same unwholesome or offensive to the county, city, town, or neighborhood thereabouts, or doing any other act or thing that would be deemed and held a nuisance at common law, is made a misdemeanor.*

The Texas law, just alluded to, indicates very well what is generally the character and effect of legislation on this subject. If any person or corporation pollutes a stream in such a way that the result would be held a nuisance at common law, or if the pollution is so great that it can be absolutely proved that water, which is taken for domestic use, has become " impure,

---

* These facts are gathered from " A Digest of American Sanitary Law, by Henry G. Pickering, Esq.," in Dr. Bowditch's Public Hygiene in America. Boston, 1877.

filthy, or unfit for use," it is, under such circumstances, possible in some cases to obtain an injunction against the offending parties. But to absolutely prove that a water is impure, filthy or unfit to use, is difficult unless one can present in court the body of some person who has died by the use of the water; and, according to certain decisions which have been made, it would seem that nothing short of this will suffice. In several States a local or a State Board of Health has some powers in these matters, but they are mostly nominal and rendered of no avail by rights of appeal. A great deal of attention has been given to the pollution of streams in the State of Massachusetts, and the two following sections from chap. 183 of the Acts of 1878 would seem sufficiently explicit :

"Section 1. No person or persons, or corporation, public or private, shall discharge directly, or cause to be discharged directly, human excrement into any pond in this Commonwealth used as a source of water supply by any city or town therein, or upon whose banks any filter-basin so used is situated, or into any river or stream so used, or upon whose banks such filter-basin is situated, within twenty miles above the point where such supply is taken, or into feeders of such ponds, river or stream within such twenty miles.

"Section 2. No person or persons, or corporation, public or private, shall discharge, or cause to be discharged, into any pond in this Commonwealth used as a source of water supply by any city or town therein, or upon whose banks any filter-basin so used is situated, or into any river or stream so used, or upon whose banks such filter-basin is situated, within twenty miles above the point where such supply is taken, or into any feeders of such pond, river, or stream within such twenty miles, any sewage, drainage, refuse, or polluting matter of such quality and amount, as *either by itself, or in connection with other such matter,* shall corrupt or *impair* the quality of the water for domestic use, or render it deleterious to health." *

It would seem that these provisions would give all necessary security, but two practical difficulties occur. Section 3 reads as follows :

"The prohibitions contained in the two previous sections shall not be construed to destroy or impair rights already ac-

---

* The italics are the author's.

quired by legislative grants, or to destroy or impair prescriptive
rights of drainage or discharge, to the extent to which they
lawfully exist at the date of the passage of this act : And nothing
in this act contained shall be construed to authorize the pollution of any waters in this Commonwealth in any manner now
contrary to law.

"This act shall not be applicable to the Merrimack or Connecticut rivers, nor to so much of the Concord River as lies
within the limits of the city of Lowell."

The deciding whether a prescriptive right exists is not always
easy, but the chief difficulty lies in the fact that while the State
Board of Health is given the power to issue orders "to cease
and desist," the parties have a right of appeal to jury. This
jeopardizes the whole matter at once, and, as the pollution
often takes place in one county to the detriment or supposed
detriment of water-users in another county, the jury are apt to
be influenced by local interests.

While it must be confessed that the present state of legislation is unsatisfactory, it must be admitted that it is practically
impossible absolutely to prevent the pollution of streams, and it
will probably always be necessary that certain streams should
serve as carriers of refuse. At the same time, the amount of
pollution should be kept within bounds, so that the water,
although it may not be fit or safe for domestic use, shall not be
an actual nuisance; while some streams are thus devoted to viler
uses, those which are reserved for purposes of water supply
should be guarded with all possible care. It is evident that
nothing is more unphilosophical than that one town should be
allowed to discharge its sewage into a water-course which is the
most available source of water supply for a town lower down on
the stream. Each river basin should be under the control of
some central authority by which conflicting interests should be
harmonized. An accurate survey should be made of the whole
area, and no town should be allowed to introduce a water supply without due consideration being given to the future of the
supply, and to the question of disposing of the sewage of the
town supplied. Moreover, while sanitary considerations are of
the highest importance, manufacturing interests must also be
considered, and no undue burden laid upon legitimate industries.

CHAPTER V.

Animal and Vegetable Life.

No surface water is free from various forms of animal and vegetable life; it is seldom, however, that any trouble arises from this cause when the water is taken directly from running streams. On the other hand, the water in lakes and ponds and in storage reservoirs is extremely liable to be disagreeably affected by the growth and decay of animal and more especially of vegetable organisms.

Animals.—The presence of fish in a source of supply is an advantage rather than otherwise. As far as known, any trouble arising from their presence is quite temporary and accidental. The sudden discharge into a stream of material injurious in itself, or which, by using up the oxygen of the water, makes it impossible for the fish to breathe, may cause their destruction in large numbers. Occasional epidemics, in some cases due to fungous growths, may affect large numbers of fish at the same time. In such cases, the sources of supply must be watched and the dead fishes removed as thoroughly and as rapidly as possible.

Among the smaller forms of animal life we have the so-called water-fleas, of which the *Daphnia pulex* (Fig. 6) and the *Cyclops quadricornis* (Fig. 7) are familiar examples. These or other similar animalcules swarm in many surface waters at certain seasons of the year, and occur more or less abundantly in all pond and river waters. They no doubt, to a certain extent, tend to purify the water by removing objectionable substances, and are in turn devoured by other animals.

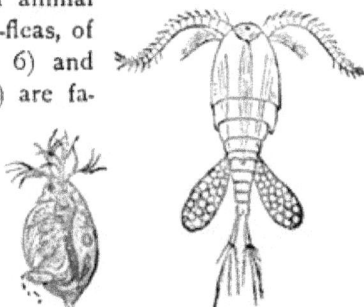

FIG. 6.—*Daphnia pulex.* FIG. 7.—*Cyclops quadricornis.*

They are easily removed by the simplest sort of filtration, but there is no probability that they are unwholesome if taken with the water. These minute crustaceans secrete an oily substance under their shells (carapaces) which some have held to be the cause of certain bad tastes which have affected water supplies, but it is extremely doubtful if this is a correct explanation of the trouble. It may be said, however, that a fishy odor has been frequently noticed on the Lake of Geneva, very perceptible to the passengers on the passing steamboats, occasionally over the entire lake. This odor is ascribed by Dr. F. A. Forel* to an unusual mortality—from some unknown cause—among the entomostraca which swarm in the lake, and which usually by day descend to a depth of 5, 10, or 20 meters, rising to the surface at night. It is possible that some of the temporary bad tastes in surface waters may be due to a similar cause.

In 1881, a portion of the water supply of Boston, Mass., was in a very bad condition. The water contained an unusual amount of organic matter and possessed a very disagreeable odor and taste. This bad condition of the water was found by Professor Remsen,† to be mainly due to the presence in one of the reservoirs of a large quantity of a *Spongilla*, or fresh-water sponge, in a more or less decayed condition. Several species of the fresh-water sponge occur in ponds and streams, and they are found even in the masonry conduits to a limited distance from the source of supply. The following cut will give a fair idea of the general appearance of the *Spongilla fluviatilis*, although the details are somewhat unsatisfactory. The sponge belongs to the animal kingdom, and the animal substance is distributed over a network of spicules. No. 2 in the figure attempts to show some of the "winter buds," or bodies by which the animal is propagated, held in a mass of spicules; No. 3 is a portion of the same enlarged. The sponge is harsh to the touch, and with a good lens something of its structure may be made out ; for confirmation, however, it is well to burn off a little on a fragment of mica, moisten with water (or better, with acid, muriatic acid or dilute *aqua fortis*) and examine with a good lens

---

* Private communication.

† Report of the Joint Standing Committee on the Impurity of the Water Supply. Boston City Document, No. 143, 1881.

or a low-power microscope (say from 50 to 100 diameters) for the spicules. The larger spicules, which are observed by examining with a low power the sponge of the Boston water supply, appear as in Fig. 9 (drawn with a power of about 150 diameters). Other spicules are covered with short spines, and the so-called winter-buds, by which the sponge is propagated, are furnished with minute spicules which are, in certain species, very characteristic : thus in *S. fluviatilis* they are *birotulate*, as shown in Fig. 10, *a*. Some of the smaller spicules of the sponge which occurs in the Boston water are shown in Fig. 10, *b* and *c*. Fig. 10 was drawn with a power of about 260 diameters.

Although the sponges have caused trouble in Boston and perhaps elsewhere, the fact that they exist in a water supply need not necessarily awaken apprehension. They probably exist in nearly all surface waters, and the spicules are among the common objects found by a microscopic examination of the sediment in natural waters.* According to Dr. R. D. Thompson, the

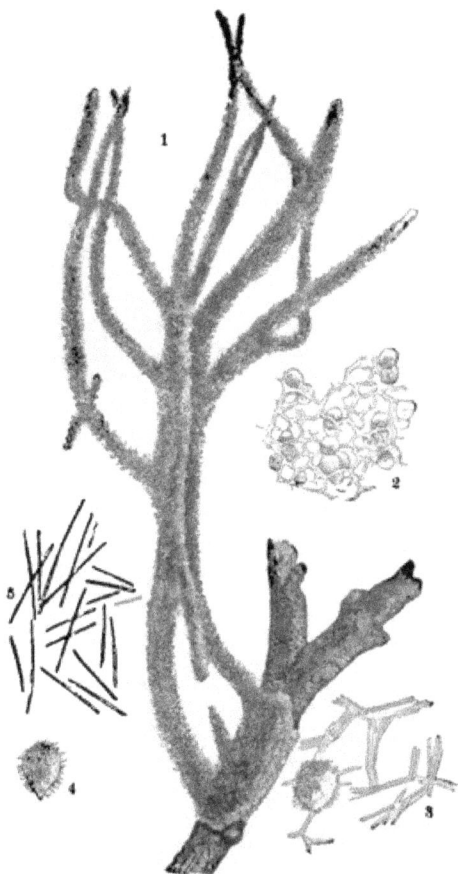

FIG. 8.—*Spongilla fluviatilis.*

---

* See for example, the plates in Hassall's Microscopical Examination of the Water supplied to the Inhabitants of London and the Suburban Districts. London, 1851. Also, Neuville, Des Eaux de Paris. Paris, 1880.

6

dried *Spongilla fluviatilis* contains 26 per cent of organic matter. This organic matter is highly nitrogenous, although no particular analyses seem to have been made of the fresh water sponges. The tissue-substance of salt water sponges—fibroin (Mulder) or spongin (Städeler)— has the following composition :

FIG 9.—*Sponge spicules.*

	Posselt.	Crookewit.
Carbon....	48.75	47.16
Hydrogen .	6.35	6.31
Nitrogen ..	16.40	16.15
Oxygen ...	28.50	26.90
Iodine	....	1.08
Sulphur ...	....	0.50
Phosphorus	....	1.90
	100.00	100.00

Among the other forms of animal life which may be here mentioned, is the *Hydra*, which is common enough in ponds, adhering to aquatic plants. The body is narrow and elongated; it is generally attached by the base to some plant or other solid object while the other extremity of the body is furnished with long slender arms or tentacles, which move about in search of the animalcules on which it feeds. It may be worth while to mention the fact that in a conduit where a gate-house admits access to the interior, the author has seen the rapidly flow-

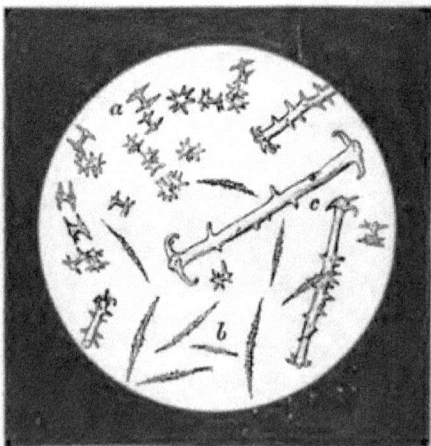

FIG. 10.—*Sponge spicules.*

ing water swarming with these creatures, so that, in dipping up a single glass of water, a dozen or twenty of the hydras would be taken at the same time. On the bottom and sides of the conduit were, no doubt, hundreds of thousands of the little animals, but no recognizable effect was produced on the water by their presence or by their death and decay, which must have followed.

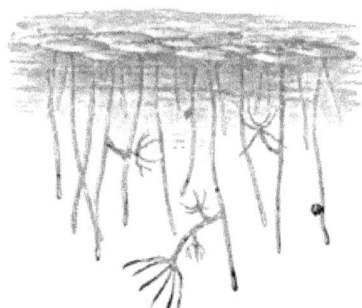

FIG. 11.—*Hydra viridis.*

Of course there are many other animal inhabitants of fresh waters, and when we descend to microscopic organisms we have a very great variety of forms. The term *Infusoria* is often used to cover all these minute animal organisms, which are grouped under orders and families and genera and species like the higher animals. Scarcely any natural water is free from these infusoria, and some of them are peculiar to impure waters, but, as they can be recognized and studied only under the microscope by those familiar with such matters, we need not dwell upon them here.

Plants.—Generally speaking, the flowering aquatic plants, such as are known as eel-grass, pond-weed, pickerel-weed, etc., are in themselves of no disadvantage, while growing, to the pond or reservoir in which they grow ; they are, indeed, of positive advantage, in oxygenating, and so, to a certain extent, purifying the water. If such plants, or portions of them, decay in a limited volume of water they produce a very offensive smell and taste. This is, in general, true of plants aquatic and non-aquatic. It is well known that the water in which flax is "retted" becomes very offensive.* In some experiments made by the author a few years ago, the worst smell obtained was from the seed-

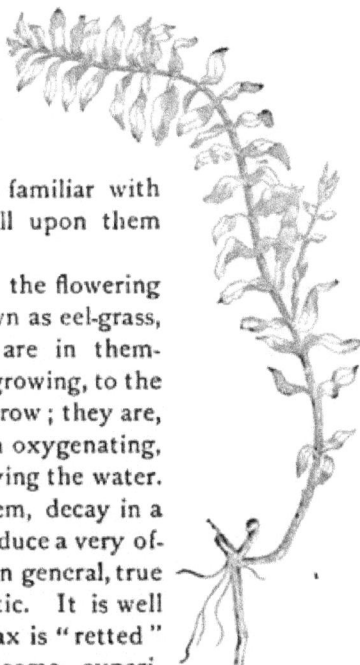

FIG. 12.—Pond-weed (*Potamogeton*).

---

* In this connection see Reichardt, E., "Schädliche Wirkung des Rostwassers von Flachs und Hanf für die Fischzucht." Arch. d. Pharm., ccxix, Heft 1, 1881.

bearing portions of a species of *Potamogeton* (a common water plant), and Professor Brewer, who has made much more extensive experiments, obtained a very *fishy* odor from the decay in water of the leaf-stalks of a pickerel-weed, *Pontederia cordata*, which grows on the margins of the pond from which New Haven receives its supply (Whitney Lake).

While the odors and tastes obtained from different plants differ from each other, in a stream or pond where the volume of water is comparatively large and the opportunity for aeration is great, the various tastes seem to *blend* into a more or less marked marshy or pondy flavor. Sometimes, even in large bodies of water, a distinctive taste is noticed; thus, in the fall of the year, the water of our ponds and lakes which are surrounded by woods acquires more of a bitter or astringent taste, which is to be referred to the dead leaves at that season most abundant.

A word or two may be in place with reference to the action of fresh water upon vegetable matter in its bearing upon impounding reservoirs. When vegetable matter decays in moist soil, it is converted into a brown or black substance generally known as *humus;* this is really a mixture of a number of different bodies, and from it chemists have isolated a variety of substances, such as humic acid and humin, ulmic acid and ulmin.* The acids of the humus, by oxidation, undergo chemical change, to be sure, being converted into crenic and apocrenic acids, which, or rather the salts of which, are found in surface waters; but when the vegetable matter is thoroughly "humified," as in the case of peat, it exerts apparently no bad effect on the water, except by giving it a brown color and a somewhat earthy taste.

When a recently felled tree is exposed to the action of the water, or when bushes or even grass and weeds are killed by being flooded with water, the sap and more soluble matters are leached out and putrefy, or, in the presence of much air, undergo other forms of decomposition. This action will take place, no matter under what depth of water the vegetable matter may be placed, but the effect will be less marked as the amount and motion of the water is greater.

---

* For a résumé of the investigations on the composition of humus, see Julien: Proc. Amer. Assoc., xxviii (1879), p. 313 and foll.

After the more soluble portions are extracted, the subsequent decay proceeds with extreme slowness, provided the remaining cellulose or woody fiber is kept continually covered with water, but alternate exposure to air and water soon causes decay, as every one knows. In a natural or artificial reservoir the inevitable variations of level are very disadvantageous. As the level is lowered, those aquatic plants which grow in shallow water die, and if the water rises after only a short interval it becomes impregnated with the products of their decay; if a considerable interval elapses, land plants grow upon the exposed surface, and, being drowned by the rising waters, tend to its contamination in the same manner.

It appears from this, that in the construction of impounding reservoirs, the mass of growing plants, as well as the soil in which they have their roots, and which of itself contains more or less soluble organic matter, should be removed as thoroughly as possible, especially if the water is to be of no great depth above it when the reservoir is flooded. If the reservoir is filled without such removal of the organic accumulations, a long time may may be required before the chemical changes have completed themselves and the water become well suited for use, but the complete removal of the soil, that is, as far as such removal is practicable, is not a guaranty that no trouble will arise from a newly filled reservoir. Occasionally the vegetable decay in a new reservoir gives rise to much offence from the formation of sulphuretted hydrogen. A marked instance of this occurred in one of the basins of the Sudbury River supply, Boston, Mass., the summer after it was first filled. The whole mass of water in the basin was permeated with the odor, which was so strong on the leeward side of the pond as to incommode the passers-by. The odor was not that of pure sulphuretted hydrogen as prepared in the laboratory, and the gas was no doubt accompanied by other chemical products. The water drawn from the depths of the pond had the odor of an antiquated privy. The presence of sulphuretted hydrogen was made very manifest by suspending in the gate-house cloths wet with a solution of acetate of lead; these became yellowish-red, and finally jet black, owing to the formation of sulphide of lead.

The formation of the sulphuretted hydrogen is readily explained. The flooding of the basin started the decay of a large

quantity of organic matter; this taking place in the presence of
the sulph*ates* contained in the water changed them into sulph-
ides, and from these sulphides thus formed sulphuretted hydrogen
is liberated by the acid products of decay. This same change
takes place to a less degree in almost all ponds and reservoirs.
The gas is formed, however, mainly at the bottom, and as it dif-
fuses upwards and mixes with the overlying water it comes into
contact with the oxygen in the water and is decomposed. The
sulphur is set free and sinks to the bottom, or in a very finely
divided state flows off with the water. In salt or brackish water
which receives sewage, these changes take place on a much
greater scale. A while ago the author had occasion to examine
a number of samples of mud from the lower part of the Charles
River, a tidal stream which receives a portion of the sewage of
Boston, Mass. In all cases sulphur in considerable quantity
could be extracted from the mud by the use of proper solvents.[*]

The plants which give the most trouble in connection with
water supplies belong to the class of cryptogamous (non-flower-
ing) plants which the botanists call *algæ*—plants which grow in the
water, or in moist places, and usually contain chlorophyll (green

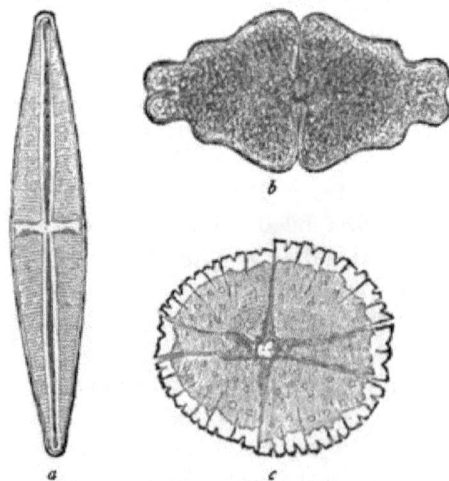

coloring matter) or some
allied substance. Not
all algæ are, however,
harmful. The so-called
confervoid growths are
made up of plants of fila-
mentous structure, grass-
green, or in some cases
bluish-green in color,
forming tangled masses
readily removed from
the water, and, when so
removed, shrinking enor-
mously in apparent bulk,
and drying away to a
grayish or colorless mass,
in some cases looking al-
most like coarse paper.

FIG. 13.—*a*, Diatom (*Stauroneis*); *b*, Desmid
(*Euastrum*); *c*, Desmid (*Micrasterias*).

* Eighth Annual Report Boston City Board of Health. (1879-80), pp. 12-18.

Plants of this character grow in almost all reservoirs or other bodies of water exposed to the light and air, both in still and running water; they either float about in masses, or are attached more or less firmly to rocks and stones and other solid objects. By their growth they do no harm to the water in which they flourish; and as they are readily arrested by ordinary wire screens, or easily removed by rakes or scoop-nets, their presence causes no serious inconvenience in water used for town supply.

Then there are the diatoms and desmids (Fig. 13), which are interesting objects under the microscope, and occur in considerable abundance and great variety; they are not, however, as far as we know, of any significance in surface waters, at least, from a sanitary point of view.

The vegetable organisms which cause the most trouble and inconvenience are those which appear as greenish specks, or minute straight or curved threads, diffused through the water— visible enough if a large quantity of water be looked at, but perhaps almost escaping notice in the small quantity which would be taken up in a single glass. It is true that the individual plants are in some cases distinguishable by the naked eye; but their form and structure can be made out only by use of the microscope. If collected together as a scum, which often happens, especially on the windward shore of a pond, the scum is not coherent, is easily broken up, either by a wind setting in the opposite direction, by a shower of rain, or by artificial agitation. The appearance has been sometimes described as that of meal or of fine dust scattered through the water. The number of individuals is almost infinite; and under favorable conditions they increase with great rapidity. Their presence gives a decidedly green or greenish yellow tinge to large bodies of water; and their death and decay often cause considerable offence to the sense of smell of those sojourning in the neighborhood, and to the sense of taste of those obliged to drink the water. The troublesome species belong, almost all, to the family of *Nostocs*, and of these the number which have been known to produce difficulty is small; this may, of course, be due in part to imperfect observation. A single species each of *Cœlosphærium* and *Clathrocystis*, two or more of *Anabæna* and one of *Sphærozyga* have been observed in considerable quantities in the neighborhood of Boston, Mass.

Fig. 14, *c* gives a general idea of the appearance of the *Cla-throcystis æruginosa* when magnified some 300 diameters. This plant is often found in much larger masses than indicated in the

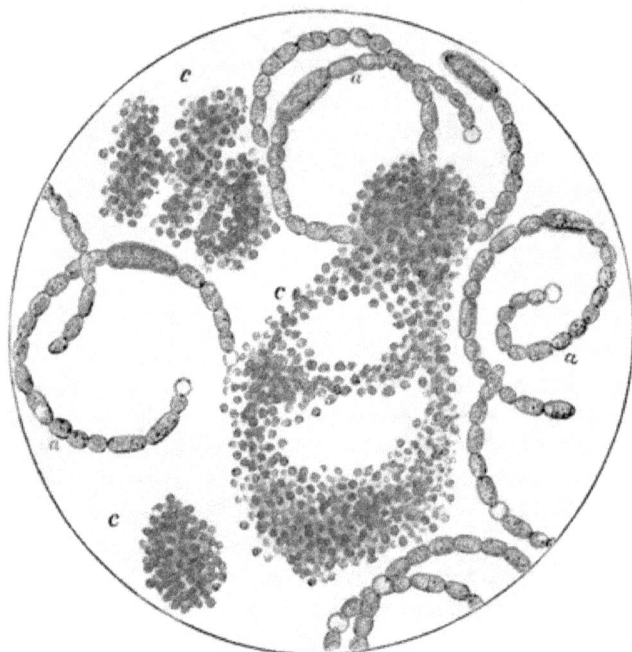

FIG. 14.

cut; in fact, the little sack-like masses are sometimes large enough to be made out by the unaided eye, although no idea of the structure can be thus obtained. Fig. 14, *a* attempts to give an idea of the *Anabœna circinalis*, one of the *Nostochineæ;* this plant occurs very frequently in ponds and in sluggish streams. Another common variety of the same genus is similar, except that the filaments are straight instead of curved; and there are other genera of *algæ* which occur in the same way as the *Ana-bœna*, and present a similar appearance.

These algæ, when present in any considerable quantity, give a repulsive appearance to the water, and when they are in a state of decay they communicate to it an offensive taste and odor. Fortunately, in most cases, the trouble which they cause is of short duration, although often recurring in the same water supply year after year. Their presence is not a sign of contamination, as they occur in natural ponds removed from all polluting influences. While, however, they do grow in pure waters and in old and clean ponds, they seem to grow more abundantly in water containing mud and vegetable extractive matter, as in newly filled reservoirs; so that, while immunity from their presence cannot be guaranteed in the case of any pond, they may with some certainty be looked for in dirty and especially in shallow ponds. A warm temperature and shallow water are perhaps of even more importance than the products of decay of higher plants, for all surface waters contain the ammoniacal and mineral salts necessary for the growth of the algæ.

Whether the presence of these minute algæ gives an unwholesome character to a water which is otherwise suited for domestic use, is an open question; but such information as the author has been able to get from various sources coincides with the statement of the Mass. State Board of Health, who investigated the matter when a certain portion of the water supply of Boston was affected in this way. They say * that the evidence "tends to show that the plant acts mechanically chiefly, perhaps like unripe fruit, when affecting the health at all, in causing diarrhœa; but that the filtered water is harmless." It is known that fish often die in ponds containing an abundance of the scum-forming algæ, probably on account of the cutting off of the supply of air; there is also one case on record where cattle have been killed by drinking pond water which contained large quantities of a species of *Nodularia*, a plant which has something of a resemblance to the *Anabæna*.† This was in Australia. No such cases have come to the knowledge of the writer here. When the algæ are alive and fresh, horses and cattle drink the water readily, in preference to spring water: when decay takes place, the water sometimes becomes so offensive that they refuse to drink it. In this condition it is manifestly unsuited for domestic use.

As far as our present knowledge extends, there is nothing that can be done to exterminate the algæ from ponds in which they occur. Sometimes in reservoirs, when the algæ have collected as a scum, it is possible to float them off from the surface

* First Annual Report of the State Board of Health, Lunacy and Charity, 1879. Supplement, p. xi.

† Nature, xviii (1878), p. 11.

by means of properly arranged waste pipes, and in reservoirs the
conditions favorable for their collection and decay may be removed by grubbing up the lilies and other pond-weeds around the
borders. Special devices sometimes avail in special cases. The
experience at Poughkeepsie, N. Y., is instructive. Here the
Hudson River water was pumped on to filter-beds, thence, after
filtration, into a small uncovered reservoir. In summer, after the
temperature of the water reached 70° F., an alga, one of the
oscillariaceæ, developed in the shallow water on the beds and in
the reservoir, and by its death and decay in the pipes caused much
trouble. The trouble occurred every summer, until the following
method of procedure was adopted by Mr. Thc. W. Davis, the
then superintendent. As soon as the temperature of the river
water approached 70°, careful watch was kept on the temperature
and on the quality of the water delivered. As soon as the taste
or odor was noticed in the city, the reservoir was shut off and
the water pumped directly from the river into the mains. In
this way all trouble was avoided and there were no complaints.

With reference to the minute organisms, animal and vegetable,
it is a curious fact that certain forms will sometimes suddenly
appear in places where for years previous they have never been
known to occur, and they may disappear as suddenly as they
came. In other cases, forms which have been known to be present to a limited extent will increase enormously, owing to conditions of which we are quite ignorant.

Odors and Tastes of Surface Waters.

Surface waters often possess peculiar odors and tastes. These
are sometimes explicable, as in the case of the odor of sulphuretted hydrogen referred to on page 85. Then there are other
odors (with accompanying tastes), which are quite certainly due
to the algæ. These odors are quite various. Mr. Fteley (Sudbury River) speaks of a *musty* odor ; at Albany it was spoken of
as a *musty* and *cucumber* odor ; at Springfield (Ludlow Reservoir),
the first summer after the reservoir was filled there was a most
distinct odor of *green corn*, perceptible for a quarter of a mile
from the pond on the leeward side. The pond was covered with
a slime of algæ, partially decayed ; and the same marked odor
was noticed at the water troughs along the line of the aqueduct.

When, under the excessive heat of summer, the algæ are collected in masses and begin to decay, a most abominable *pig-pen* or *horse-pond* odor is sometimes noticed in the ponds; but this is seldom noticed in the water drawn from the service pipes, although a foul odor similar to that common in "dead-ends" does occur when water containing the algæ stagnates in the pipes.

Besides the tastes and odors which may with reasonable certainty be ascribed to the growth or decay of organized beings, there have been certain conditions of the water in the case of many water supplies which are very enigmatical, and for which no satisfactory explanation has been offered. The so-called " cucumber " taste, and the other tastes characterized as " fishy " or " oily," occur when the water is of its ordinary purity and in waters naturally pure. Some have maintained that the tastes ought to be due to the presence or to some peculiar condition of the algæ, but as it is impossible to discover any unusual amount or condition of those algæ, which are, so far as we know, harmless, and which are always present, and as none of those algæ which are known to produce bad tastes and odors are found, it is rather difficult to accept this explanation. Since Professor Remsen has found reason to believe that the recent condition of the water in Farm Pond is due in part, at any rate, to the decay of a sponge, it has been suggested that we have here the cause of the various difficulties heretofore unexplained. While it seems to be undoubtedly true that the sponge may, under certain circumstances, produce what is properly spoken of as a " cucumber " taste, there are many cases on record where it is difficult to believe that this can be the cause ; and with reference to such cases, for the present, we can only say, " We do not know."

Temperature of Surface Waters.

One of the great disadvantages to which surface water is subject is the variation in temperature. The water in winter is but a few degrees above the freezing point, and in summer the temperature is so high that the water is not agreeable as a beverage unless artificially cooled. The use of ice is so general in the United States that much less stress is laid upon this point than in other countries, but, of course, a considerable proportion of the inhabitants in the thickly settled parts of our cities are unable to

supply themselves regularly with ice. Of late years iced water
has been supplied at several public fountains in New York, and
perhaps in other cities. It would be difficult to isolate the effect
of the temperature of the water on the public health from the
general effect of the hot weather, of eating unripe and decayed
fruit, and of other causes, all of which affect particularly the
poorer class of the population. In England, the increased death-
rate of the warmer months has been connected directly with the
temperature of the water supply. Thus, in the report of the
Registrar General for July 22, 1878, we find:

"The high mortality of the week is due to diarrhœa, which
becomes fatal in London when the temperature of the Thames
rises above 60° F. Thus the Thames temperature, which had
been 60°, rose in the last week of June to 65°; in the following
weeks it was 68°, 66°, 67° F. The weekly deaths from diarrhœa
and simple cholera, which had been 23, rose to 78, 156, 256, 349
in corresponding weeks." To show that this increase was not
due simply to the increased atmospheric temperature and its
attendant discomforts, it is stated that "the deaths from diarrhœa are differently distributed in the fields of the water companies; thus the deaths in the last four weeks were 786 in the
districts supplied by the Thames and Lea waters, whereas the
deaths in the districts supplied with water drawn from the chalk
by the Kent company were 19; out of the same population, the
deaths in the former were to the deaths in the latter as 3 to 1."
The temperature of the Kent company's water at the wells was
uniformly 52° F.; at the same time it must be noted that the
waters differed not simply with respect to temperature. The
water of the Kent company is harder, and, what is perhaps more
important, it contains but little organic matter.

Baldwin Latham, while believing that "the summer diarrhœa
is governed by the influence of the temperature of our water
supply, as invariably the disease becomes epidemic when the
water, whatever be its source of supply, reaches a temperature
of 62° F. (16°.7 C.)," attempts to show that the temperature of
the water delivered to the consumers is much less dependent
upon the original temperature at the source than is usually supposed, and that if the water is carried for any considerable distance in the mains, it approaches or acquires the temperature of
the ground in which the pipes are laid, as appears from the

following table.* Here the Kent water, alluded to as having a uniform temperature at its source, appears, when delivered, as variable as the water of the Thames. He asserts† that the general mortality in London from diarrhœa is practically the same in the districts supplied from the rivers as in those supplied by the Kent Water Company, but that the water in the latter region does not reach its highest temperature until later in the season, owing to the advantage which the lower initial tempera-

TABLE X.—TEMPERATURE OF LONDON WATER SUPPLIES.

[The degrees are Centigrade.]

DATE.	KENT COMPANY'S WATER.		THAMES WATER IN THE MAINS.	THE GROUND AT A DEPTH OF METERS	
	In the wells.	In the mains.		0.838.	1.448.
July, 1873......	10.59	16.80	18.39	17.66	15.47
August, ...	10.67	16.62	17.70	17.16	16.05
September, ...	10.71	14.78	14.92	15.28	15.04
October, ...	10.68	12.90	12.87	12.53	13.05
November, ...	10.61	8.17	7.47	6.98	9.04
December, ...	10.50	5.98	5.14	3.72	6.12
January, 1879......	10.45	5.06	4.77	2.80	4.68
February, ...	10.40	5.45	5.72	3.58	4.66
March, ...	10.35	6.30	7.20	4.97	5.54
April, ...	10.44	8.38	8.20	6.80	6.85
May, ...	10.42	9.36	10.20	7.32	8.31
June, ...	10.57	12.63	14.25	13.01	11.23

ture gives to it. It will be understood that Latham's figures have reference to the temperature acquired in the service pipes;‡ the water passing through the main conduit or even through the large iron mains suffers much less change of temperature than Table X would indicate.§ Latham has patented an apparatus for "tempering" the water, which consists "of a vertical tube driven or screwed into the ground to a depth of about 25 feet, the water being admitted at the top and withdrawn at the bottom, and special arrangements being adopted for the protection of the ascending pipe." With such an apparatus interposed in the service connection of the house, "the range of temperature in

---

* Quoted from Journal für Gasbeleuchtung und Wasserversorgung, xxii (1879), p. 756.

† Journal of Society of Arts, Sept. 17, 1880.

‡ The temperatures given in the reports of Dr. Frankland to the Registrar General were taken in the company's mains at Deptford, near the source of the water.

§ This matter is discussed at length and mathematically by Perissini: Journ. für Gasb. und Wasserv., xxiii (1880), pp. 608 and 644.

the water required for dietetic purposes need not exceed 3° F. throughout the year, when drawn from a 3-inch tube at a rate not exceeding one gallon every half-hour."

The question of temperature is an important one in bodies of stored water, as the troublesome algæ already alluded to seem to require a somewhat elevated temperature (approaching 70° F.) for their rapid and abundant development; when collected as a scum they are killed and enter into decay when the water becomes strongly heated in midsummer. While it is, of course, impracticable to cover ponds and impounding reservoirs, it is of advantage to cover the smaller storage reservoirs which are frequently used in connection with water-works to contain a reserve supply, or a supply for a limited number of days, and thus to prevent, to a certain extent, the elevation of temperature to which

TABLE XI.—Observations of Temperature in Fresh Pond, Mass.*

Date.	Temperature (expressed in Centigrade degrees) at		
	Two feet from surface.	Eighteen feet from surface.	Thirty-five feet more or less from surface.
	°	°	°
May 4, 1878	16.5	12.5	8.5
" 14,	14.5	14.5	8.5
June 4,	19.	16.5	8.8
" 12,	17.3	16.8	8.6
" 19,	20.5	16.8	8.7
" 25,	22.2	16.6	9.2
July 2,	28.0	16.7	9.3
" 9,	26.0	15.4	9.2
" 16,	25.3	16.8	9.6
" 23,	24.0	16.8	9.9
August 6,	24.0	17.3	10.1
" 13,	24.0	20.1	10.0
" 20,	24.0	20.0	10.2
" 27,	22.3	20.0	10.0
November 7,	9.5	9.2	8.7
December 7,	4.5	4.3	4.5
January 2, 1879	0.5	1.0	1.0
" 14,	0.7	1.3	1.7
" 22,	0.9	2.0	1.8
April 14,	6.0	5.0	4.4
May 13,	18.5	13.0	8.3

* First Annual Report of Mass. State Board of Health, Lunacy and Charity, 1880. Supplement, p. 98.

a small and comparatively shallow body of water is subject under a summer's sun.

Table XI shows the variation in temperature of the surface water in a pond near Boston, Mass. (lat. about 42°), which is used as a source of city supply; and also the variation at different depths.

For making observations on the temperatures of bodies of water, especially below the surface, thermometer makers supply instruments surrounded by a copper tube in which some of the water is brought to the surface. Where samples for analysis are taken at the same time, a chemical thermometer may be inserted in the bottle used for the collection of the water. The bottle having been sunk to the required depth, the stopper is withdrawn, and after the bottle has filled it is allowed to remain until it is certain that the whole apparatus has acquired the actual temperature of the water. It is then drawn up and the reading of the thermometer is taken quickly while still surrounded by water. This method answers very well, with care, up to depths of 80 feet.

A very convenient instrument for taking temperature at various depths is the " New Standard Deep Sea Thermometer," made by Negretti and Zambra, London. The construction of the thermometer is shown in Fig. 15, c. To protect it against pressure, this thermometer is inclosed in a glass tube, hermetically sealed, the portion which surrounds the thermometer bulb being filled with mercury. The object of the mercury is to furnish a good conductor of heat between the outer wall and the thermometer bulb, and it is confined in place by a partition cemented on to the neck of the bulb. The whole apparatus is inserted into a hollow wooden frame containing a quantity of lead shot. When the thermometer is lowered to any depth, it descends as shown in Fig. 15, a, and the bulb of the thermometer is downward; it is allowed to remain at the required depth for a few minutes in order that the thermometer may acquire the temperature of the place, the mercury rising or falling in the capillary tube as in an ordinary thermometer. Finally, a sudden pull is made on the line, and the instrument, owing to the resistance of the water and the consequent displacement of the center of gravity (the shot falling to the other end of the frame), will turn over and be drawn upward with the thermometer in the position shown in Fig. 15, *b*.   When the thermometer is inverted, the mercury column breaks at the constriction *A*, and falls to the other end of the tube, from which the degrees are read off, as shown in the figure, with the bulb of the thermometer upper-most.

As with any thermometer, it is necessary to determine the

DESCENDING.   ASCENDING.

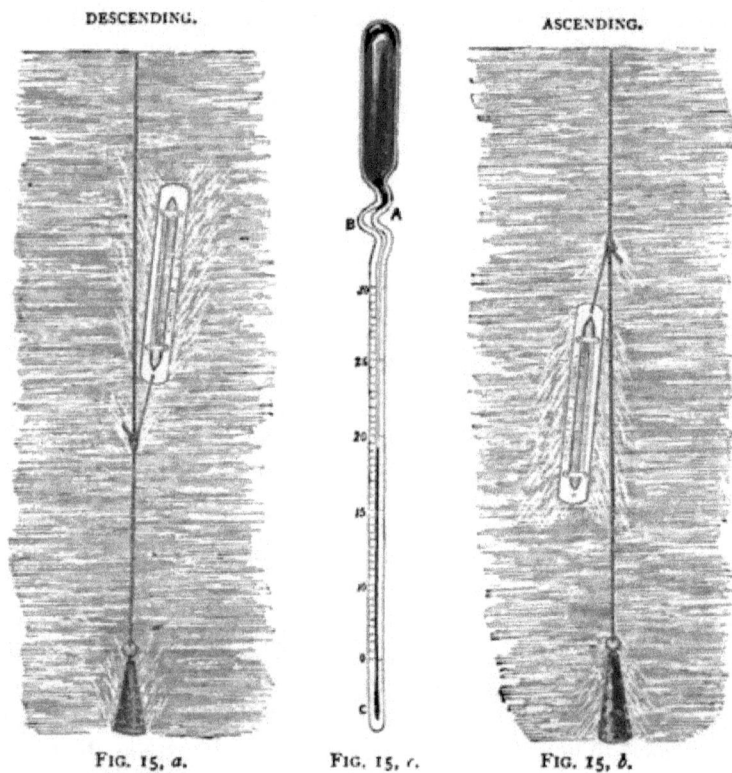

FIG. 15, *a*.   FIG. 15, *c*.   FIG. 15, *b*.

error of graduation once for all, and the error of the zero point from time to time.   For very nice work, a correction should also be made for the temperature of the mercury column at the time of reading, but in ordinary work this is not neces-sary.

Examination of Surface Waters.

In choosing a surface water as a source of supply, there are certain concessions which must be made. In the first place, the water will be, almost inevitably, somewhat colored, especially if taken from a pond or lake; in the second place, there will usually be a slight "pondy" taste, even in the best of surface waters. Considered simply as *drinking* water, surface water will always be at a disadvantage by the side of a pure, soft spring water, but, as stated on previous pages, a surface water may often be, *on the whole*, the best suited for a general supply.

In examining as to the suitability of any source of surface water, after determining whether a sufficient amount can be obtained directly or by means of storage reservoirs, the desirability of the source can be ascertained better by a survey of the drainage area, and by a knowledge of the present population and sources of pollution, and the probable increase in the future, than from the results of chemical examination of the water, the interpretation of which is sometimes attended with difficulty. It may be possible, it is true, to state from the chemical examination of a single sample that no considerable or no appreciable contamination exists; it is impossible to recommend a water for drinking without knowing something of the situation and surroundings of the source from which it is taken.

The principal difficulties in the way of the satisfactory chemical examination of surface waters are three in number: In the first place, the volume of water is generally so large that, even when polluting matter is known to be present, the dilution is so great as to prevent the detection of unmistakable evidence of contamination. In the second place, all surface waters contain more or less of organic substances—substances containing carbon and nitrogen—which it is impossible to refer definitely to animal or vegetable sources, or otherwise to distinguish as harmless and harmful. In the third place, the water of such streams and ponds is subject to very considerable variation, so that the examination of a single sample is of comparatively little value. With reference to the second point something has already been said in the chapter on water analysis. It may be said further that the substances which form the most offensive part of the soluble vegetable matter are *albuminous* in character, and the chemical effect on the water is to increase the amount of what is designated as "albuminoid ammonia;" that is, they contain nitrogen, which, under the analytical treatment, is evolved and

7

measured as ammonia. It is unfortunately impossible by analytical means to distinguish whether this "albuminoid ammonia"
is to be ascribed, in any given case, to vegetable or to animal
origin. No doubt the excrement of fishes, their dead bodies so
far as they are not consumed by their living comrades and by
the animalcules, and the bodies of the animalcules themselves
add to the nitrogenous organic matter in our surface waters. As
a rule, in waters not contaminated by sewage, the animal matter
forms only a trifling proportion of the entire organic matter, but
the recent investigation of Professor Remsen shows that in some
instances the animal matter (as from sponges) may be appreciable and of practical importance.

In the case of a bad condition of the water arising from the
decay of an unusual amount of animal or vegetable matter on
the bottom or sides of a reservoir, or from the presence of algæ,
the water is ordinarily characterized by an abnormal amount of
soluble organic matter, which shows itself in the common method
of analysis as "albuminoid ammonia," or in the Frankland
method as "organic carbon" and "organic nitrogen." But, in
order to judge whether the amount is abnormal or not, it is necessary to have an extended series of analyses, and this is seldom
at hand. The effect of algæ may be well seen by a study of the
weekly analyses of the Springfield water for the years 1876 and
1877, and of the Mystic during 1879, as shown in the respective
water reports.*

As, in this country, waters have been and are most frequently
examined by the "ammonia" process, attempts have been
made to fix the limit of "albuminoid ammonia" which may be
allowed in a surface water. Wanklyn, as stated on page 41,
looks upon 0.010 part of "albuminoid ammonia" in 100,000 as
suspicious, and upon 0.015 part as sufficient to condemn a water,
and some analysts are inclined to adopt this standard for our surface waters; such an absolute standard is, however, impracticable, and would exclude many waters which are known to be free
from contamination and to be perfectly well suited for domestic
use. With reference to this matter Dr. Smart says: †

---

* See Annual Reports of the Water Commissioners of the City of Springfield
(Mass.), 1877 and 1878. Also, First Annual Report of Massachusetts State Board of
Health, Lunacy and Charity. Supp., pages 119, 120.

† Buck's Hygiene, ii, p. 128.

" The waters of the purest mountain streams in our unsettled West, where animal contamination is an impossibility, contain 0.014 part per 100,000 of albuminoid ammonia.   At other times they may yield 0.020, 0.025 or more, and yet be regarded as comparatively innocent."

Dr. Smart found the Black's Fork, Wyoming, to contain 0.014 part in 100,000 when most free from surface admixture, and 0.028 part when swollen by melting snows.   The Little Wind River, Wyoming, a stream running over a rocky bed and containing only about 3.75 parts of total solids in 100,000, gave 0.034 part of "albuminoid ammonia."   The North Platte River yields from 0.030 to 0.050 part in 100,000 at different times.   The question may be pertinently asked how it is that our surface waters contain so much more organic matter than the waters of Great Britain?   Dr. Smart says: " These streams ought to be pure, if pure water is to be found in nature, as they run through no populous districts and are thus free from the sources of contamination against which sanitary officers are most on guard.   They spring from a cleft in the rocks, are mostly rapid in their course until they reach the plains, and are fed by the rainfalls and melting snows.   There seems nothing left by way of explanation but the wildness of the country through which they run.   In England the fields are fenced in and the soil cultivated to the very banks of the stream, the woods are well kept, and the swamps are drained and reclaimed ; but here there is no cultivation ; vegetation lives, and, instead of being garnered up, dies and decays.   The forest trees fall and rot where they fall.   I have been up in the Uintah Mountains, where are the sources of the Black's Fork, and among the pines covering the slopes of the ridge there are more fallen trees in all stages of decay than living ones in those untouched forests.   Through such dead vegetation the streams have to force their way, and it would be singular indeed if they did not take up a portion of the soluble organic matter.   But, in addition, in the tangled willow growths of the valleys, where, as in the forests, the growth of to-day rises from the decay of ages, the beaver dams up the stream, and vast masses of water are stagnated, to dissolve the dead vegetable tissues and find their way by slow degrees back into the beds of the running water."

" That the dissolved organic matter is vegetable in its origin, is also shown by the absence of chlorides and nitrites, and that it is recent, by the frequent absence of ammonia."

It must not be understood that the presence of an excess of vegetable matter is absolutely a matter of indifference. Waters thus charged may be the cause of diseases of the digestive organs, without doubt. Whether they may also cause any of the so-called zymotic diseases or give rise to specific diseases of peculiar type, is doubtful.

Dr. Smart, whose opinion is entitled to much weight, ascribes the "mountain fever" of the West to this cause (compare page 52). He says:

"As animal matter, in certain stages of its decomposition, or enveloping specific germs, gives expression to its presence in the system by the development of typhoid fever, so vegetable matter, in certain stages of its decomposition, or enveloping specific germs, gives rise to an adynamic remittent, for which the writer has suggested the name of *aquamalarial fever*. Viewed in its connection with this affection, the organic ammonia should not exceed 0.016 part in 100,000, for when 0.020 is reached, the disease makes its appearance, and becomes more pernicious in individual cases as the amount increases. Not that aquamalarial developments are to be expected in every case where the organic ammonia exceeds this limit, but that experience shows a greater probability of their occurrence with a water thus impregnated—malaria being more likely to be present with a large than a small vegetable contamination."

With reference to the third point alluded to above as affording difficulty in the interpretation of the results of chemical examination, it may be said that the results of a single examination are to be received with a good deal of caution, and such results must be interpreted somewhat according to the season of the year in which the sample is taken. The very considerable variation to which streams are subject, as far as the suspended matter is concerned, has been shown in Table VII, on page 57. The state of things is similar with reference to the matter in solution, especially with streams in which the volume of water is subject to much variation. Thus the Hooghly, at Calcutta, is stated to carry:

21.68 parts in 100,000 of "total solids" in May,
11.30 "   "   "   "   "   "   " October.

The rainy season greatly increases its purity, and the melting of the snow on the Himalayan Range helps in the same direction, so that the water is most pure in October.* Further illustration of the variation to which surface waters are subject, particularly with regard to the organic matter, may be seen from the following tables. Table XII shows the variation in the sum of the "organic carbon" and "organic nitrogen," and also in the "albuminoid ammonia," as observed in the case of the Mystic water, which is supplied to a portion of Boston, Mass.

TABLE XII.—EXAMINATION OF MYSTIC WATER.

[Results expressed in Parts in 100,000.]

DATE.	NO. OF SAMPLES.	SUM OF THE ORGANIC ELEMENTS.	"ALBUMINOID AMMONIA."
June, 1879	Average of 2 samples	0.478	....
July	" " 4 "	0.775	0.035
August	" " 4 "	0.605	0.026
September	" " 3 "	0.448	0.020
October	" " 5 "	0.333	0.014
November	" " 2 "	0.393	0.011
December	" " 1 "	0.297	0.011
January, 1880	" " 2 "	0.364	0.012
June 19 to July 3	" " 3 "	0.486	....
July 10 to Aug. 7	" " 4 "	0.852	0.034
Aug. 14 to Sept. 11	" " 4 "	0.526	0.022
Sept. 18 to Jan. 15	" " 12 "	0.375	0.014

In this case, the large variation was partly due to the presence of an abundant growth of algæ, the trouble being at its height in the latter part of July and during August. But, in the absence of any such growth, the variation is often very great. Weekly examinations of the Cochituate supply of the city of Boston from July, 1876, to July, 1877, showed a variation

in the ammonia.................... from 0.0005 to 0.0056 part in 100,000
in the "albuminoid ammonia"..... from 0.0099 to 0.0176 "   "   "
in the total solids. .... from 3.72   to 5.58   "   "   "

Further illustration of this point is afforded by Tables XIII and XIV.

Table XIII contains the results of monthly examinations of the water of Glasgow, Scotland, as reported by Professor Gustav Bischof of the Andersonian University. The water comes from

---

*Proc. Inst. Civ. Eng. Gr. Br., lxiv, p. 361.

TABLE XIII.—Examination of Glasgow Water by Professor Bischof.

[Results expressed in Parts in 100,000.]

Date.	Organic Carbon.	Organic Nitrogen.	Sum of Organic Elements.
May 12, 1873.....................	0.204	0.017	0.221
June 16, ...	0.181	0.016	0.197
July 18, ...	0.192	0.008	0.200
Aug. 1, ...	0.209	0.011	0.220
Sept. 1, ...	0.156	0.047	0.203
Oct. 14, ...	0.256	0.028	0.284
Nov. 24, ...	0.177	0.035	0.212
Jan. 15, 1874.....................	0.154	0.021	0.175
Feb. 5.	0.251	0.008	0.259
March 10, ...	0.185	0.007	0.192
April 1, ...	0.169	0.003	0.172
May 5, ...	0.235	0.011	0.246
Average.....................	0.197	0.018	0.215

an unpolluted Highland lake, Loch Katrine, and flows some
thirty-six miles in a masonry conduit. Table XIV, which, like
No. XIII, is compiled from the Sixth Report of the Rivers Pollution Commission, shows the variation in the water of the several companies which supply London with filtered river water.
These are not *monthly averages*, but the results of the examination of single samples taken at monthly intervals.

TABLE XIV.—Variation in Monthly Samples of London Water, 1873.

Name of Company.	Organic Carbon.			Organic Nitrogen.		
	Maximum at any one time.	Minimum at any one time.	Mean of 12 Samples.	Maximum at any one time.	Minimum at any one time.	Mean of 12 Samples.
Chelsea....................	0.447	0.121	0.197	0.067	0.013	0.034
West Middlesex.........	0.341	0.114	0.173	0.055	0.015	0.028
Southwark..............	0.396	0.118	0.186	0.060	0.020	0.030
Grand Junction..........	0.412	0.117	0.183	0.050	0.016	0.032
Lambeth	0.449	0.130	0.206	0.065	0.021	0.040
New River..............	0.257	0.059	0.107	0.032	0.010	0.018
East London............	0.333	0.109	0.175	0.082	0.015	0.035

It may be said, in general, that no source of surface supply
should be adopted on the strength of examinations made in the
winter season, and in the case of ponds and lakes the examination should include a careful survey of the shallow portions
during the hot weather, with a view of discovering the possible
presence of noxious algæ. Negative results in this direction will
not, however, *guarantee* future immunity.

As already intimated, the preliminary examination of a surface water, from a sanitary point of view, concerns itself chiefly
with the present and probable future pollution, and this must be
considered with reference to the volume of water with which the
polluting substances will be diluted, taking care to err rather on
the side of safety: the chemical examination should not, however, be omitted, as the results, if properly interpreted, may be
of great value. Tables XV and XVI will furnish data for comparison in the case of surface waters.

TABLE XV.—EXAMINATION OF SURFACE WATERS.

[Results expressed in Parts in 100,000.]

GEOLOGICAL FORMATION.	TOTAL SOLIDS.	ORGANIC CARBON.	ORGANIC NITROGEN.	AMMONIA.	NITROGEN AS NITRITES AND NITRATES.	TOTAL COMBINED NITROGEN.	PREVIOUS SEWAGE OR ANIMAL CONTAMINATION.	CHLORINE.	Temporary.	Permanent.	Total.	NO. OF SAMPLES.
									HARDNESS.			
Igneous rocks	5.15	0.278	0.033	0.001	0.002	0.035	0	1.13	0.1	2.0	2.1	18
Metamorphic, Cambrian, Silurian, and Devonian	5.12	0.293	0.024	0.002	0.006	0.031	3	0.92	0.3	2.5	2.8	81
Yoredale and Millstone Grit, and non-calcareous Coal-measures	8.75	0.377	0.033	0.003	0.010	0.050	6	1.05	0.4	4.3	4.7	47
Calcareous portion of Coal-measures	22.79	0.346	0.033	0.007	0.016	0.056	33	1.52	4.0	8.3	12.3	26
SURFACE WATERS FROM CULTIVATED LAND.												
Non-calcareous districts	9.52	0.276	0.034	0.007	0.089	0.128	635	1.49	0.6	4.3	4.9	31
Calcareous districts	30.03	0.268	0.053	0.005	0.257	0.314	2,306	2.24	12.4	8.2	20.6	12

In Table XV are presented the results obtained by the Rivers
Pollution Commission from the examination of a large number
of samples of surface water from various geological regions, the
organic matter being indicated by the determination of the " organic carbon" and "organic nitrogen." In Table XVI are
brought together the results of the examination of various American surface waters, mostly in actual use as sources of supply,
the organic matter being indicated by the "albuminoid ammonia."

---

* Sixth Report of Rivers Pollution Commission.

TABLE XVI.—PARTIAL ANALYSES OF SURFACE WATERS.

[Results expressed in Parts per 100,000.]

LOCALITY.	DESCRIPTION.	DATE.	NO. OF SAMPLES.	TOTAL SOLIDS.	AMMONIA.	ALBUMINOID AMMONIA.	CHLORINE.	AUTHORITY.
Boston, Mass	} Main Supply, Lake and River {	July, '76-July, '77. July, '77-April, '79.	43 40	4.3 ...	0.003 0.004	0.014 0.015	0.4* ...	W. R. Nichols. " "
" "	Mystic Lake	Oct., '79-June, '80.	17	9.8	0.019	0.015	2.0*	" "
Plymouth, Mass	Pond	June, 1877.	1	3.0	0.008	0.017	0.7	" "
" "	"	March, 1880.	1	2.6	0.001	0.010	0.8	" "
New London, Conn	"	December, 1879.	1	3.9	0.006	0.008	...	" "
Springfield, Mass	Reservoir.	Jan.-Dec., 1876.	45	4.9	0.017	0.052	9.1†	G. H. Cook.
Jersey City, N. J	Passaic River.	August 1876.	1	27.2	0.013	0.022	1.0‡	" "
" "	"	"	1	11.2	0.010	0.019	6.1†	" "
Newark, N. J	"	"	1	16.0	0.010	0.015	0.4‡	" "
" "	"	"	1	10.0	0.012	0.020	0.8	" "
Philadelphia, Pa	Schuylkill "	January, 1875.	1	12.0	0.015	0.037	0.8	C. R. Cresson.
Wilmington, N. C	Cape Fear River.	January, 1880.	1	10.3	0.021	0.044	1.3	C. W. Dabney.
"	"	June, 1881.	1	5.6	0.004	0.017	0.6	" "
"	"	August, 1881.	1	5.6	0.008	0.016	0.4	W. R. Nichols.
Cincinnati, Ohio	Ohio	1880.	6	14.2	0.011	0.048	0.8	C. H. Stuntz.
Louisville, Ky	"	1880.	1	11.7	tr.	.....	0.6	T. C. Van Nuys.
Evansville, Ill	"	1880.	1	18.6	0.012	.....	0.9	" "
Indianapolis, Ind	White	1880.	2	28.0	0.003	.....	0.4	" "
Minneapolis, Minn	Mississippi "	1877	1	18.6	0.003	0.015	1.1	S. F. Peckham.
Fray Bentos, S. A	Uruguay "	September, 1877.	1	8.6	0.003	0.020	0.2	—
Higueritas, S. A	"	"	1	8.7	0	0.014	0.2	—

* These amounts of chlorine are approximate—not averages.   † High Water.   ‡ Low Water.

CHAPTER VI.

GROUND WATER AS A SOURCE OF SUPPLY.

A PORTION of the water which falls as rain or snow sinks into the earth, and where the surface deposit is gravel or other porous material overlying some impervious rock, the water collects to constitute the ground water of the locality, the water-table of the engineer. The rivers which flow through such a deposit, or the ponds and lakes which are situated in it, determine the level of the ground water in their banks; but as we recede from the banks the water level is found to rise more or less regularly, according to the character of the porous stratum. Although subject to fluctuation, the ground water often maintains a very uniform relative level over large areas: its height and fluctuations are important factors in the sanitary condition of any locality.

The cause of the rise of the ground water as we recede from the wells—a fact which has been established by numerous observations in this country and in Europe *—is evident : the water falling upon the whole water-bearing area would naturally raise the level of the ground water ; that level cannot be permanently higher than the water in the natural drainage channels in their immediate neighborhood, as there is a continual passage of water through the porous material to the visible streams or lakes. Owing to the resistance of the material through which the water passes, the surface will be an inclined one, and the amount of inclination will depend upon the resistance encountered. On Long Island, N. Y., the inclination is quite uniform from the

---

* A great many profiles resulting from actual measurements, and showing the inclination of the ground water, may be found in the Berlin and Munich reports, the titles of which appear on pages 217–218. In the latter the profiles include the surface levels, the level of the ground water, and the level of the underlying impervious stratum, and are very instructive. See also, The Brooklyn Water-Works and Sewers, New York, 1867.

central ridge to the ocean or to Long Island Sound, and averages
about seven feet to the mile. In the valley of the Sacramento
the general slope is about four feet in a mile. In some localities
the inclination is much greater than this for limited distances;
thus, in the neighborhood of the Taunton (Mass.), Water Works
there is a fall, in what seems to be a continuous water-table, of
about 14 feet in 1,000. Besides the slope towards a visible
stream, there is often a fall in the ground water in the direction
of the mouth of the stream, and a corresponding flow. It will
be understood, however, that the "flow" has reference generally
to a rather slow passage through the interstices of the ground:
sometimes, however, on account of a lack of homogeneousness in
the water-bearing stratum, veins of water occur, in which the
flow may be quite rapid.

The water obtained by sinking a well into a stratum of sand
or gravel which has not been artificially disturbed, is, as a rule,
bright and clear, and free, or nearly free, from organic matter.
Although originally coming from the atmosphere, in its slow
passage into and through the ground, the water has been subjected to a long process of sedimentation and filtration, combined with processes of oxidation. In this sense, the water may
be said to have been purified by *natural* filtration: the process,
however, is not brought about by the means taken to collect and
utilize the water, but has been practically completed before the
demand is made upon it.

Utilization of the Ground Water.

The most simple method of making the ground water available, and the one earliest adopted, is to sink a well, covered or
open, into the water-bearing stratum, and to pump therefrom.
Such a well, which draws its supply from the ground water proper,
is generally called a shallow well, in distinction from a deep well,
which may extend into a rocky stratum, and obtain its supply from
a water-bearing fissure; and in distinction also from an artesian
well sunk to a considerable depth into underlying strata which
have no connection with the ground water of the particular
locality. This method of obtaining water from shallow wells has
been practised from time immemorial for the supply of single
families and small communities, and is, nowadays, used on a large
scale for furnishing town supplies. In many places the well, from

its dimensions and shape, may more properly be called a basin, and, like the ordinary circular wells, these basins may be either open or covered.

A second method of collecting the ground water is by means of a covered gallery or tunnel constructed in part of porous material; often the top and sides are built of tolerably impervious masonry or brickwork, while the bottom is of an open character, so that the water which rises into the gallery shall come mainly from beneath. An example of this now quite common mode of collection is at Lowell, Mass.* The "filtering gallery" is situated on the northerly shore of the Merrimack River and parallel with it, about 100 feet from the water's edge. Its length is 1,300 feet, width 8 feet, and height (inside) 8 feet. The side walls have an average thickness of $2\frac{3}{4}$ feet and a height of 5 feet, and are constructed of heavy rubble masonry, laid water-tight in hydraulic mortar. The walls support a semicircular brick arch,

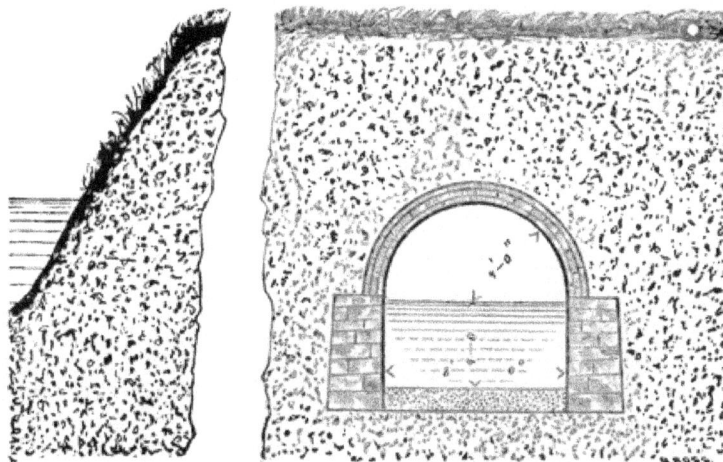

FIG. 16.—FILTER GALLERY, LOWELL, MASS. (FROM FANNING.)

one foot thick, made water-tight. Along the bottom, stone braces, one foot square and eight feet long, are placed, ten feet from

---

* A full description of the works is given in the Fifth Annual Report of he Mass. State Board of Health. Also, in the Third Annual Report of the Water Commissioners of the City of Lowell, 1873.

center to center, between the walls, to keep them in position.
The water comes in at the bottom, which is covered with screened
gravel and small stones.

One of the best examples of a filtering gallery in this country
is that which supplies the city of Columbus, Ohio. This gallery
is a brick and cement conduit, 36 by 42 inches, and is shown in
process of construction in Figure 17. It is in all 5,715 feet in

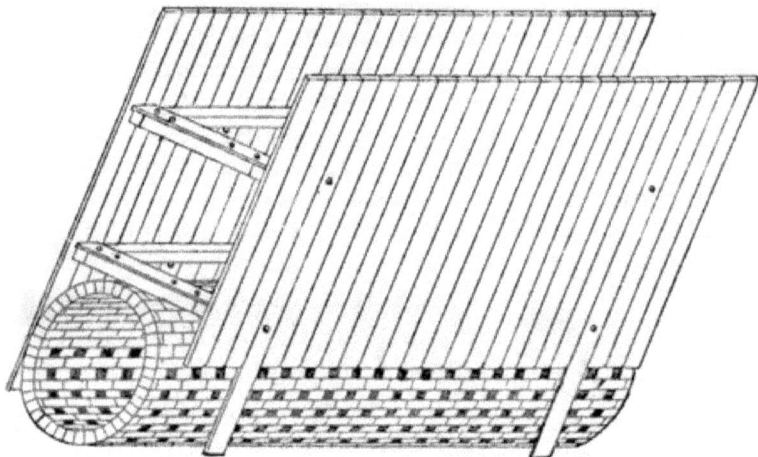

FIG. 17.—FILTERING GALLERY, COLUMBUS, OHIO.

length, and is situated in the gravel deposit at the junction of
the Scioto and Olentangy rivers.* This method of construction
has been followed also at Taunton, Mass.

A third method is to substitute for the collecting gallery a line
of iron pipes, i.e., practically water-mains, cast with a great number
of narrow longitudinal slits, and laid with loose joints. These
pipes collect the water, and conduct it to receiving wells, from
which the supply is pumped. In filling the trench in which the
pipes are laid, the pipes are surrounded on all sides with coarse
material, of too large a size to fall into or through the slits, and
the trench is then filled with screened material of decreasing size.
Works of this kind are in use in various places in Germany, at
Dresden, Hanover, etc. At Halle, glazed clay pipes are em-

---

* Tenth Annual Report of the Trustees of the Water-Works, Columbus, O., 1880.

ployed, 47 c.m. in diameter and 2.8 m. long; the total area of the slits in a single pipe is equal to the area of the cross section of the pipe. (See Fig. 18.)

Still a fourth method consists in the use of the "driven well," which is described on page 112 and following pages, but as wells of this description are frequently sunk through a layer of clay into a stratum of water below the ground water proper, they partake also of the character of "artesian wells," which will be considered in the next chapter.

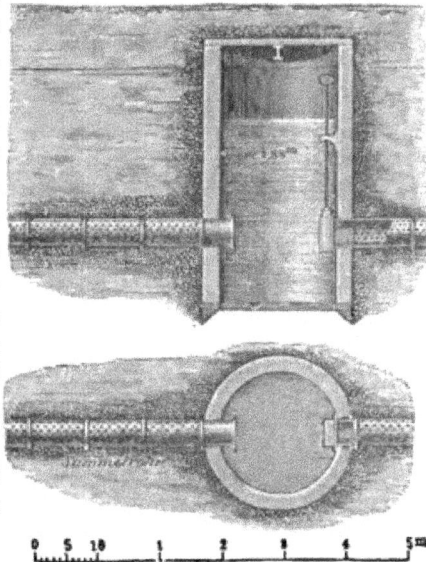

FIG. 18. (FROM FISCHER.)

The Effect of Pumping upon the Ground Water.

For the purposes of this discussion, we will suppose that the water-bearing deposit into which a well is sunk is perfectly homogeneous. When no water is removed, by pumping or otherwise,* the water in the well stands at the same level as in the ground; when pumping begins, the water falls at first rapidly, afterward more

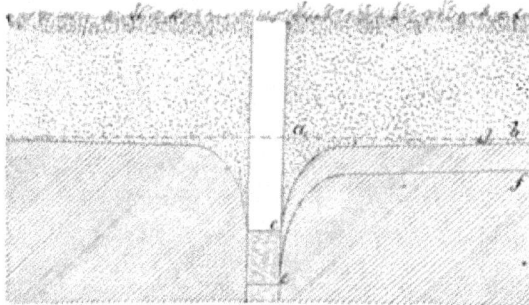

FIG. 19.

slowly, until—if the discharge of the pump be uniform—a point

---

* If, as is exceptionally the case, the water is delivered by gravity, the effect on the ground water is essentially the same as if the water were removed by pumping.

is reached where the water is supplied at exactly the same rate as delivered by the pump. Suppose, in Fig. 19, that the water stood originally at *a b*, and that an equilibrium has been established when the water in the well has fallen to *c*. The water flows from the gravel into the well by virtue of the head or difference of level *a c*, but its flow is impeded by the resistance due to interstitial friction against the particles of sand or gravel, and the water surface assumes somewhat the form indicated by the line *c d*. The line *c d* approaches *a b* until it finally coincides with it; that is, there is a point beyond which no measurable influence is exerted on the natural level of the ground water, and its distance from the center of the well depends upon the circumstances of each particular case. In certain experiments made by Salbach in the alluvial deposit on the banks of the Elbe, above Dresden, it was found that when the water in an experimental well was, by pumping, kept constantly 2.5 meters below its normal level, the height of the ground water was measurably affected in every direction for a distance of some 60 meters (say 200 feet). In experiments made by Piefke, at Berlin, the influence of the well was felt to a distance of some 300 meters in wet weather, and to over 700 meters at other times; but, while the effect could be traced to that distance, it was very small at the extremity of this radius. With the water in the well 2.33 meters below the normal level of the ground water, there was a lowering of only 0.35 meter at a distance of 50 meters, of 0.17 meter at a distance of 100 meters; and at a distance of 260 meters the lowering was through only 0.10 meter. In the Berlin locality the natural movement of the ground water was very slow, and 524 meters from the river the water stood only 0.63 meter above that in the stream.

Where the ground is homogeneous, or ·nearly so, and the water can come from one direction as easily as from another, we have what may be called a circle of influence, with the center of the well for the center of the circle; but if the deposit is not homogeneous, as is often the case, the water comes more easily from one direction than another, and the effect of pumping is felt to unequal distances from the well. As appears from Fig. 19, the effect of the flow of water into the well is to form a sort of crater from which the water is drained. This is often spoken of as a " cone," but it is not a cone, strictly speaking. The exact form of the curve $c\,d$ will depend upon circumstances, but it will always lie above the straight line joining the points c and d.

Returning again to our well, if pumping ceases, the water will gradually flow into the well until finally it has found its level and stands as in the surrounding ground. If, on the other hand, starting with the water in the well at c, a larger quantity be pumped than before, the level in the well will fall, and as c sinks to e, the water in the ground also falls and the surface will be indicated by $e\,f$. In order that this new and larger quantity should be obtained, the circle of influence must become also enlarged, that is, a larger area must contribute to the supply. The absolute quantity of water which can be obtained from any well depends upon the amount of rainfall which finds its way into the ground water of the region from which the well draws its supply. If the deposit were in a basin, and no water came from the rain, the effect of pumping would be to gradually exhaust the water: thus, if the water in the well were kept at *a constant level*, say at c, the quantity of water delivered in a given time would grow less and less, and finally the surface of the ground water would be a horizontal plane passing through c; if, on the contrary, a *constant quantity* were pumped, the water in the well would sink lower and lower until the bottom was reached, and the further delivery of the same quantity would be impossible. Practically, wells are not sunk in such a deposit, but in one where the ground water is continually receiving accessions from the rain or melting snow, or, in some cases, from a neighboring stream. The amount which can be obtained from any deposit depends finally on the amount received, and no such well, however great its diameter or its depth, can be *inexhaustible*, although practically it may never be called upon to furnish more than it can supply.

A good illustration of the effect of a constant draught in permanently lowering the level of the ground water is afforded by the well in Prospect Park, Brooklyn, N. Y. The well was constructed in 1869.

The elevation of water table as first found, Nov., 1868, was...15.6 ft. above tide level.
Elevation of water table, May, 1879.......................15.2   "   "
Elevation of water table on completion of the well, Dec., 1869. 14.55   "   "

Pumping began regularly on June 5, 1870; the effect has been as follows:

Year.	Average Number of Gallons per Day.	Average Elevation of Water Table.
1870	300,000	14 15
1871	272,000	13.03
1872	437,000	10.56
1873	288,000	11.29
1874	333,000	10.70
1875	294,000	9.83
1876	235,000	9.83
1877	252,000	9.21

It is seen here that an average draught of only 304,000 gallons per day has lowered the water table five feet in eight years, and also that the yield is diminishing, for while in 1873 a daily draught of 288,000 gallons permitted the water table to rise five inches, in 1876 a draught of 235,000 gallons was just equal to the supply, and in 1877 a draught of 252,000 gallons again lowered the water.*

In the previous discussion we have spoken of a single well of ordinary diame-

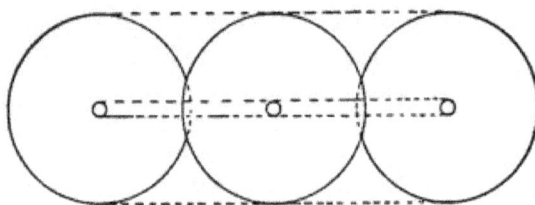

FIG. 20.

ter. If a series of wells be located near each other, the effect will be essentially the same, except the circle of influence will become approximately an ellipse, as would be the case if several wells were connected so as to form an open basin or a covered gallery. In locating a series of wells, reference should be had to the character of the water-bearing deposit, in order that they may not be placed unnecessarily near together.

Driven Wells.

"Driven" wells, "tube" wells, or as they are sometimes called abroad, "American" or "Abyssinian" wells,† are formed by forcing wrought-iron (or galvanized iron) tubes, such as are used for gas or water pipes, down into the stratum from which

* Croes and Howell, Newark Aqueduct Board : Report on Additional Supply, 1879, p. 61.

† Also called "Norton" wells, the English patent having been taken out by a Mr. J. L. Norton.

the water is to be taken. The pipes are generally from 1¼ to 2 inches in diameter, and furnished at the lower end with a wrought-iron or steel point ; above this point the pipes are perforated for some distance with holes to admit the water. The pipes with point attached may be driven with a mallet or falling weight, and when the top of one tube has reached the surface of the ground, a second length is attached to it with a common coupling, and the driving continued to the desired depth. In many localities it is better to first drive down a suitable steel-pointed rod or drill until water is reached, and to insert the well-tube in the hole thus made.* In the perforated points for such wells, the greatest variety exists, it being stated that about 150 patents have been issued for points and cognate portions of the pipe. The figure represents that known as Andrews' Patent.

FIG. 21.—DRIVEN WELL POINT.

Although pipes of larger dimensions than those mentioned are sometimes driven, it is usual when a large amount of water is required—as for manufacturing purposes or for town supply—to drive a number of wells in the same limited area, and connect them to a common suction pipe leading to the pump. The driven well partakes of the character of the shallow well when its source of supply is the ground water, but it often partakes of the character of the artesian well, as when it is driven through a layer of clay or other impervious material underlying the ground water into another water-bearing stratum below.

When a driven well is forced into the ground water, and water is removed by pumping, the effect is essentially the same as has already been described (pages 109-112) with an open well. The driven well is valuable as a means of obtaining water on account of facility of construction, but it involves no princi-

---

* Both methods of constructing the driven well are covered by the Reissue Letters Patent (No. 4,372) granted to Nelson W. Green, May 9, 1871, and the validity of the patent has been affirmed by several legal decisions. It is claimed, however, that the patent is antedated by a U. S. Patent granted to James Suggett, March 29, 1864, and by British Letters Patent granted to John Goode, Oct. 16, 1823.

8

ple which is new as far as bringing the water to the surface is concerned.

It is asserted that a driven well differs from an ordinary well in two essential respects. In the first place, the well, which is always of very small diameter, is not dug or bored, but sunk *without removal of the earth* * in the manner already described, either directly or by first driving down an iron rod, and after its removal, inserting the well tube; in either case the result is a narrow well with air tight walls, fitting closely in the earth about it: *the tube is the well.* It is further asserted that when a suction pump is attached to the pipe a new element is introduced, and peculiar effects are produced by "exhausting the air," or "producing a vacuum," and that thus the water is drawn to the pump by a force independent of gravity, and to which gravity is, in this case, but auxiliary.

These claims are, however, fallacious. The diagram, Fig. 22, may represent the suction pipe of a pump inserted in a narrow open well, the normal level of the ground water being at *ab*. Now, although with a driven well much stress is laid upon the "air-tight" tube, it is the tube alone that is air-tight, as any suction pipe must practically be. The soil, even if compacted about the tube, is not air-tight,

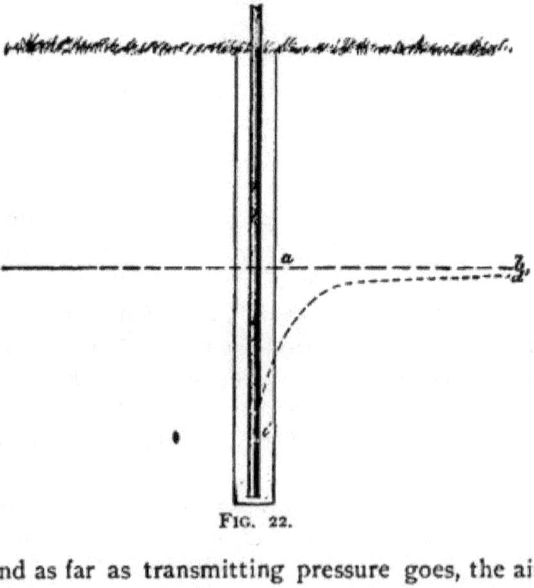

FIG. 22.

and as far as transmitting pressure goes, the air which is about

---

* This is Col. Green's method, but well tubes are also driven into the earth at the same time that their passage is facilitated by forcing into the tube, which in this case, is open at the bottom, a stream of water. This water washes out and brings to the surface the sand and clay from the bottom in advance of the driving.

the tube in Figure 22, and which rests on the surface of the water at *a*, is in no different condition whether the tube be in natural ground, or in a dug well, as indicated in the figure. The air circulates freely in the ground; it responds at once to any change in the barometric pressure, and at once takes the place of any water which may be removed from the interstices of the soil. Again, below the water-level, the water, like the air above, circulates, although less freely, owing to interstitial friction, and, of course, fills all the pores of the ground close up to and around the pipe. The statement that *the pipe is the well*, is misleading. If we start (Fig. 22) with the tube as a suction pipe in an open well, and imagine the well to be gradually narrowed in diameter by filling in around the circumference, the tube will continue to be practically a suction pipe, even when the well has been finally filled up—the well finally having become a hollow cylinder of water, of the thickness of a mere film if the soil is very compact. It is quite inconceivable that the filling of the well with gravel or sand, no matter how closely compacted the sand may be, could produce any other effect than that due to the increased resistance to the passage of water in the annular space about the suction pipe.

To show further the fallacy of the claims alluded to, let us return to Fig. 22, in which the normal level of the ground water is represented at *a b*. If, now, a given quantity of water be taken continually from the point *c*, in a given interval of time, the slope *c d*, which the water surface will assume, will be precisely the same whether the water is drawn in buckets, or by a tube in an open well, or by a driven well, because the same amount of water must reach the same point *c* in the same time, and starting from the same original position. If the claim be true that more water can be obtained by one method than by another, it follows that the water must be supplied faster in one case than in the other, and there are two necessary consequences: first, if the point *c* remains unchanged, this increased rapidity of flow must result in *an alteration of the slope of the water surface*. On the other hand, if the quantities pumped in the same time are made equal, then in the first case the point *c* will not fall as low as in the second.

While we should reject, *a priori*, the consequences to which these assumptions necessarily lead, recent experiments made by

Mr. J. C. Hoadley [*] show that the slope is the same whether the
given yield of water be from an open well or from a driven tube;
and that, with the same delivery, the level of the water in the
well or pipe is lowered to the same point. The particular experiment alluded to was performed as follows: A 3-inch open pipe
was driven in pervious soil, into, and considerably below the surface of the ground water, forming an open well—the earth being
removed from within.   Into this pipe a suction pipe of 1½-inch
diameter was dropped and wedged into position, so as not to

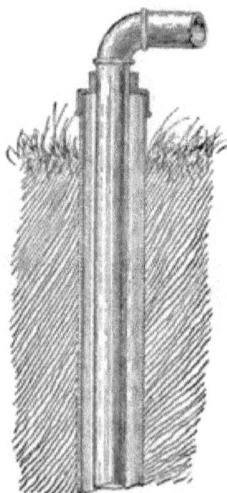

close the opening of the 3-inch pipe. Water
was pumped for a certain time, as much as
the well would supply. Subsequently, by
means of a cap, the suction tube was se-
cured in the 3-inch pipe and the opening of
the latter pipe hermetically sealed. The
suction pipe thus became, practically, a
driven well. Under these circumstances,
every other condition being unchanged, the
yield of water was approximately the same
as in the previous case, the slight difference
which existed being in favor of the open
well.

It should be noted that in what has been
said above, the yield of a driven well is compared with that of a dug well of no great
diameter. If the well be increased in di-

Fig. 23.

ameter to 30, 50, or 100 feet, so that the distance $c\,c'$ (Fig. 22),
becomes considerable, the limit of measurable effect on the ground-
water level will be removed farther from a, and the yield of the
well will be appreciably greater—or, in other words, with the
same delivery, the point c will not fall so low.

With regard to the absolute amount of water which can be
utilized in a given locality, common sense, as well as science, tells
us that the amount of water which a given deposit can furnish
must be a definite quantity, although to us unknown; and although the driven wells may enable us to obtain this water more
conveniently than other methods, the absolute amount obtainable is no greater, and the supply cannot be inexhaustible, as

---

[*] Private communication: this statement is *absolutely* true only when the wells
are of the same diameter.

some of the enthusiastic advocates of the driven-well system would have us believe. One great advantage which the driven wells possess is the facility with which they may be sunk for experiment or temporary use. For example, they were extensively used by the British army in the Abyssinian expedition, 1867-68 ; and hence, in England, they are frequently called Abyssinian wells.

It should also be noted that the driven well ordinarily takes its water from a lower point than that to which a dug well would be sunk in the same locality. For this reason, a driven well may continue to furnish water when a neighboring dug well has become dry, and thus the impression that the driven well is inexhaustible gains ground.

On this account also, the driven well is somewhat less liable to pollution than a dug well in the same locality, as the polluting material may be rather more diluted in the mass of the ground water. Moreover, as has been said, the driven well often passes through an impervious stratum of clay, so that the water obtained is entirely distinct from the ground water of the locality. In this way good water may sometimes be obtained where the surface conditions are very unfavorable, but there is always an element of risk involved in sinking a well among sources of pollution.

"Natural Filtration."

The ultimate source of the ground water is the rain, and that the rain is the proximate source of the water obtained from a well sunk into a gravel deposit far removed from any stream or pond, scarcely any one can doubt. Such a well is that in Prospect Park, Brooklyn, alluded to on page 111. This well is nearly two miles from tide-water, and, although the natural level of the water has been lowered by pumping, it is still a number of feet above tide level. Generally, however, a gathering well, basin, or gallery is located near a lake or river. This location is chosen mainly because at such a place there is almost always a decided movement of the ground water toward, or in the same direction as, the stream ; but such a location is also chosen in order that the river may make up any deficiency caused by the removal of the ground water.

It was formerly supposed, and is so even now, by many per-

sons who have not made a study of the subject, that in such
cases the water is derived directly from the river, and filtered by
passing through the intervening sand and gravel.   Undoubtedly,
in some cases, a considerable proportion is thus derived, but, as a
rule, the contrary is true, and, where the location is such that
most of the water must come from the visible body of water,
the supply generally proves inadequate.   The beds of ordinary
streams furnish a poor filtering surface, and the experience with
artificial filters shows how soon an originally clean surface becomes clogged.*

That the view just expressed is correct, appears from a variety of considerations.   From the discussion of the effect of
pumping on the ground water (pages 109–112), it is evident that,
from a well situated near a stream, a certain amount of water
can be drawn without calling upon the stream at all for supply;
if, however, the circle of influence includes a portion of the
stream, some of the water may come from this source, unless, as
is indeed generally the case, it is easier for the water to come a
greater distance through open water-bearing deposits than to
force its way through the silted-up and more or less impervious
bed of the stream.

If we consider the character of the water, there are certain
general facts that are at once and readily noticeable : the water
thus obtained is generally clear and colorless ; it is of a quite
uniform temperature, cool therefore in summer, and in winter
much warmer than the water of neighboring ponds and rivers,
which, of course, approach in temperature very close to the
freezing point; the water also differs in chemical character from
that of neighboring streams or ponds, generally being somewhat
harder.

With regard to the temperature, the difference is very marked,
even where the water is collected in an open basin and thus
exposed to the heating (or cooling) influences of the air.   For
instance, in the filtering gallery at Lowell, Mass., during the
month of September, 1873, the highest temperature was 50° F.,
the lowest 49° F. ; during the month of October, observations

* The term natural filtration is objectionable only so far as it implies that the
water is obtained from the lake or stream by a process of filtration : that the rain falling upon the ground may be said to be filtered naturally by passing through the interstices of the water-bearing deposits is, of course, true.

were made on thirteen different days showed identically the same temperature, namely, 50° F. Between September 6 and January 1, the highest recorded observation is 52° F., on November 8, and the lowest is 47° F., December 31. There is no corresponding record of the temperature of the river, nor is such necessary, as every one knows that river water varies with the temperature of the surrounding air, and in December must have been nearly at the freezing point. At Waltham, Mass., where the water is taken by means of an open shallow basin, more marked differences have been observed between the temperatures at different seasons. Thus in winter, when the river was frozen, the temperature in the basin was about 44° F., and the average of nineteen observations made at intervals from August 23 to August 26, showed for the river an average temperature of 74°.1 F., and for the basin water an average temperature of 62°.8 F. Such instances might be multiplied indefinitely, and it seems quite impossible to account for the observed differences by the continuous passage of water through 100 feet or so of gravel. In fact where no such differences are observed, it may be a sign that the water does come from the stream, and the water is likely to be otherwise unsatisfactory ; thus the city of Toulouse, in France, is supplied by a number of filtering galleries in a gravel deposit on the banks of the Garonne. The original gallery was built in 182– at a distance of about 60 meters (200 feet) from the river. This furnished water acceptable in quality, but deficient in quantity ; an increase of the length of the gallery failed to furnish a corresponding increase in quantity of water obtained. A second filtering gallery, or rather series of connected wells, was constructed nearer to the river, at a distance, in fact, of only ten meters. In this case, the water obtained manifestly did come, in part at any rate, from the river : the water was somewhat turbid, and what is very instructive, the passage through a bank of thirty feet, and admixture, of course, with some ground water, failed to bring the water to anything like the uniform temperature of the other galleries. The temperature fell in winter to 2° C. (35°.6 F.), and in summer rose above 21° C. (70° F.).* This gallery was therefore abandoned, and others constructed at a greater distance from the stream. These

---

* D'Aubisson. **Annales des Ponts** et Chaussées, 1838.

furnish water which is satisfactory, except when in time of flood the river covers the whole territory in which the galleries are built, and the galleries become filtering galleries in the true sense.

As marked differences as in the matter of temperature are also observed in the chemical character of the water. This often appeals to the eye by the absence of color in the (so-called) filtered water, while the water of the river may be strongly colored ; or, if the gallery be alongside of a pond, the latter may be filled with algæ in a state of decomposition, without producing the slightest effect on the gallery water. It is, however, the *hardness* of the water which generally attracts attention, being noticed where the water is used for washing or in steam boilers. Usually the ground water is harder than the surface water of the same region, but occasionally the reverse is true. Belgrand gives a number of examples from French localities, from which may be cited the following : *

Water of Rhone, at Lyons.	16°
Water of filtering gallery at Lyons.	17.94
Water of Loire, at Nevers.	4.96
Water of collecting well.	20.70
Water of Loire, at Blois.	7.76
Water of the gallery (which is beneath the bed of the river).	14.45

Sharples has found † that the water in the filter gallery near Little Pond, Cambridge, contains nearly twice as much lime as that of the pond, and instances might be multiplied indefinitely. In the case of the Dresden water supply the river water is harder than that obtained from the collecting wells. ‡

Even when the gallery or well is sunk directly in the bed of the river, or in an island surrounded on all sides by the river or pond, the ground water still contributes largely or wholly to the supply. Many experiments have shown that the water in a gravel deposit directly beneath a river differs essentially from that of the stream itself.

The belief that a well or gallery located near a pond or stream

* La Seine, etc., pp. 463 and following.

† Twelfth Annual Report of the Cambridge Water Board, for the year 1876. Boston, 1877 ; page 30.

‡ Salbach. Das Wasserwerk der Stadt Dresden ; 3r Theil, page 7.

does not necessarily derive its supply from the visible body of fresh water, finds confirmation in the well-known fact that springs are often observed to issue from the sand along the sea shore, even below low-water mark,* and fresh water is often obtained by sinking wells very near the shore. Generally, in such cases, the surface of the ground and the water table rise as they recede from the shore, the ground water, derived from the rain, passing with more or less resistance to the sea. In such wells, the water rises and falls with the tide, as the water must enter the sea under the pressure of a varying height of salt water, but the salt water itself does not penetrate the soil and reach the well itself. From such wells a certain amount of water can be pumped. If the amount pumped exceeds that which the ground water can furnish, salt water may then be drawn into the contributing area, and the water become brackish. Even where the ground near the sea is level, the mere effect of the rain falling upon the sandy area is sufficient to create a deposit of fresh water which may crowd out or prevent the entrance of salt water. Darwin, in the voyage of the "Beagle," discovered this to be the case in low coral islands of the Pacific, close to the sea ; and in Holland, Amsterdam, the Hague and Leyden obtain their water from collecting canals in the sand-dunes which form an almost barren strip of country from 2 to 5 kilometers wide, having only a few elevations of surface. Sometimes fresh water overlies the salt, so that shallow wells furnish fresh water, while deeper wells give brackish or salt water. McAlpine has made the interesting observation that where, as on Long Island, N. Y., the water table slopes down to the sea, the underlying deposit of salt water slopes away from the sea—the higher and consequently heavier column of fresh water at some distance inland being able to displace the salt water to a greater depth : thus, the vertical section of the body of fresh water, in the direction of its flow, would be that of an elongated wedge. Salt water has been found underlying the fresh water in other localities—

---

* A remarkable example of this occurs at the four iron forts at Spithead, Eng. Here wells are sunk on artificial islands, at a considerable distance from the shore, and, although two of them are over 550 feet deep, they pass entirely through sand and gravel. In spite of this location, the water of the wells contains only a small proportion of chlorine (18.6, 11.4, 4.1, 7.6 parts in 100,000 respectively), showing that almost no sea water finds its way into the wells.—*The Analyst*, April, 1883.

for instance, at Hull, in England *—where the salt water is supposed to be due to the infiltration of sea water, and not to the
mineral character of the rock.

Preliminary Examination of a Proposed Ground Water Supply.

The least satisfactory point in connection with ground-water
supplies is that the amount of water to be obtained in any one
locality is limited in amount, and it is very difficult to tell in
advance how large an amount a given region can be relied
upon to supply, except as a result of thorough surveys and long-
continued experiments.

The effect of pumping upon the level of the ground water
and information as to the direction of its flow may be obtained
by driving a number of iron pipes with perforated " points " at
regular distances, preferably in two lines at right angles to each
other, intersecting in the experimental well. Observations should
be made on the natural level of the ground water before pumping is begun ; and the pumping is best conducted by keeping the
level of the water in the well at a constant distance below the
natural level of the ground water, or below the level of the water
in the pond or stream. Although absolute equilibrium cannot
be established for a considerable time, unless the water comes
very freely, and in the absence of rain, sufficient indications can
be obtained to form judgment, within limits, as to the probable
yield of the well. In locating a gallery or elongated basin, reference will be had to the direction of the greatest movement of
the ground water, which is sometimes in the direction of the flow
of the visible stream and sometimes at right angles to it.

A preliminary examination with reference to a future supply
should include a careful survey of the entire drainage area, and
in all cases the preliminary examinations should be made by
those conversant with the matter, as there is great liability to
overestimate the probable yield of water. As a rule, the amount
obtained from any such well is greater at first, as it requires time
to drain out the water naturally occupying the territory which
hereafter is to flow into the well. On the other hand, the effect
of the draught of water toward a single point is to open channels in the porous material so that in some cases the yield

* Proc. Inst. Civ. Eng. Gr. Br., lv, p. 257.

increases with time. Besides an assurance that the quantity of
water obtainable is and will be sufficient, it is necessary to know
that the water is satisfactory in quality. As far as the character
of the water is concerned, it is in New England generally good
when sufficiently abundant ; it is almost always harder than the
river water, but in most localities this difference in hardness is
small, although appreciable. In limestone regions, however, the
ground water is often so hard as to be unsuited for use ; and
sometimes the presence of streaks or beds of clay or of ochre
makes it impossible to obtain clear water.

The absence of such injurious deposits should be ascertained,
not only at the point at which it is proposed to locate the actual
well or gallery, but also in the immediate neighborhood, especially in the direction in which the gallery is likely to be extended or where additional wells may be sunk.

Leipzig, in Germany, has had a ground-water supply since
1866. The water, which was of good quality, proved insufficient
for the wants of the city, and the supply was increased (1871–72)
by the construction of an additional collecting gallery. Apparently the work was done without sufficient preliminary examination, for the works were scarcely opened before trouble was
experienced, and it was found that the locality into which the
gallery had been extended was generally unsuitable. There was,
however, one peculiar and instructive difficulty. The gravel of
the deposit in which the gallery was located contained—as grav-
els frequently do—oxide of iron. This ordinarily would give no
trouble, but the gallery intersected an old river-bed containing
many partially decayed stumps and other organic matter which,
in the presence of water, reduced the oxide of iron to the pro-
toxide condition, forming soluble protosalts of iron. These compounds dissolving in the ground water, found their way into the
collecting gallery in large quantity. As soon as these soluble
protosalts of iron come into contact with the air they are oxidized, and a deposit of the red hydrated oxide is formed. In
Leipzig the oxidation generally took place before the water
reached the consumers, and the complaint was with reference to
the muddy, red appearance of the water when drawn; this was
easily overcome by filtration. Sometimes, however, the water
reached the consumers before the oxidation was complete, in
which case the filtered water tasted " like ink," and on standing

deposited a further quantity of a red sediment.* It may be
stated that the remedy in this case consisted in seeking a new
supply in a more favorable locality.

As we have seen, even where a well or gallery is located near
a stream or pond, the proportion of water received from the
visible stream or pond is usually small; therefore, to obtain information as to the character of the water to be obtained, it is
much more important to examine the ground water than the
water of the river. The examination of the latter should not,
however, be neglected, and it would scarcely ever, if ever, be
advisable to locate " natural filtration " works on the banks of a
stream which was seriously polluted.

Further, although there is less liability to pollution than in
the case of small shallow wells sunk near dwellings, slaughter
houses, factories, or stables, it must be remembered that the
ground water is fed by the percolation into it of the atmospheric
water, and that it is possible to pollute even a large body of water.
This fact should be taken into account in choosing a locality for
the collecting wells.

TABLE XVII.—EXAMINATION OF GROUND WATER.

[Results expressed in Parts per 100,000.]

LOCALITY.	TOTAL SOLIDS.	AMMONIA.	" ALBUMINOID AMMONIA."	CHLORINE.	AUTHORITY.
Ayer, Mass., 1880, ...	3.3	0.008	0.008	0.1	W. R. Nichols
Newton, Mass., basin near Charles River, 1877.....	3.9	0.	0.002	0.3	J. M. Merrick
Taunton, Mass., basin, Aug., 1877	5.6	0.009	0.010	....	W. R. Nichols
" " river, " "	5.8	0.005	0.021	....	"
Waltham, Mass., basin, Dec., 1873...............	6.5	0.005	0.006	0.4	"
" " river, " "	5.7	0.006	0.016	0.4	"
Lowell, Mass., gallery, Jan., 1874	6.4	0.006	0.003	0.3	"
" " river, "	4.5	0.005	0.010	0.2	"
Cambridge, Mass., gallery, Dec., 1876	18.6	0.080	0.005	3.1	S. P. Sharples
" " pond, " "	14.0	0.070	0.016	1.7	"
Chautauqua, N. Y., filter chamber, ...	10.2	0.	0.005	0.7	S. A. Lattimore
" Lake	7.0	0.001	0.006	0.8	"
Indianapolis, Ind., well, 1880	34.0	0.003	....	0.05	T. C. Van Nuys
" " White River, "	29.0	0.005	....	0.2	"

* Hofmann, Dr. Franz: Die Wasserversorgung zu Leipzig. Pph. 8vo, pp. 62.
Leipzig, 1877.

In Table XVII are given the results of the partial analyses of some ground-water supplies, together, in most cases, with the analysis of the neighboring pond or stream. The chemical examination of a water under discussion directs itself, mainly, to proving the freedom from organic matter and other signs of pollution, and to ascertaining that the hardness is not excessive.

In this connection we may mention a peculiar trouble which has occurred at several foreign water works.*

Since September, 1877, a portion of the Berlin water supply has been taken from the neighborhood of the "Tegeler See," by means of a series or line of 23 wells running parallel with the shore of the lake.

Shortly after the introduction of the water, complaints arose as to its quality, and investigation proved the difficulty to be twofold. It is frequently noticed that water—and especially water from a driven well—although apparently clear when first drawn, becomes turbid on standing and deposits an ochreous sediment. This is generally due to the presence in solution of the protocarbonate or to some organic protosalt of iron, which—on exposure to the air—becomes oxidized and changed to an insoluble hydrated sesquioxide. This was the cause of the trouble which occurred at Leipzig, and this was one of the difficulties with the Tegel ground water, but the microscope showed that the ochreous sediment which settled from samples of the water, and which accumulated in the reservoirs and in the pipes, especially in " dead ends," was by no means made up wholly of amorphous mineral matter, but consisted very largely of *algæ*, dead and alive.

Most noticeable among the *algæ* was the *Crenothrix Kühniana* (*Crenothrix polyspora*, Cohn). This plant was first discovered by Kühn in 1852, in the drains of a cultivated field in Silesia, but has since been found in wells in various parts of Europe, and is probably very widely distributed.

In Berlin, it was found in the wells, in the reservoirs and in the service pipes, in various stages of development and decay. The spores are minute spherical or oblong bodies from one onethousandth to six one-thousandths of a millimeter in diameter. From these spores, and by other means of development, the

---

* This is abridged from an account of the trouble given by the author in the Journal of the Franklin Institute, March, 1882.

plants grow into comparatively long threads, each of which on
examination is seen to be made up of a number of individual
cells, end to end, inclosed eventually in a gelatinous sheath. The
general appearance of a mass of these threads is shown in the
figure, and the masses are sometimes a centimeter or more in diameter.

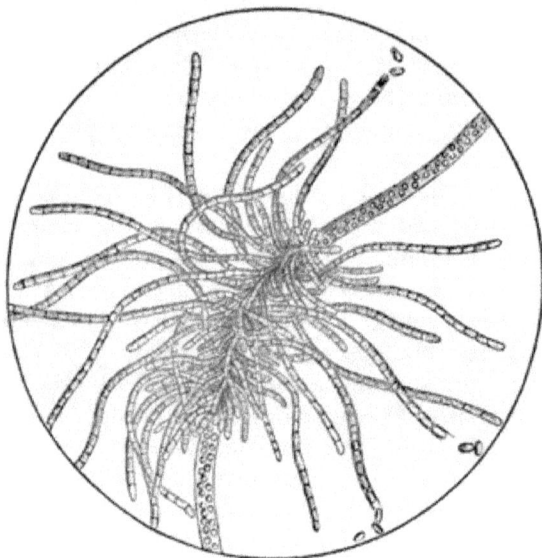

FIG. 24.—CRENOTHRIX KÜHNIANA. 450 : 1.

The threads are at first, like the spores, transparent and
colorless, but by the absorption of iron in some form or other
they become colored from olive-green to a dark brown. They
eventually, in many cases, become incrusted with the hydrate of
iron to such an extent that their structure becomes invisible,
but it may be made evident by dissolving away the hydrate of
iron by very dilute chlorhydric acid. Under favorable circumstances the plants may develop with great rapidity, and Professor Kühn speaks of their having frequently stopped up agricultural drain pipes. Also, the pipes in which water is taken from
a well ten meters deep, in the neighborhood of the Plötzensee,
near Berlin, have in summer been choked and nearly filled up by
the multiplication of the same organisms. In the reservoirs and
in the "dead ends" of the service pipes they seemed to accumu-

late by growth as well as by deposition. While the plants develop more rapidly in the warm season, they are found at all times of the year in all stages of development.

It may be remarked, in this connection, that the *Crenothrix* has great vitality; thus, Dr. Zopf exposed a quantity in water out-of-doors from the first of January to the middle of February. The water was, of course, frozen, and during the time the temperature fell as low as to $-8°R.$ ($11°F.$), but after being thawed out the plants had, in a few weeks, contrary to all anticipation, revived again or new ones had grown from the spores.

The *Crenothrix* seems to live and develop in the ground itself, and in an examination which was made of the water from a number of wells in different parts of Berlin, the same plant was found in many cases, in one instance at a depth of more than 24 meters from the surface.

Whether its presence would be revealed in the preliminary examination of a ground water is doubtful, but it ought certainly to show itself if pumping experiments were carried on for any considerable length of time.

There seems to be no remedy for this trouble. It was found possible in Berlin to filter the water artificially through sand— after exposing it to the air—so as to obtain the supply perfectly clear; but, of course, the filters were very much fouled, and, on account of the difficulty of washing the sand thoroughly and the risk that the spores of the plant would eventually find their way into the lower part of the filters and thence into the service, it was thought best by those in charge of the works to abandon the wells altogether, and to make use of water taken directly from the lake and filtered in the usual manner. The same trouble occurred in Halle, and it is stated that it was overcome by sinking other wells in a different locality. In the second locality the water was much harder and free from the *Crenothrix ;* in fact, when it was mixed with water from the previous source it brought about the extermination of the plant ; hence it has been inferred that the presence of a considerable amount of carbonate of lime is fatal to the plant, but this is very doubtful in view of what follows.

The same trouble has occurred recently at Lille, in France. The source of supply is here a subterranean reservoir in marl and water-bearing chalk lying near the surface. The water comes to

the surface in actual springs which originate at no great depth.
The hardness of the water is about 25° (French), and the examination made in 1864 showed 44 parts of total solids in
100,000, a large proportion being carbonates of lime and magnesia. The water was then considered of good quality,* but for
some time there has been complaint of a red color and of an unpleasant taste and odor. The matter becoming very serious in
the spring of 1882, led to the discovery that the trouble was
mainly due to the *Crenothrix.* The previous winter had been
very dry, and the water level had been lowered about five meters.
The rains of the spring raised the water level, and seem to have
washed out the plants into the sources of supply ; † it is possible
also that contamination of the overlying soil had increased the
amount of soluble iron salts which are necessary to the growth
of the *Crenothrix.*

The Pollution of Domestic Wells.

In isolated dwellings and in villages and small towns not yet
provided with a public water supply, drinking water must, as a
rule, be obtained either by collecting the rain water and storing
it in tanks and cisterns, or else by sinking wells. On account of
the clearness and nearly uniform temperature of the ground water, the latter method is usually preferred when practicable. In
the majority of cases the location of the well is dictated simply
by convenience, and it frequently happens that it is in close prox-
imity to a privy, or to cesspools, or to a barn or stable. The result
is that the well is very liable to pollution, and, more often than
not, it is simply a question of time when the water shall become
unfit for use. The pollution of the well generally takes place
gradually. The ground gradually becomes charged with the
soakage from the privies and manure heaps, and percolating rain
water carries the impure matter into the ground water from
which the well draws its supply. In other cases, actual channels
are formed, by which the foul liquid trickles or flows into the
well itself, or a leaky drain, laid near the well, may be the source
of the trouble.

Whatever views may be held of the effect upon the human

---

* Masquelez : Ville de Lille. Établissement de la Distribution d'Eau, Paris, 1879.
† Alf. Giard : Comptes rendus, xcv (1882), 247-249.

system of drinking such water, there is no question whatever as to the pollution itself, and although the water may appear clear and bright, and be inoffensive to the senses, chemical examination may show that it is highly charged with the products of decomposition. Moreover, there are hundreds of cases on record where sickness has been coincident with the use of polluted well water, and, although the evidence is of necessity circumstantial (see Chapter I), it is too striking to be disregarded. In the present state of knowledge, it must be said that the continued use of a well water proved to be polluted is as unjustifiable as suicide generally is.

It is often difficult to persuade the owner of a polluted well to abandon its use. The water tastes good and has been used for years without producing any bad effects. Meanwhile, however, in these years the neighborhood has become thickly settled, the various possible sources of contamination have increased, and the whole ground water of the region has felt the effect. At the same time, in urging the abandonment of the well, one cannot say that, in spite of the pollution, it may not be used for years more without noticeable ill effects. Under what conditions the water may become injurious, and when, no one can say.

It is also difficult to realize the distance from which the pollution may come. Until the water of the well becomes contaminated to a very great extent, the taste gives no evidence of contamination, but occasionally accidental evidence is furnished of the distance from which communication with the well may exist.

An illustration of this point, and a further illustration of certain chemical changes which have been already alluded to is the following. In Wernigerode, Germany,* a certain well which had always been nearly free from iron, suddenly began to furnish a chalybeate water. Clear when drawn, the water soon became turbid, and deposited on standing a copious ochrey sediment. It was finally discovered that this sudden change was due to the emptying of several casks of spoiled beer into the ground at a distance of some 35 meters (115 feet). The organic matter thus introduced into the ground acted as a reducing agent on the ferric oxide contained in the soil, and the iron, dissolved as

---

* Wockowitz, E.: Wernigerode's Trinkwasser. Wernigerode, 1873.

9

protocarbonate, found its way into the body of water from which the well was supplied.

In some places, owing to the very nature of the locality, shallow wells are to be rejected as sources of supply. Thus, Dr. Smart * says, with reference to New Orleans: " The well waters of New Orleans are unfit for use. They are but little less impure than the sewage water carried off by the drainage canals, yet they are reported as being employed for family use, in bakeries, and for stock, especially in summer, when the cistern supply fails. The site of the city is waterlogged to within a few feet of the surface. One well, on Chestnut street, the least impure of those examined, is only 10 feet deep, and contains 7 feet of water. The saturated soil is of great depth, and the ground water is practically stagnant. The filtration into the wells is insufficient even to free the water from turbidity. Organic matter is unaffected by the process. The water contains alkaline carbonates, chlorides, large amounts of free ammonia, but no nitrates or even nitrites. In four wells examined, the ammonia from organic matter amounted to 0.039, 0.041, 0.044, 0.080 part ; while in the sewage from the Orleans canal it only reached 0.120 part. These samples are so impure that the use of well water in New Orleans should be interdicted.† Even careful filtration should not be relied on to purify such waters. Filtration is not a process by which dangerous waters may be utilized, but simply a guard against the possibility of danger in doubtful waters."

We have thus far spoken only of wells which are sunk into the ground water. These are the most common, but many wells are sunk into a more or less compact rock, and the water comes through fissures in the rock. In such cases it is often difficult to tell where the water does come from, and the well is liable to contamination from distant sources. The pollution is liable to be even more serious than in wells sunk into the ground water, because the contaminating substances carried by the stream of water do not have the same opportunity to be oxidized as they do when the water passes with comparative slowness through a body of sand or gravel.

---

* Bulletin National Board of Health, April 17, 1880.
† Such use is now prohibited by law, 1883.

Of the well waters which are submitted to chemical examination a limited number show by the absence of ammonia, nitrog-
cnceous organic matter, and chlorides in appreciable quantity,
that they are free from all contamination; on the other hand, a
considerable proportion (not, however, one-half according to the
experience of the author) may be condemned at once; the remainder can only be considered doubtful or suspicious. In the
cases of those suspicious wells which cannot be absolutely condemned, the proper course is to have, for a time at least, somewhat frequent examinations made of the water to see whether
the impurity is on the increase. For this particular purpose, it
is usually sufficient to follow a single ingredient, say, for example, the chlorine existing as chlorides. If the amount of chlorine
increases to any considerable extent, the source of impurity
should be ascertained and the water be protected therefrom, if
possible, or else be rejected from use.

It may be said, in a general way, that a good well water
should not contain over 0.005 part of ammonia in 100,000, or
over 0.010 part " albuminoid ammonia," and, in most places, not
over 1.0 part of chlorine (as chlorides). The amount of solid
matter in solution depends necessarily upon the locality, and
what might be a reasonable amount in one region would be very
abnormal in another. The presence of nitrates is also suspicious,
but, unless the quantity is very considerable, cannot alone condemn the water. Dr. Charles Smart, U. S. A., accepts 0.010
albuminoid ammonia in 100,000 as suspicious, and 0.015 as a limit
in the case of well waters " in the denser settlements, and in every
case where an animal origin to the organic matter is indicated by
careful survey or chemical analysis."

In the case of doubtful waters, the greatest satisfaction may
be obtained when it is possible to find in the same immediate
neighborhood a well of whose freedom from contamination there
can be no doubt. The comparison of the waters of the two
wells will probably enable one to decide the question as to the
contamination of the first well. The next most satisfactory
course of procedure is to throw a quantity of salt (or brine) into
the various cesspools, drains, etc., and to determine at frequent
intervals the amount of chlorine (as chlorides) in the water of
the well. As instances in which this method was used with good
results, the two following may suffice :

In No. I, the well was located 100 feet from the privy ; a bushel of coarse salt was put into the privy-vault October 24, and a bushel of fine salt on October 31. This caused an evident increase of the amount of chlorides in the well, as appears from the figures. In case No. II, two bushels of salt were put into a cesspool which was 75 feet from the well. A sample of water was then taken and afterward at intervals of three days. The effect on the well water was not as marked as in No. I, but the results were confirmed by a subsequent examination of the locality :

I. Date of Examination.	I. Chlorine, expressed as Parts in 100,000.	II. No. of Sample.	II. Chlorine.
October 17	3.3	1	1.4
26	3.9	5	1.5
29	3.9	3	1.6
November 2	4.0	4	1.7
5	4.4	5	1.7
8	3.5	6	1.9
13	3.4	7	2.6
17	3.4	8	2.0
20	3.3	9	2.0
23	3.1	10	1.9

In Table XXIII are brought together the results of the examination of a few well waters from various localities. The table might be extended to an indefinite length, as the reports of boards of health and water committees would, in almost every case, contribute to the list.

TABLE XVIII.—EXAMINATION OF WELL WATER.

[Results expressed in Parts in 100,000.]

LOCALITY.	TOTAL SOLIDS.	AMMONIA.	"ALBUMINOID AMMONIA."	CHLORINE.	QUALITY.	AUTHORITY.
Saugus, Mass	7.3	0.001	0.002	1.1	Good.	W. R. Nichols.
" Another	21.0	0.002	0.002	3.1	Suspicious	"
Williamstown, Mass	19.3	0.002	0.009	1.7	"	"
" Another	63.1	0.006	0.015	10.2	Polluted.	"
" Another	112.1	0.005	0.013	40.0	"	"
North Adams, Mass	31.7	0.014	0.009	2.2	"	"
Gloucester, Mass	68.6	0.230	0.029	9.5	"	"
Watertown, N. Y	37.4	0.002	0.005	9.3	Good.	E. Waller.
Croton Falls, N. Y	13.2	0	0	0.8	"	"
Lockport, N. Y	96.8	0.001	0.007	8.9	Doubtful.	"
Southampton, L. I	45.0	0.006	0.018	4.0	Bad.	"

CHAPTER VII.

WHILE a portion of the rainfall which soaks into the ground soon encounters an impervious stratum, above which it collects to form the ground water of the locality, much of the water precipitated from the atmosphere falls upon the edges of upturned rocky strata, or upon rock deposits which are either themselves porous or so fissured that they afford a more or less free passage for water. When the pervious stratum has an outcrop at some lower level, the water may issue in the form of springs, more or less copious. Where the course of the water has not been too long, and it has not, consequently, taken up a large amount of mineral matter, such springs furnish one of the best sources of drinking water, although the water is very often, in fact usually, less well-suited for technical purposes, on account of its hardness. The advantage of spring water over surface water for drinking is considered by some so great as to justify the incurring of very considerable expense in order to procure it. Thus, the city of Vienna constructed extensive water works for the sake of bringing water from springs which are sixty miles distant.

Artesian Wells.

When the water precipitated from the atmosphere is absorbed by a pervious stratum which is situated between two impervious strata, the water may exist under considerable hydrostatic pressure. The occurrence of a "fault" in the strata may allow the water to rise to the surface of the ground as springs, but often the water can be utilized only by sinking or boring artesian wells.

An artesian well is a well which is sunk or bored through an impervious stratum so as to reach a water-bearing stratum in which the water is under hydrostatic pressure; so that, as soon as the well is opened, it rises through the impervious stratum and often to, or higher than, the surface of the ground. Artesian wells may, therefore, be regarded as artificially opened springs. The term *artesian* is frequently applied to non-flowing deep wells, but, while the question of flowing or non-flowing may be unessential, the term is improperly applied to wells, however deep,

FIG. 25.—ARTESIAN WELL.

when the water is taken from the deposit into which the well is bored or sunk, and where the water collects from the fissures and cavities of the rock itself. Thus, in England, there are many deep wells in the chalk or in the new red sandstone which collect and utilize water from the chalk or from the sandstone itself, and which are not properly to be characterized as artesian. In this country, driven wells are often called artesian wells, and they may be properly so designated if they pass through a stratum of clay, so that the water rises from an underlying deposit not in communication with the ground or surface water of the same locality : driven wells, however, as we have already seen, often utilize simply the ground water where they are driven.

Although, within modern times, improvements have been made in the methods and apparatus employed for boring wells, wells of this description are of great antiquity. They are found in China, and many such wells have existed for a long time in North Africa, in the oases of the Sahara. Here, until recently, they were excavated by hand, the earth and other material being drawn up in baskets. Finally, a thin stratum of rock was reached beneath which experience had shown that water existed. This rock stratum was cautiously perforated, and as soon as it was pierced the workman was drawn up rapidly—and not always safely—as he was sometimes overtaken by the rush of water. The French in the province of Constantine (Algeria), between the years 1856 and 1878, bored over 400 wells. The flowing wells numbered 158, with an average depth of 85.5 meters; the temperature of the water was generally betwen 21° C. and 26° C., and the total solids between 300 and 600 parts in 100,000.*

There are a great many artesian wells in various parts of the

* Les Forages artésiens de la province de Constantine (Algérie). Résumé des Travaux exécutés de 1856 à 1878. Par M. Jus. 8vo, pp. 97. Paris, Imprimerie Nationale, 1878.

United States. Thus, Professor Winchell, in 1856,* mentions as many as 74 such wells in a single and somewhat circumscribed region of middle Alabama, and, of late years, many wells have been sunk in the southwestern part of the country with favorable results.

The sinking of artesian wells is attended with great uncertainty as regards both the quality and the quantity of the water to be obtained, and many wells have been sunk which have failed to reach water at all, or from which only water unfit for any domestic use has been obtainable. To judge of the probability of success in sinking a well in a new locality, a knowledge of the geological character of the underlying strata is essential. At Charleston, S. C., where are several successful artesian wells,† the possibility of obtaining such wells was inferred from a knowledge of the geology of the region. More than 100 miles from the city, starting from Augusta, Ga., and proceeding northeastwardly, a granite ridge rises to the surface of the earth, exposed to view in favorable positions, elsewhere covered with superficial drift sands and clays. The line may be followed northward through North Carolina, Virginia, and Maryland. On the broad surface of this granite ridge, and on its seaward slope, the sands drink in the rain water that falls. The streams from the up country that cross the ridge may also supply their quota. The water thus imbibed sinks down by the force of gravity, ever seeking the lowest attainable position. Now, the tertiary beds of the Charleston Basin, the cretaceous beds under them, and any other sedimentary beds beneath the cretaceous, must rest against this eastern slope of the granite ridge, and their sandy layers must drink in the water filtering through the sands. As all of these beds have a gentle slope toward the coast, the water will follow them down in their course. These formations, no doubt, continue their course under water for many miles, and, indeed, there is evidence that the water contained in them finds a discharge into the sea. To this cause are attributed the springs of fresh water that have been observed to rise, bubbling up at times in notable quantity through the salt water at points along the coast, fifteen or twenty miles from the shore. Moreover, in all the deep wells in

* Proc. Amer. Assoc., x (1857). p. 83.
† Municipal Report of the City of Charleston, S. C. Artesian Wells, 1881.

Charleston, varying from 60 to 1,260 feet in depth, the level or
head of water in the pipes has been observed to oscillate at tidal
intervals to an extent varying from 4 to 6 inches. The explanation is simple. In issuing from its natural vent under the sea
the fresh water must lift the column of salt water above, the
weight of which acts as an obstruction. When the tide at sea
is high, this column is greater than it was at low tide. The consequence is a diminution of the escape of water by that channel,
and a compensating increase of the discharge through other
channels not so obstructed, and an increase in the head of water
in the wells.*

One disadvantage of sinking artesian wells for town supply
is the great uncertainty as to the quality of the water, and
the fact that water from considerable depths is often of elevated temperature, and therefore not fit to drink unless cooled.
Moreover, the water is apt to be charged with a large amount
of mineral matter derived from the strata through which it has
flowed or percolated, or in contact with which it has remained
for a long period of time. The widely-known well at Gre-
nelle, Paris, which is about 1,800 feet deep, has a temperature of
27° C. (80°.6 F.), and contains only about 14 parts in 100,000 of
dissolved solids, whereas a well in St. Louis, Missouri, sunk at
the sugar refinery of Belcher and Brothers to a depth of over
2,000 feet, and at an expense of $10,000, furnishes about 75 gal-
lons per minute of water emitting a strong odor of sulphuretted
hydrogen, and containing 879.1 parts of dissolved matter in
100,000 parts; this water is entirely useless for the purposes of
the refinery or for domestic use. As already stated, the artesian
wells in Algeria contain from 300 to 600 parts of dissolved
solids in 100,000 parts of water, and would, in most localities, be
at once rejected even for purposes of irrigation. In the absence,
however, of better water, such wells as these are regarded as
godsends by the inhabitants.

The fact of a considerable amount of dissolved solids does
not necessarily prove that an artesian water is unfit for use,
although usually the salts present are objectionable in character.
Sometimes the dissolved matter, in the absence of lime, magne-

---

* The above statement is condensed from the Charleston Municipal Report
already cited.

sia and sulphates, may be unobjectionable in character, although the large amount present may be undesirable. For example, the water of the Wentworth Street artesian well in Charleston, S. C., which contains 273.66 parts of total solids in 100,000, has been used for years. In this case the dissolved matter is almost entirely common salt and carbonate of soda, and the use of the water is held to be beneficial in dyspepsia and kindred diseases. The water of the more recent Citadel Green well contains only 111.55 parts in 100,000 of solid matter, likewise consisting mainly of these two salts. The water is considered wholesome as a drink, and, for washing, the presence of the carbonate of soda makes it an excellent water; the principal objection found to it is that the carbonate of soda gives to rice, hominy and other farinaceous articles cooked in it a light golden tinge, owing to the action of the carbonate of soda on the starch in such articles. In the laundry, also, it cannot be used in the mixing of the starch for the same reason.

It may be here noted that the quantity of water obtained from an artesian well is often seriously diminished by the sinking of other wells into the same water-bearing stratum. This has been the experience in many localities. With reference to wells in the neighborhood of London, Eng., De Rance says :

"The outcrop of the lower London tertiaries is about 100 feet above the Thames, whilst their depth below it varies from 200 to 300 feet, the only notch in the rim of the basin being the valley of the Thames at Deptford and Greenwich, where the outcrop is 100 feet lower than the remainder of the margin of the basin ; the sectional area of the depressed portion being much less than the elevated portion, far less water can escape than can be absorbed by the sands, which are practically water-logged by the overlying, impermeable clay, through which borings were carried to a depth of 80 to 140 feet at the beginning of the century ; at that time the liberated water flowed up the bore-holes, and rose permanently above the level of the Thames until the supply was over-pumped, and it has fallen to 70 feet below Trinity high-water mark. To supply the deficiency, most of the artesian wells in London have been carried down to the chalk beneath, to intercept the water which circulates freely in the fissures and lines of joints. The level to which water will rise is steadily decreasing."

Deep Wells.

In certain geological formations, the nature of which does not
admit of the construction of artesian wells proper, water may
often be obtained in large quantities by sinking shafts, in which
the water collects and from which it may be raised to the surface
by pumps. Horizontal tunnels may be carried from the shaft, at
one or more levels, so as to intercept the water flowing through
the fissures or along the planes of stratification. Sometimes, indeed, the water may be obtained solely by means of a horizontal
tunnel, the opening being made in the face of a bluff. Thus,
Dubuque, Iowa, is supplied from a tunnel or adit penetrating the
bluffs and extending for about a mile in length at a depth, from
the surface of the ground, of from 100 to 200 feet.

Deep wells are used as sources of public supply, to some
extent, but the greater number the world over are sunk or bored
for private establishments, notably for breweries. It is stated
that in the city of New York there are as many as 40 wells
on Manhattan Island, although some of them are not now in use.
Nearly one-half this number are owned by breweries. The wells
vary in depth from 26 to 2,000 feet. Eighteen are 500 feet or
more in depth. The diameter also varies, being from $2\frac{1}{2}$ to 10
inches, although the majority are 6 or $6\frac{1}{2}$ inches. The capacity
of the wells ranges from 2,000 gallons to 126,000 gallons in 24
hours ; and the temperature of the water, so far as noted, is
between 50° and 59° F. As might be expected from the geological formation of the island, the wells are, in most cases, bored
in gneiss and mica schist.[*]

In England, where deep wells are used to a considerable extent as sources of town supply, the water-bearing capacity of the
various geological formations, and the character of the water to
be obtained therefrom, has probably been studied more carefully
than elsewhere.[†] Of the water supply of Liverpool, 5,500,000
(imperial) gallons are daily pumped from the wells in the new red
sandstone, and London receives daily some 8,000,000 (imperial)
gallons from deep wells in the chalk.

---

[*] Sanitary Engineer, October 12, 1882.

[†] See Sixth Report of Rivers Pollution Commission ; also, the various (annual)
reports of the Underground Water Committee of the British Association ; also, De
Rance, Water Supply of England and Wales.

Fig. 26 shows a well which is sunk in the new red sandstone, at Whiston, England.* Two wells, each 9 feet in diameter and 12 feet apart, were sunk to a depth of 135 feet and then continued to a depth of 225 feet as a single well, 30 feet long and 9 feet broad. The bottom of the well is 25 feet below mean sea level, and when first sunk, supplied some 400,000 gallons in 24 hours, with a depth of about 9 feet of water in the well. The manner in which the well cuts the strata of the sandstone is evident from the figure, the water having a natural tendency to flow along the planes of stratification toward the fault shown at the left, which presents a barrier to its farther progress. The works were subsequently extended by sinking and boring the auxiliary well in the right of the figure, and connecting the two wells by means of a tunnel. The supply obtained from the combined wells, was, in 1876, about 900,000 (imperial) gallons in 24 hours.

The capacity of a rock for storing and absorbing water varies with its texture and character; and when, after long continued rains, the rock has become fully saturated, no more water can be absorbed, and all additional supplies pass off as floods, as absolutely as if the precipitation took place on an impermeable formation. Many rocks thus contain, in their natural and undisturbed condition, water which was derived from the atmosphere long ago, and in some cases the rocks may contain saline solutions which have filled their pores from the time of their formation.† When a well is sunk into such a deposit, the water may be gradually forced out by the pressure of the water accumulated in other parts of the same stratum, or in communicating strata, but it may take a very long time to exhaust the subterranean reservoir. In some cases, near the sea, there may be communication with the ocean, which may thus produce the hydrostatic pressure, but which may not contribute by its waters directly, or at least not for a long time after the well is opened. Some deep wells near the sea gradually become more brackish, probably from the fact that the purer water which originally filled the pores of the rocks, and perhaps subterranean reservoirs, is gradually exhausted, and other water—in this case sea water—comes in to replace it.

Some idea of the vast amount of water stored below the sur

* Proc. Inst. Civ. Eng. Gr. Britain, xlix (1877), p. 221.
† See Hunt's Chemical and Geological Essays, p. 104 and elsewhere.

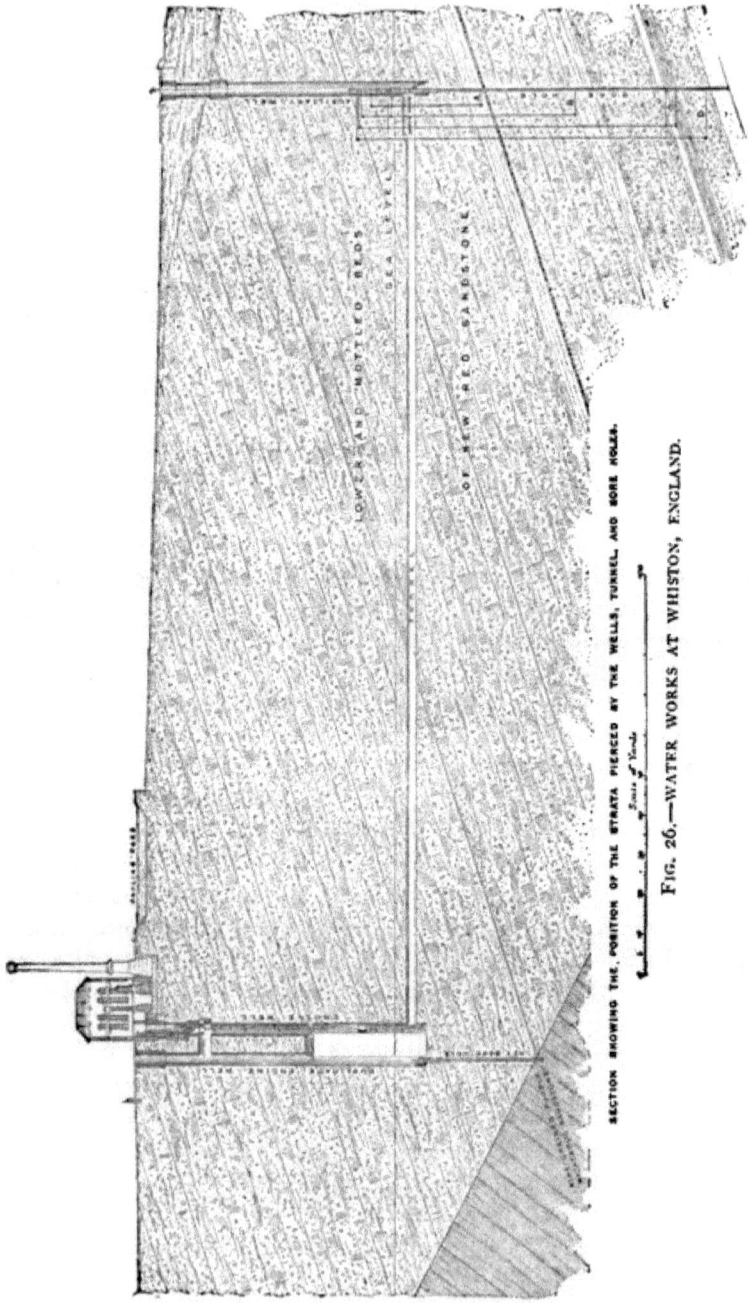

SECTION SHOWING THE POSITION OF THE STRATA PIERCED BY THE WELLS, TUNNEL AND BORE HOLES.

Scale of Yards

FIG. 26.—WATER WORKS AT WHISTON, ENGLAND.

face of the ground may be obtained from the following extract (De Rance):

"In the Thames and east coast district are not less than 4,000 square miles of pervious cretaceous rocks, receiving not less than 5 inches of rain annually, or a daily absorption of 800,000,000 gallons. It is readily understood with these figures, how the dry weather flow of the Thames is kept up by chalk springs; one-fifth of the yield is sufficient for 4,000,000 people, and taking the oolite supply, the total volume of water absorbed by underground sources in the Thames and east coast river basins may be taken as 1,125,000,000 gallons—a supply equal to the wants of 22,000,000 people, or nearly that of the total inhabitants of England, supposing that the whole of the 5 inches of rainfall absorbed could be pumped up."

It is, of course, impossible to utilize all the water actually contained in any rock. From a compact rock like chalk or limestone, a portion of the water is furnished by cracks and fissures, and this is readily given up; another portion passes through the rock itself, and although the water may be received and absorbed with great rapidity, it is delivered with extreme slowness, and a struggle is maintained, as it were, between capillarity and gravity.

Baldwin Latham * has called attention to the influence of the barometric pressure on the volume of water discharged by springs (or yielded by deep wells). When the barometer falls, the air confined in the fissures of the rocks tends to expand and force out the water, and the volume of the springs increases; when there is a rise in the barometer, there is a diminution of the flow. A more or less marked coincidence between barometric changes and variations in the amount of water discharged by mineral springs was noticed long ago, and various explanations have been offered to account for the phenomenon.†

When a well is opened in a water-bearing rock, the level of the water, or plane of saturation, will be found to vary within certain limits, being governed by the amount of rainfall absorbed. This level, after extensive pumping, is artificially and locally lowered, but, on the cessation of pumping, the original level is restored by a sufficient interval of rest, provided the volume

---

* Nature, September, 1881.

† See, for example, Alois Nowak: Ueber die barometrischen Ergiebigkeits-Schwankungen der Quellen in Allgemeinem. Prag, 1880.

abstracted annually is not more than is supplied by the rainfall. If the demand upon a deep well is greater than the supply received directly or indirectly from the rainfall, the well will show signs of exhaustion; the supply may, however, be kept up by deepening the well, that is, by taking the water from a lower level. Many wells gradually furnish less and less water, because in the beginning there was a quantity of water stored in the rock, which has gradually become exhausted. On the other hand, some wells furnish a supply increasing in abundance, owing to the fact that the passages through which the water comes become less obstructed and of larger size. Thus, according to the Rivers Pollution Commission, every 1,000,000 (imp.) gallons of water drawn from the chalk carries with it, in solution, on an average 1¼ tons of chalk through which it has percolated, causing an additional storage room for 110 gallons of water; so that the yield of a well draining a given area in the chalk, other things being equal, ought to gradually increase until the maximum limit of permeability is reached. As a further example of the same thing, it may be mentioned that, during the construction of the tunnel at the Whiston water works, upward of 350 tons of sand were in a few years washed from the fissures of the rocks, thus increasing the storage capacity of the rock.

Characteristics and Examination of Deep-seated Water.

The questions of the amount of water to be obtained from springs and deep wells, and of the probability of procuring water by means of artesian wells in any given locality are questions for the engineer and geologist. The fact that all such waters are liable to contain an excess of mineral matter has been sufficiently noticed: the chemical examination concerns itself mainly with the amount and nature of the dissolved salts. These deep waters are characterized, in general, by an absence of organic matter, but that even deep wells are liable to pollution may be easily realized by an inspection of Figure 26. It is very evident that any polluting matters in the soil might easily find their way into the well, being carried downward by the water passing along the planes of stratification. In the case of the water works at Whiston, all the wells in the immediate neighborhood were affected, most of them losing their water altogether. This in-

fluence was felt at least 1½ miles to the southeast and more than
a mile to the south. Where the water flows underground
through cracks and fissures the polluting substances do not have
the opportunity to become oxidized and harmless, as when the
water passes slowly through a gravel deposit. Mr. Baldwin
Latham has connected the periodic outbreaks of fever in the
parish of Croydon, England, with the intermittent appearance
of springs called the *Bourne*. The water which is reabsorbed by
the chalk lower down, is supposed to carry the objectionable
substances to the wells in the center of the old town. When
the springs are low and the Bourne begins to run, after a sudden
and copious rainfall, the water line under the town is elevated
and an outbreak of enteric fever results. Even with artesian
wells there is not perfect security, for many such wells—espe
cially when first opened—throw out fragments of vegetable substances, and even living fish and other small aquatic animals,
showing that they must have a more or less direct communication with the surface.

Signs of pollution in such waters must be sought mainly in
the "organic matter" as variously determined : chlorides are
often present in considerable amount, but are not evidence of
impurity ; nitrogen in the form of nitrites and nitrates is also
often present in notable quantity in water of deep wells, especially in the chalk, and is no sign of contamination ; ammonia
may also be allowed in amounts which would be suspicious in
shallow wells.

While the artesian wells often furnish water the temperature
of which is objectionably high, the water of many springs and of
ordinary deep wells is usually of nearly uniform and of comparatively low temperature. In fact, the sinking of deep wells in
connection with breweries is partly due to the fancied necessity
for hard water in brewing certain kinds of beer, and partly to
furnish an abundance of cold water for cooling purposes.

It is a curious fact that the hard water from springs and deep
wells, though clear and bright when first obtained, becomes
covered with a confervoid growth when exposed to the sunlight
in open reservoirs, and the tubes of some artesian wells become
lined with a growth of algæ. If it is necessary to store the
water from deep wells, this should be done in covered reservoirs ;
this is, of course, desirable also as a means of avoiding elevation

of temperature in summer if the water remains in the reservoir for any considerable time.

Table XIX contains some details with reference to artesian

TABLE XIX.—EXAMINATION OF ARTESIAN AND DEEP WELLS.

LOCALITY.	DEPTH IN FEET.	TEMPERATURE IN CENTIGRADE DEGREES.	HARDNESS: PARTS IN 100,000.	TOTAL SOLIDS: PARTS IN 100,000.	AUTHORITY.
Artesian Wells.					
Grenelle, Paris.........................	1,806	27	....	14.2	Peligot, 1857.
Passy, Paris	1,914	28	....	14.2	Poggiale & Lambert, 1862.
Boston, Mass..........................	1,750	....	....	1878.7	J. M. Merrick.
Chicago, Ill..........................	700	14	....	....	
Louisville, Ky., Dupont's Well......	2,086	24.5	....	1570.0	J. Lawrence Smith.
St. Louis, Mo....	2,199	23	....	879.1	A. Litton, M.D.
" Mo., Asylum Well.........	3,843	40.5	....	....	C. C. Broadhead.
Charleston, S. C., Wentworth Street	1,260	30.7	....	273.7	C. U. Shepard, Jr.
" " Citadel Green....	1,970	37.5	....	111.6	S. T. Robinson, Jr.
" " Chisholm Mill....	425	....	....	369.7	Wm. Robertson.
Coosaw, S. C....	760	....	....	82.7	F. F. Chisholm.
Deep Wells.					
Birkenhead, Eng	527	....	5.7	14.2	Rivers Pollution Com.
Birmingham, Eng	300	10.2	15.8	31.3	" " "
" Another...............	400	10.8	15.1	19.3	" " "
Bradford, Eng.........................	360	12.8	14.1	55.4	" " "
Brighton, Eng	1,285	9.9	4.4	35.4	" " "
Liverpool, Bootle Well.............	312	10.4	12.6	34.4	" " "
London, Trafalgar Square.........	383	....	5.9	83.4	" " "
Jersey City, N. J., Secaucus Works.	600	...	...	117.7	G. H. Cook, Geol. Rep.
Newark, N. J., Celluloid Works.....	250	...	...	213.0	" " "
" " Lister Bros	615	13.0	....	262.0	" " "
Paterson, N. J., Burton Brewing Co.	200	...	....	20.6	" " "

and deep wells in various localities. Although there are so many of these wells in the United States, the author has found it extremely difficult to obtain reliable information with reference to the chemical character of the water. The depth of the well, whether the water is palatable or undrinkable, how it acts toward soap and in steam boilers—these observations, which do not require the aid of an expert or involve additional expense, usually complete the stock of available information. Table XX contains the results of more complete analyses obtained by the Rivers Pollution Commission of Great Britain from the examination of a large number of deep-well waters from various geological formations. In the same table also—for convenience of arrangement—are inserted the results obtained by the same commission in the examination of unpolluted waters of various descriptions and from many different localities in Great Britain. Table XXI contains results derived from the examination of the water from wells and springs in the different geological formations in Bohemia,* the total number of analyses being about 125.

* Bělohoubek: Ueber den Einfluss der geologischen Verhaltnisse auf die chemische Beschaffenheit des Quell- und Brunnenwassers. Pph. 8vo, pp. 46. Prag, 1880.

TABLE XX.—Examination of Deep-Well Waters and of Unpolluted Waters from various Sources.

[Results expressed in **Parts in 100,000**.]

Geological Formation.	Total Solids.	Organic Carbon.	Organic Nitrogen.	Ammonia.	Nitrogen as Nitrites and Nitrates.	Total Combined Nitrogen.	Previous Sewage or Animal Contamination.	Chlorine.	Hardness.			No. of Samples.
									Temporary.	Permanent.	Total.	
Deep Wells.												
Devonian Rocks and Millstone Grit....	32.68	0.068	0.012	0.005	0.294	0.310	2,671	2.70	8.8	8.6	17.4	7
Coal Measures.	83.10	0.119	0.034	0.044	0.207	0.278	2,243	18.05	15.1	20.6	35.7	9
Magnesian Limestone.	61.14	0.076	0.030	0	1.426	1.456	13,037	4.31	16.9	26.9	43.8	3
New Red Sandstone....	30.61	0.036	0.014	0.003	0.717	0.734	6,895	2.94	7.4	10.5	17.0	28
Lias.	70.98	0.146	0.027	0.001	0.389	0.417	3,730	4.42	21.9	8.2	30.1	2
Oolites.	33.60	0.037	0.010	0.022	0.625	0.654	6,118	2.69	13.8	6.8	20.6	5
Hastings Sand, Green Sand, and Weald Clay.....	45.20	0.068	0.014	0.016	0.196	0.223	1,864	5.38	16.8	10.5	27.3	20
Chalk.	36.88	0.050	0.017	0.001	0.610	0.628	5,801	2.76	21.2	6.5	27.7	66
Chalk beneath London Clay.	78.09	0.093	0.028	0.048	0.068	0.135	797	13.02	9.7	8.7	18.4	13
Thanet Sand and Drift.	53.84	0.113	0.020	0.072	0.116	0.202	1,517	6.32	14.4	7.6	22.0	4
Unpolluted Waters.												
Class I. Rain Water......	2.95	0.070	0.015	0.029	0.003	0.042	42	0.82	0.4	0.5	0.3	39
Class II. Upland Surface Water.....	9.67	0.322	0.032	0.002	0.003	0.042	10	1.13	1.5	4.3	5.4	193
Class III. Deep Well Water	43.78	0.061	0.018	0.012	0.695	0.522	4,743	5.11	15.8	9.2	25.0	157
Class IV. Spring Water....	28.20	0.056	0.013	0.001	0.383	0.396	3,595	2.47	11.0	7.5	18.5	198

TABLE XXI.—Bohemian Well and Spring Waters.

[Results expressed in Parts in 100,000.]

Geological Formation.	Results.	Total Solids.	Sulphuric Acid (SO_3).	Chlorine.	Hardness.*
Azoic............	Max. and Min.	2.8- 28.0	0.2- 2.4	0.1- 0.8	1.3- 6.8
"	Usual Limits.	4.6- 14.3	—	—	2.5- 4.9
Huronian	Max. and Min.	19.8- 55.0	1.3- 5.9	0.9- 2.4	7.7- 13.9
"	Usual Limits.	30.5- 55.0	—	—	—
Silurian...........	Max. and Min.	14.5-150.2	2.8- 48.6	0.5-12.8	4.7- 57.3
"	Usual Limits.	66.0-120.0	—	—	22.6- 45.4
Carboniferous......	Max. and Min.	38.5-374.0	2.4-101.6	0.8-25.2	—
"	Usual Limits.	—	—	—	10.3-124.9
Permian	Max. and Min.	4.5- 29.7	0.1- 1.5	0.1- 1.3	19.9- 22.8
"	Usual Limits.	6.5- 9.0	—	—	1.3- 13.3
Chalk.............	Max. and Min.	4.0-109.0	0.3- 28.3	0.1- 6.8	2.1- 3.5
"	Usual Limits	21.5- 75.7	—	—	1.3- 27.1
Neogen...........	Usual Limits.	37.0- 49.7	0.7- 6.8	1.8- 4.6	19.2- 21.3
Diluvium and Alluvium }	Usual Limits.	19.1- 75.5	0.6- 5.7	1.8- 2.3	7.9- 24.5

* The hardness is in German degrees.

CHAPTER VIII.

ARTIFICIAL IMPROVEMENT OF NATURAL WATER.

NATURE sometimes furnishes water which leaves nothing to be desired in respect to quality, but, unfortunately, the best water—such as is sometimes derived from springs and not unfrequently from the ground water—is apt to be limited in amount, and, very generally, a supply sufficient in quantity can be procured only from a source possessing some undesirable qualities. Although a water which is polluted to any considerable extent by sewage is not capable of purification by any process practicable on the large scale, so that it can safely be used for domestic supply, the character of many natural waters may be sensibly improved by proper treatment. Again, there are circumstances under which it becomes absolutely necessary to use a bad water or none at all, and in such cases purification must be accomplished if possible.

We shall consider various methods of improving potable water under the following heads:

1. Sedimentation and storage.
2. Filtration (on the large and on the household scale).
3. Clark's process for softening hard water.
4. Other (chemical) processes.
5. Distillation.

Sedimentation and Storage.

When a stream or other body of surface water is used as a source of supply, the best way—speaking solely from a sanitary point of view—is to pump directly from the source into the distribution without the intervention of settling basins and reservoirs. This is not, however, generally practicable. In some cases the general or occasional turbid character of a stream renders sedimentation necessary, and in other cases storage basins are necessary in order that the stream may furnish a sufficient quantity of water during the dry season.

Sedimentation.—The particles of suspended matter which render a stream turbid or muddy, regularly or in times of flood, are of a greater specific gravity than the water itself, and settle out more or less completely if the water be allowed to stand quiet for a time. Lakes and ponds are natural settling basins, and have this advantage over running streams, that they are much less liable to be rendered turbid by freshets ; they are not, however, usually entirely free from floating particles, but the suspended matter in this case cannot be removed except by filtration.

Some figures have been already given in Table VII to show the various amounts of suspended matter in certain rivers. It is well known that the water of many of the rivers in this country, especially in the West, is not, in its natural condition, acceptable, if indeed it can be regarded as at all suitable for use. It is said* that the sediment in the Mississippi (or rather the Missouri) at St. Louis amounts at times to 1.8 per cent of the bulk of the water. About 94.5 per cent of the sediment is deposited within 24 hours in still water at ordinary stages of the river, but for two months in the year, during floods, there is so much fine sediment that no amount of settling will clarify the water.

It is desirable to remove the suspended matter, not simply on æsthetic grounds, because it renders the water less acceptable to the eye, but also because particles of gritty mineral matter, or even of clay, often cause diarrhœa, especially in the case of persons not in the habit of using the water, to which many persons do become accustomed by use. Where thorough filtration is for any reason impracticable, sedimentation serves a useful purpose.

There are now at St. Louis four settling basins, 600 × 278 feet, and 19 feet deep. The floors are paved with brick on edge and slope toward the center and the river side. The basins are used alternately, one being drawn from, one filling and two settling, or one settling and one being cleaned. The sediment is removed from each basin about once in four months, some 16 inches being collected in that time. The sediment is floated off with a stream of water, at a cost of from 0.84 cent (1879) to 1.05 (1878) per cubic yard.

---

* Engineering News, 1881, p. 142.

As an accompaniment of a scheme of filtration, settling basins are in many cases essential. Where a stream is subject to sudden and transient periods of turbidity, besides serving in their proper capacity, they may also serve as storage basins and make it possible to avoid altogether taking water from the stream when it is at its worst.

In following the variations of a turbid water, or in tracing the progress of sedimentation, estimation of the amount of turbidity is usually made by simply looking through a certain depth of the water in a tube or other glass vessel. Several attempts have been made to reach more accurate results, and Grahn and Salbach[*] have proposed to apply the principles of photometry to the solution of the problem.

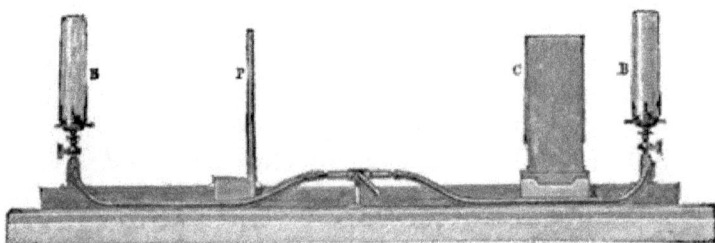

FIG. 27.—SALBACH'S PHOTOMETER, ELEVATION. (FROM FISCHER.)

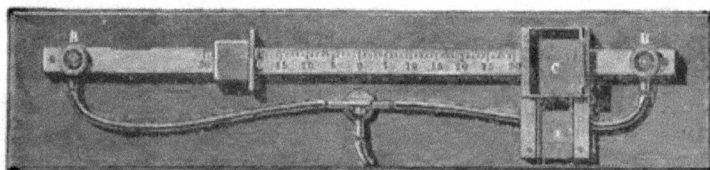

FIG. 28.—SALBACH'S PHOTOMETER, PLAN. (FROM FISCHER.)

Figures 27 and 28 represent Salbach's arrangement of the photometer. P carries a disk of paper on which a spot has been made transparent by means of oil or stearine; at the beginning P is set at the zero point of the scale, and the burners, B B, regulated so as to give an equal amount of light. C is a leaden box the glass sides of which are exactly parallel, and 100 millimeters apart. When C is filled with turbid water a portion of the light given by the right-hand burner is cut off, and the screen P must be moved nearer to this weakened source of light in order that the illumination on both sides may be equal. From the distance through which the screen must be moved, it is possible to calculate the loss of light, and thus to obtain an expression for the amount of turbidity of the water.

Storage.—Some of the disadvantages to which stored water is subject in ponds and impounding reservoirs have already been indicated—such, for instance, as undesirable increase of temperature, growth of noxious algæ, etc. On the other hand, there are certain advantages in storing surface waters in clean deep basins exposed to the sun and air. When strongly colored surface waters are thus stored, the dissolved organic matter undergoes chemical change, and a portion of it, being removed from solution, settles out as a sediment ; at the same time the color becomes less marked.

In order to compare and estimate the depth of color of various waters, or of the same water at various times, an instrument was invented and used by a medical commission which investigated a number of sources of water supply proposed for the city of Boston.* "The instrument consists of two tubes, B and D (Fig. 29), sliding water-tight one within the other, the lower end of each tube being closed with a disk of plate glass. Into the large tube, B, just above the plate glass disk, is inserted a small piece of tubing which terminates in a funnel - shaped receiver, A. Water poured into this receiver will therefore pass into the space between the two glass disks, entirely filling the outer tube when the inner tube is withdrawn, and again

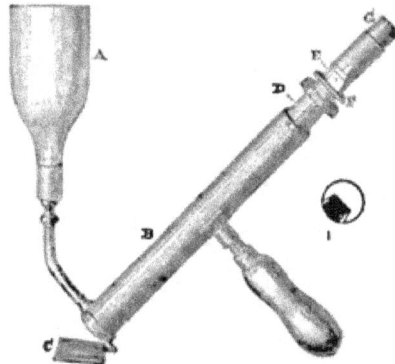

FIG. 29.

returning to the receiver when the inner tube is pushed down so that the glass disks come in contact with each other. Through

---

* Report of the Medical Commission upon the Sanitary Qualities of the Sudbury, Mystic, Shawshine and Charles River Waters. City Document, No. 102. Boston, 1874.

an opening near the upper end of the smaller tube, *D*, is inserted one end of a rhombic prism, *E*, in which total internal reflection takes place twice.

" This prism extends half way across the inner tube, *D*, so that an eye, looking through the eye-piece, *G*, sees the field of vision nearly half filled by the surface of the prism. This appearance is represented at *I*. The eye-piece, *G*, contains a single lens, which is focused upon the upper surface of the prism. The position and angles of the prism are such that a ray of light outside of, and parallel to, the tube *B*, is reflected, first directly into the tube *D*, and then parallel to its axis, thus emerging from the prism and entering the eye-piece alongside of the rays of light which have passed through the two plate glass disks. It will thus be seen that the conditions for comparing the color and intensity of these two sources of light are as favorable as possible. A piece of white card, *C*, fastened at the lower end of the larger tube, throws a uniform white light through the tubes *B* and *D*, and also along the outside of the tube *B*, into the prism *E*.

" In using this instrument, a piece of brownish-yellow glass, *F*, is placed in front of the prism *E*, and the water, whose color is to be determined, is poured into the receiver *A*. The inner tube is then withdrawn until the column of water between the two glass disks is sufficiently long to give to the light passing through it a color equal to that imparted by the colored glass *F* to the light passing through the prism *E*. The length of this column of water, which will, of course, vary inversely with the depth of color, can be determined by means of the scale on the inner tube *D*. By this means, the relative intensity of color of various specimens of water may be determined with considerable accuracy."

Aeration.—Although a water colored by vegetable matter loses color when exposed to sunlight in closed vessels, it is probable that the changes which take place in storage basins are due partly to the action of the air. There is no doubt that the passage of the water over natural falls or artificial dams tends to its improvement, or that the stagnation of water in "dead ends," or in small reservoirs without circulation, tends to its deterioration. In the larger reservoirs and ponds the winds play an important part in agitating and aerating the water, but it is very doubtful if any scheme for artificially aerating the water would accomplish enough to pay for the outlay involved.

Filtration.

The filtration of water on the large scale has been practised in England and on the continent of Europe for many years, and has become very general in cases where the supply is taken from streams or ponds. From statistics which were laid before the Düsseldorf meeting of the German Public Health Association (in 1876) by Engineer Grahn,* it would seem that in Germany, since 1858, there has been no town of considerable size supplied with unfiltered river water, while the increase with reference to other sources of supply may be seen from the following data :

TOTAL NUMBER OF INHABITANTS IN 80 TOWNS OF GERMANY, GERMAN–AUSTRIA, AND SWITZERLAND

SUPPLIED WITH	1858.	1876.
Unfiltered river water........................	460,000	460,000
Filtered river water...............................	1,060,000	1,697,000
Spring and ground water (by gravitation)............	25,000	1,519,000
Spring and ground water (by pumping).............	45,000	1,719,000

In the United States very little has yet been done in the way of systematic filtration on the large scale, although, in some localities, attempts have been made to improve the condition of the water by intercepting some of the suspended matter.

Filter beds, as usually constructed, are water-tight basins some ten feet or more in depth, the sides built of masonry, and the bottom puddled or made of concrete, or paved with brick and cemented. The area may be from 20,000 to 50,000, or in some cases even 150,000 square feet. In building up the filtering bed, provision is first made for the ready collection of the water by constructing upon the floor of the basin drains or channel-ways of stone or brick laid dry; then follows a layer of broken stone, the fragments being three or four inches in diameter. This is succeeded by gravel screened so as to be of uniform size, a layer of coarse being followed by one or more layers of finer material; upon the gravel rests sand, likewise separated

---

* See the Deutsche Vierteljahrsschr. für öffentl. Gesundheitspflege, ix (1877), p. 108.

into layers of uniform size. The exact thickness of the different layers, and the extent to which the separation into the different sizes is carried, are subject, of course, to considerable variation.

The water stands several feet deep over the surface of the sand, and is allowed to flow down through the filter at such rate as experience shows to be most advantageous. Naturally, when the sand is clean, a greater quantity of water can be passed in a given time than when the sand has become clogged; practice differs as to the maximum rate, but it is seldom over six inches, vertically, per hour, and often less. At the rate mentioned, each square foot of surface would deliver 12 cubic feet (or 89¾ United States gallons) per day.

When the beds become clogged so as no longer to filter with sufficient rapidity, the water is drawn out from the beds, and the upper layer of sand, for a depth of one-half or three-quarters of an inch, is removed. When by successive parings the thickness of the sand has been considerably reduced, that which has been removed is washed and replaced so as to restore the original thickness, the waste of washing being made up with fresh sand.

Principles of Sand Filtration.

Having thus stated briefly the main features of ordinary sand filtration, we will proceed to discuss the principles which govern filtration in general, and afterward consider certain special points with reference to the successful carrying out of the process. For this purpose we shall consider the "impuri- . ties" of ordinary water as divided into three classes: first, the suspended matters, whether of mineral, animal or vegetable origin; second, the dissolved mineral or saline matters; third, the dissolved organic matters.

The action which takes place when an ordinary water is passed through a sand filter is threefold. In the first place, the most obvious action is the arresting of suspended particles of solid matter which are too large to pass through the pores of the filter. The second action partakes something of the character of sedimentation, and may be well illustrated by the following experiment:

Take two jars of equal size, and fill one of them with fragments of broken rock as large as half a fist, or with very coarse gravel, arranging the material so that a syphon can be inserted

as shown in the figure.   Prepare now a quantity of a turbid liquid
by stirring up
some fine clay in
water and allow-
ing the coarser
particles to sub-
side.   With this
turbid water fill
both jars and al-
low t h e m to
stand for twelve
or fifteen hours.
Then, by means
of syphons reach-
ing to the same
depth in t h e

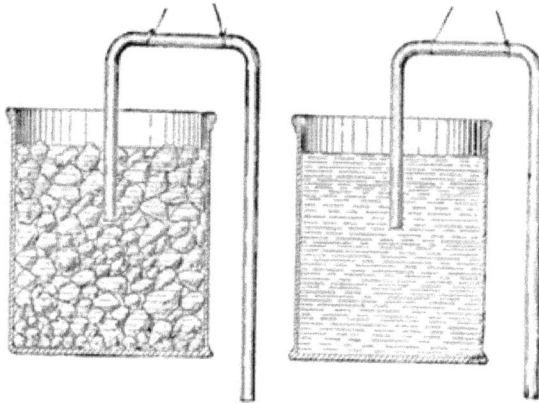

FIG. 30.

jars, carefully remove a quantity of water from each.   It will be
found that the water from the jar containing the broken stone is
perceptibly clearer than the other.

The same thing may be shown by allowing a turbid water to
flow *very slowly* through a trough filled with broken stone.   In
these cases the interstices between the fragments are so many settling chambers, as it were, and the particles of the clay deposit
not only upon the floor of these chambers, but also on the sides
and roof, being drawn thereto by a sort of attraction.   In the
case of a sand filter, the interstices are small and very numerous.

The third sort of action which takes place in the porous
material of a filter is the removal of substances which are actually
dissolved in the water.   As far as the mineral or saline matters
are concerned, this action is trifling, although not inappreciable
with certain filtering media: with sand filters we can say that
there is, practically, no effect on the dissolved mineral matter,
unless there is opportunity for a chemical change to take place.
Thus, it seems to be well attested, that a hard water containing
bicarbonate of lime may deposit carbonate of lime in the filter,
owing to the escape of carbonic acid.*   Sometimes the amount

* See, for example, Lefort, Chimie Hydrologique, pp. 165, 200. It has also
been shown by Schloesing (see Assainissement de la Seine, 2ième partie, Enquête. p.
191), that at some depth in soil which had been irrigated with sewage, there were
formed crystals of carbonate of lime, owing to the escape of carbonic acid from the
sewage water, which contained a small proportion of bicarbonate of lime in solution.

of mineral matter may be greater in the filtered than in the unfiltered water, if the material of the bed, the gravel and stones,
contain, as they often do, soluble ingredients.

With reference to the dissolved organic substances, it may
be said that a small but appreciable amount may be removed by
a well-conducted sand filtration; the action may be explained in
two ways.   In the first place, most porous substances possess
the power of removing certain kinds of organic matter by something which may be called *adhesion*.   The absorptive power for
any substance is limited and soon reached, and the substance
thus removed may by appropriate means be again brought into
solution.   Quartz sand, as we should infer, possesses the power
to a slight degree only.   In the second place, dissolved organic
matter is removed in the sand filter by oxidation.   The substance is actually burned more or less completely, in part by the
oxygen held in solution in the water, and in part by the air entangled in the interstices of the sand.   Although in filling the
beds with water, great care is taken to displace the air gradually,
and as completely as possible, there must always some remain in
the concavities of the individual grains of sand and otherwise
entangled.   The extent of the action of a sand filter in this
direction depends not only on the fineness of the filtering
medium, and the rate at which the filtration takes place, but also
and in considerable measure upon the frequency with which the
filter is cleansed.   The cleansing of the filter not only removes
the accumulation of organic matter, which, if allowed to remain,
would tend to injure the water, but also involves the aëration of
the sand, at least to a considerable depth.

Details of Practice.

We now proceed to some more particular details of the practice of sand filtration.   The quality of the sand employed is by
no means a matter of indifference, and in the case of waters
which usually or occasionally carry finely divided clay in suspension, a great deal depends upon having proper sand and a slow
rate of filtration.   It may be said, in general, that the sand employed should be made up mainly of grains from $\frac{1}{3}$ of a millimeter to 1 millimeter in diameter, and the more uniform the size

of the grains the better.* A considerable proportion of larger grains does no harm, but the smaller particles should be washed out before the sand is used ; as a rule, sand that has been used and washed is better than fresh sand. As the fineness of the sand increases, its efficiency as a filter increases, but the difficulty and cost of filtration increase likewise, and more frequent cleansing is necessary. To obtain the best and most economical results with a given water, special experiments should be made with reference to the sand best fitted for that water—although, to be sure, it is not always possible to command that which would be absolutely the best.

While it is, in general, true that the upper layer of sand does most of the work in intercepting the various floating matters in the water, it does not do the whole under the conditions which occur in ordinary practice. Examination shows that the sand is somewhat affected to a greater depth, and it may occasionally be necessary to renew all the sand. The very fact, which will appear presently, that in all actual works there are times when the water is imperfectly clarified, shows that the interior of a sand filter must in time become more or less foul.

It may perhaps be asked, why, if the work is practically done by the first few inches of sand, it is necessary to bestow such care on the construction of the beds, and on the arrangement of the materials employed.

In the first place, it is a well-recognized fact, that the worst possible filter is one in which the portions of material of different sizes are indiscriminately mixed. " The different degrees of fineness in the materials beneath the sand, and their several thicknesses, were intended first to prevent the fine sand from following the water downward into the drains, and next to insure the presence of such a body of clean water below the surface of the filter as would penetrate the numerous joints and openings of the drains, and keep them full, without creating anywhere currents or veins of water of any perceptible difference of velocity.

" With the drains much nearer to the body of the sand, it will be understood that the tendency of the water would be to flow through the filtering material more rapidly just over the

* Mr. Charles Greaves, of the East London Works, says " sand that would go through a screen consisting of 32 or 33 No. 10 wires in 6 inches," is the best, according to English experience.

pipe than at five feet on either side of it. The distance through which it had to travel might be so short as to induce its concentration. The low velocity at which the water flows through the filter, the uniformity of fineness in the sand, and the distance of the collecting drains from its surface, all work together to produce that regularity of action over the entire filter bed upon which its perfection depends."[*]

The rate of filtration must be determined by the character of the water and the condition of the filters. The maximum rate given on page 152 as $89\frac{3}{4}$ U. S. gallons per square foot in 24 hours would be equivalent to about $3\frac{3}{4}$ cubic meters per square meter of surface. The practice of most works falls considerably below this as an average rate; thus at Altona, where, to be sure, the constantly turbid water of the Elbe is filtered, the average rate is only 1.5 cubic meters per square meter of surface in 24 hours. It is stated that the sand here employed is coarser than necessary, and that with somewhat finer sand a more rapid rate of filtration would be possible.[†]

There is considerable difference in practice as to the depth of water kept upon the surface of the beds and the head under which filtration takes place. Moreover, the *head* under which the water is filtered varies at any works according to the condition of the sand. The clear-water well is generally so arranged that the height of water in it can be lowered at pleasure; and the head under which the water is filtered is the difference between the level in the bed and in the clear-water well, as may be seen, in the accompanying cut, where the head is measured by the distance between a and b. While the beds are clean, a difference of from 9 to 12 inches suffices to cause a proper rate of flow; as they become clogged a

FIG. 31.

much greater pressure is required, but it is not desirable to in-

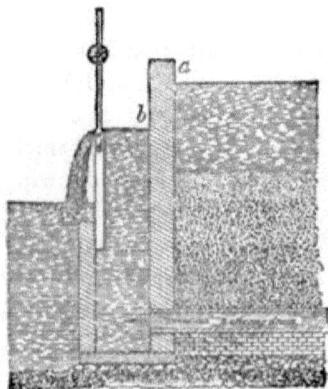

---

[*] Kirkwood, Filtration of River Waters, p. 10.
[†] Samuelson, Nachschrift to German edition of Kirkwood's Report. Hamburg, 1876.

crease the pressure to too great an extent, as the sand is thereby fouled to a greater depth and compacted more than is desirable.

The frequency with which it is necessary to cleanse the beds depends upon circumstances. In the worst stages of the English rivers a filter bed has to be cleaned once a week, rarely oftener. When the rivers are free from turbidity, cleansing may not be necessary more than once a month, or in some cases once in two months. The general method of cleaning has already been indicated. In some places the practice is different. At Zurich, in Switzerland, it is the custom to clean the beds by forcing the water in a reverse direction through the filters. Workmen, clad in rubber clothing, then stir up the upper surface of the sand with forks, and the collected slime is washed off and floated away. This requires an abundance of water, and the ability to command the requisite pressure. One would suppose also that it would involve some danger of disturbing the arrangement of the filtering material.

Certain recently published details of the manner in which the filtration works at Berlin* are conducted, are of considerable interest, as the condition of things is similar to that which exists in some of the surface waters of our Eastern States. The water of the Spree, besides being somewhat polluted by sewage and being in a constant roily condition, possesses, especially in time of flood, a deep brownish-yellow color, and, at times, a peculiar *poady* taste due to vegetable extractive matter. Moreover, from spring until fall, a more or less copious growth of *algæ* adds to the disagreeable character of the water, similar to those described and figured on page 86.

The filter beds are construced on the English model and are eleven in number—three covered and eight uncovered—having a total area of 37,000 square meters. The filtration is carried on at a very slow rate. The water is used, of course, in varying quantities from hour to hour, and, on account of the small size of the clear-water reservoir, a constant rate of filtration is impossible ; the maximum rate is, however, not over 0.1 meter downward per hour. For the greater part of the time 1 square meter

---

* Mittheilungen über natürliche und künstliche Sandfiltration. Nach Betriebs-resultaten der Berliner Wasserwerke vor dem Stralauer Thor, bearbeitet von C. Piefke, Betriebs-Ingenieur. 8vo, pp. 75. Berlin, 1881. A review and abstract of this pamphlet appeared in the Journal of the Franklin Institute, December, 1881.

of sand surface is not required to furnish much more than one cubic meter of water in twenty-four hours. This would be at the rate of only 24½ U. S. gallons per square foot, and very much less than is the practice in many other places. The head under which filtration takes place is seldom more than 0.5 meter (say 20 inches), but even with this low pressure and slow delivery it has been found impossible, with clean sand alone, to filter the water satisfactorily. If the unfiltered water be allowed to stand a fortnight or so, although the larger of the suspended particles will have settled to the bottom, the water still retains a milky appearance, and sand alone cannot remove the exceedingly fine particles to which this appearance is due. On this account the water from a freshly cleaned filter is not used at once, but is allowed to stand on the bed and then to pass through very slowly until a thin coating has formed on the surface of the sand. This coating is essential to the removal of the finest particles from the water subsequently filtered. Of course, as the coating becomes thicker the filtration becomes more difficult until it partially stops and the filter is " dead."

As has been hinted above, the great trouble in summer is from the abundance of small algæ which soon clog the filter. When the algæ are absent, a square meter of surface usually filters 20 cubic meters before cleaning is necessary ; but in summer the capacity is not over 10 cubic meters to the same area, and when a slimy coating of decayed algæ covers the surface of the sand it becomes impossible, under the pressure commonly employed, to pass more than 2 cubic meters of water through 1 square meter of sand surface. In the Berlin beds the thickness of the sand is 600 millimeters (about 2 feet). At each cleaning the sand is removed for a depth of about 10 millimeters, but fresh sand is not returned to the bed until only about 200 millimeters of the original thickness remain. The foul sand is allowed to stand exposed to the air until, by decay, the organic matter has lost its slimy character ; it is then washed and eventually replaced upon the beds. When the filters are emptied the water is drawn completely off, and by successive and systematic stirring nearly the entire thickness of the sand is exposed to the air, in order that the small amount of organic matter which was not retained at the surface may be oxidized and destroyed. With the same object in view, the air is allowed to circulate freely, for several days if possible, through the coarser underlying material. These filters are filled from below with filtered water, and then the water is passed through slowly and is allowed to waste for several days.

Practical Results of Artificial Filtration.

As far as the suspended matter is concerned, the chief difficulty in obtaining a bright and clear filtered water lies with the finely divided clay which forms the turbidity of many streams, especially at times of high water. The Berlin experience has already been alluded to. The following table, taken from the Sixth Report of the Rivers Pollution Commission (p. 215), will give an idea of the efficiency of the filtration as practised by the various London companies. The observations being made on monthly samples, the statements of the table will perhaps hardly give a just idea of the results obtained day by day; but they will serve to indicate the fact that the mere possession of filter-beds does not secure perfectly clear water at all times.

TABLE XXII.—Thames and Lea Water—Comparative Efficiency of Different Rates of Filtration during the years 1868 to 1873, inclusive.

NAME OF COMPANY.	Maximum rate of Filtration expressed in inches per hour.	NUMBER OF MONTHLY OCCASIONS WHEN—			
		Clear.	Slightly Turbid.	Turbid.	Very Turbid.
THAMES.					
Chelsea........................	7.27	49	15	5	6
West Middlesex...............	4.71	75	0	0	0
Southwark and Vauxhall.......	6.00	41	24	5	4
Grand Junction...............	6.97	55	14	7	0
Lambeth	12.00	42	11	12	10
LEA.					
New River....................	5.00	70	4	0	0
East London.................	3.85	51	18	3	2

As already explained, in addition to clarification of the water, ordinary filtration does remove an appreciable amount of organic matter previously held in solution. In addition to the explanation given on page 153, it may be said that a part of the effect which has been observed may be ascribed to the oxide of iron,[*] and perhaps other minerals, which exist in the sand used for filtration, the sand being seldom or never pure quartz.

The effect of filtration on the water of the Thames and Lea

---

[*] This is the view of Thomas Spencer, the inventor of the so-called "carbide of iron," used sometimes as a filtering medium. See page 166.

has been made the subject of experiment by the Rivers Pollution Commission and others. The following table includes some of the results obtained:

TABLE XXIII.—Observations on the Water of the various London Companies.

[Results expressed in Parts per 100,000.]

COMPANY.	DATE.	UNFILTERED OR FILTERED.	TOTAL SOLID RESIDUE AT 120°–130° C.	ORGANIC CARBON.	ORGANIC NITROGEN.	AMMONIA.
NEW RIVER. New River, Stoke Newington	1873. Jan. 25..	Unf..	31.98	0.350	0.084	0.004
		Filt'd.	30.16	0.246	0.042	0
New River, New River Head	Jan. 27..	Unf..	31.96	0.330	0.061	0.004
		Filt'd.	31.56	0.242	0.043	0
THAMES RIVER. Southwark, Hampton	Jan. 31..	Unf..	32.00	0.321	0.063	0.001
		Filt'd.	31.56	0.273	0.042	0
Chelsea	Jan. 31..	Unf..	31.36	0.325	0.046	0.003
		Filt'd.	31.10	0.256	0.032	0
Lambeth	Jan. 31..	Unf..	32.96	0.273	0.067	0.004
		Filt'd.	32.74	0.256	0.038	0.001
Grand Junction	Feb. 3..	Unf..	31.42	0.262	0.042	0.004
		Filt'd.	30.68	0.231	0.032	0.001
Southwark, Battersea	Feb. 5..	Unf..	31.80	0.239	0.047	0.005
		Filt'd.	30.90	0.226	0.035	0.001
West Middlesex	Feb. 7..	Unf..	31.22	0.209	0.071	0.005
		Filt'd.	30.56	0.198	0.043	0.001
RIVER LEA. East London	Feb. 1..	Unf..	34.68	0.363	0.082	0.004
		Filt'd.	34.70	0.305	0.041	0.001

From this table it appears that the filtration effects an appreciable decrease in the amount of organic matter as judged from the "organic carbon" and "organic nitrogen." In ordinary practice this effect is trifling, and sand filtration is not sufficient to remove the color which many surface waters possess, nor to completely remove the unpleasant taste which sometimes affects such waters. On these points the author has satisfied himself by abundant experiments, and this is also the experience at Berlin. Here, as has been mentioned, the Spree water often possesses to a marked degree the brownish-yellow color common to streams which flow through marshy or peaty regions, and to the water of most impounding reservoirs. This color, with the taste which at times accompanies it, gives rise to general complaint, but even very slow filtration fails to remove it to any considerable extent. The slight action which has been observed in this connection, Piefke, resting on experiments made with prepared cellulose, ascribes rather to the sediment containing vegetable fiber, than to the sand itself. Table XXIV contains the results of a few examinations of water from certain American localities: here the amount of organic matter is indicated by the " albuminoid ammonia," and this, when the filter beds are in good working order, is appreciably less in the filtered than in the unfiltered water.

TABLE XXIV.—Examination of Water from Poughkeepsie and Hudson, N. Y.

[Results expressed in Parts in 100,000]

DATE RECEIVED.	LOCALITY.	AMMONIA.	" ALBUMINOID AMMONIA."	SOLID RESIDUE.		TOTAL SOLIDS AFTER FILTRATION THROUGH PAPER.	REMARKS.
				" Organic and Volatile."	Total at 212° Fahr.		
1877.	POUGHKEEPSIE.						
Nov. 13,	River............	0.0109	0.0117	1.7	12.1	10.1	Very turbid.
Nov. 13,	Clear-water basin.	0.0077	0.0139	1.1	9.1	9.0	Clear.
Nov. 19,	River............	0.0104	0.0157	1.5	10.5	8.6	Very turbid.
Nov. 19,	Clear-water basin.	0.0112	0.0155	1.3	9.4	9.0	Slightly turbid.
	HUDSON.						
Nov. 27,	River............	0.0059	0.0152	1.13	8.21	....	Turbid.
Nov. 27,	Filtered water....	0.0040	0.0123	....	....	....	Slightly turbid.
Dec. 10,	River............	0.0051	0.0152	0.72	8.40	....	Turbid.
Dec. 10,	Filtered water....	0.0056	0.0131	1.02	8.14	....	Slightly turbid.
1878.							
Jan. 18,	Top of filter bed, i.e., unfiltered..	0.0123	0.0133	1.12	10.64	10.00	Turbid.
Jan. 18,	Filtered water ...	0.0237	0.0163	0.92	11.12	10.60	Slightly turbid.

Sand Filtration in the United States.

Up to the present time there has been very little done in this country in the way of systematic filtration of water supplies, partly, perhaps, from indifference and lack of information, but

11

mainly on account of the expense. The numerous complaints which arise in the case of almost every city and town supplied with surface water render the question of filtration an important one, and attempts have been made in various places to accomplish the desired object with a less expensive and elaborate plant than that required by the English system.

Poughkeepsie, on the Hudson River, in the State of New York, was the first city in the Union to adopt a scheme for the artificial filtration of the entire water supply. The filtering works consist * of a settling-basin 25 × 60 feet in plan and 12 feet deep, in three compartments, arranged with reference to the deposition of the heavier particles of mud before the water passes on to the beds. The two filter beds are each 200 by $73\frac{1}{2}$ feet in plan, and 12 feet deep, built with vertical walls ; each has, therefore, 14,700 square feet of filtering area. The 6 feet of filtering materials, beginning at the top of the bed, are disposed as follows :

```
24 inches of sand.
 6   "    " ¼ inch gravel.
 6   "    " ½  "     "
 6   "    " 1  "     "
 6   "    " 2  " broken stone.
24   "    " 4 to 8 in.  "     "
 ———
Total, 72 inches.
```

The beds have a concrete bottom or floor 12 inches in thickness, upon which are arranged open stone culverts to conduct the filtered water to the intermediate basin. The flow of water from each bed to this intermediate basin is controlled by a gate, so that while one bed is being cleaned the other may be used. The filtration is conducted in the usual manner, as is also the cleaning and renewal of the sand, an inch or so of sand being removed at a time, and the sand being washed and replaced only when the upper layer has been much reduced in thickness.

The intermediate filtered-water basin is 6 × 85 feet in plan, and 16 feet deep. This retains the filtered water until it is allowed to pass into the filtered-water reservoir. This reservoir is 28 × 88 feet in plan, and 17 feet deep, and from it the water is pumped to the uncovered distributing reservoir from which the

---

* See Fourth Annual Report of the Water Commissioners of the City of Poughkeepsie for the year ending Dec. 31, 1872.

service pipes are fed. Sluice gates and drain pipes permit the lowering of the water on the beds in any or all of the basins.

The city of Hudson, N. Y., is also supplied from the Hudson River. The river water is pumped to the summit of a hill overlooking the town, on which are situated the filter bed and the distributing reservoir. The filter basin [*] is $13\frac{1}{2}$ feet in depth, is built with sloping sides, and has an area, at the surface of the sand, of 9,081 feet.

The filtering material is six feet deep, and is arranged precisely as in the Poughkeepsie works which have been already described. The fragments of broken stone rest upon a concrete floor six inches in thickness, having a slight inclination toward the middle or axial line, and this line toward the outlet. Along this line runs an openly-laid stone culvert 18×24 inches, which is connected by a cast-iron pipe under the division embankment with the clear-water well. From the clear-water well the filtered water passes over a gate or weir, where it is measured and its flow regulated, to the clear-water basin or distributing reservoir. Thence it passes ordinarily into the effluent chamber through fine copper-wire screens to the 18-inch supply pipe; but the clear-water well can be connected directly with the supply main, so that the city may be supplied from the bed without passing the water through the basin or distributing reservoir. The distributing reservoir is 20 feet deep; its capacity is 3,200,000 gallons. Chemical examinations of the water from these localities have been given in Table XXIV.

Advantages of Covered Filter Beds.

The exposure of a comparatively thin layer of water on the surface of the filter beds has at least two disadvantages. In the first place, in summer the water becomes heated and is, consequently, in a condition to favor the growth of the lower orders of plant life; in the second place, in winter there is likely to be inconvenience from the freezing of the water. In the climate of England neither of these difficulties is as serious as in countries which are either much warmer or much colder, and the filter beds are universally uncovered. On the Continent, however,

---

[*] See Third Report of the Water Commissioners of the City of Hudson, 1875.

the beds and the clear-water reservoirs are sometimes covered as at Berlin, Magdeburg and other places. With reference to the first point—vegetable growth—some trouble is experienced even in England, and the beds become clogged with a confervoid growth, which forms, as it were, a sort of carpet on the surface of the sand, and this, when the beds are cleaned, can be raked off or rolled up in a coherent sheet. This trouble might be lessened somewhat by the use of covered beds, but where the water to be filtered contains an abundance of minute algæ, as is the case with the water of the Spree, at Berlin, there is no perceptible difference in the condition of the covered and uncovered beds.

With reference to the second point alluded to above—the freezing of the water in winter—the European practice, in locations where the ice freezes to any thickness, may be learned by the following quotation from Kirkwood's account of the Berlin works: "The long and severe winters here made special care and precaution necessary in the use of filters during the months of severe frost. The filter beds cannot be laid bare in midwinter; for the frost would in that case penetrate the body of the filter and render it useless. All the filters are, in consequence, during the winter months, kept constantly covered with their maximum depth of water, four feet. Luckily the river water during the winter months is in its best state as regards freedom from turbidity, and also as regards freedom from vegetable discoloration or impurity. The filters, therefore, have comparatively little to intercept, and the river water is flowed continuously upon them, and passes through them without very sensibly impairing their efficiency. To make provision, however, for an unusually long winter, or for an exceptional condition of the river then, which may occasionally occur, it is evident that a larger filtering surface is desirable than would be necessary in a milder climate.

"The ice forms upon the filter beds 15 inches thick, and sometimes, though rarely, 24 inches thick. To protect the enclosing walls of each filter from damage, the ice is kept separated from the walls, 6 to 12 inches, by attendants appointed to that duty; and, so long as the cake of ice is kept floating in this way, the masonry is safe from any danger by its thrust. That this service has been well performed, is demonstrated by the condition of the walls, which are in the best of order, and nowhere out of line, or abraded, that I could perceive."

Since the date of Mr. Kirkwood's report, covered filter beds have been built, and it is stated that the uncovered beds are not cleaned during the winter, the burden of the work being thrown upon the covered beds. At Poughkeepsie and at Hudson, the filtering area is not sufficient to deliver the water throughout the winter without occasional cleaning. The ice has therefore to be broken up and thrown, or rather, dragged out.

There is no question but that water once filtered should be distributed as soon as possible to the consumers. If it is necessary that the water should be stored, it should be in covered reservoirs of small size, which can be readily emptied and cleaned in case of necessity. Apparently, the spores of certain algæ are not removed by filtration: at any rate, it has been found that if, after filtration, the perfectly clear Spree water is allowed to stand for eight or ten days, algæ are developed. This fact is of no practical consequence in a case like that of Berlin, where the clear-water reservoir is too small to hold a single day's consumption, and where, consequently, the water is delivered at once into the service mains.

Expense of Sand Filtration.

The most valuable accessible data of the expense of filtration, as drawn from actual experience, are found in the reports of the Poughkeepsie Water Works. From these data it seems that the expense may be set at from $2.50 to $3.50 per million gallons, not allowing for the interest on the plant or for the cost of pumping. The original cost of the beds was $54,000, the interest on which would exceed the cost of maintenance. In 1879, Mr. J. P. Davis, City Engineer of Boston, Mass., estimated the cost of constructing and operating artificial filters for the Mystic water supply of the city—10,000,000 gallons daily. He allowed for seven beds, each with an area of 33,000 square feet, and estimated that the cost of pumping and of operating the filters would be about $5 per million gallons, and the interest on the necessary works, at five per cent, would be nearly $6.00 per million gallons, making the total cost about $11.00.

Filtering Materials other than Sand.

Many other substances have been proposed from time to
time as suitable to replace the sand wholly or in part, and to
accomplish more than sand can by chemical action on the impurities of the water filtered.   The so-called carbide of iron, of Mr.
Thomas Spencer, is used in several towns of England with some
success.   The carbide of iron is prepared by roasting a mixture
of hematite iron ore and sawdust, and is held to consist mainly
of the magnetic oxide of iron : it is, no doubt, an efficient purifying agent.   It is, however, expensive, and could hardly be prepared for less than $20 or $25 per ton, and for the best effect
should be preceded by a rough sand filtration.   At Wakefield,
England, where, to be sure, the water is extremely filthy, and
the bed confessedly overworked, the Rivers Pollution Commission found that "the water, owing in part to putrescent fermentation and subsidence, and in part to filtration, was chemically less
contaminated than might be expected, yet on both occasions it
contained a large proportion of nitrogenous organic matter.   It
was of a greenish-yellow color, and on one occasion very turbid."

Various attempts have been made to use iron as a filtering
medium since Medlock, in 1857, patented the process for purifying water by allowing it to stand for some time in contact with a
considerable quantity of metallic iron.   It is claimed that "spongy
iron " is now being used with success at Antwerp.*   This material, which was introduced as a medium for household filters a
few years ago by Prof. Bischof, is prepared by reducing hematite ore, and is in a peculiarly porous or spongy condition.   The
filters at Antwerp are said to have been laid out to treat over
two million gallons per day, but it does not appear that anything
like that amount is yet treated.   The works went into operation
in June, 1881, and after twelve months Dr. Frankland was re-
quested to examine and report on them.   The following is taken
from his report :

" The water, which was abstracted from the river Nethe, about
fifteen miles above Antwerp, is first impounded in two reservoirs,
where it is allowed to subside for from 12 to 24 hours ; from these
reservoirs it is pumped on to the spongy iron filters, whence it
flows by gravitation upon sand filters.

---

* Circular of " The Spongy Iron Water and Sewage Purifying Company," London.

"The spongy iron filters consist of two layers of bricks loosely laid upon a bed of concrete. On the bricks rests a layer 3 feet in thickness, formed of 5 m.m. gravel mixed with one-third of its bulk of spongy iron. Then comes a layer 3 inches thick of fine gravel, and lastly a stratum of sand 2 feet deep, making in all 5 feet 3 inches of filtering material.

"The sand filters are similarly laid upon bricks and concrete. They consist of a layer of 5 m.m. gravel 1 foot thick, covered with 3 inches of fine gravel and topped with 2 feet 6 inches of sand, making altogether 3 feet 9 inches of filtering material.

"The area of filtering surface of each filter amounts to 7,302 square feet, and the rate of filtration varies from 300 to 500 gallons per minute, or from 60 to 100 (imp.) gallons per square foot per 24 hours.

"The result of the analysis of the three samples of water show that even after subsidence for nearly 24 hours, the water of the Nethe is exceedingly impure, being still turbid and loaded with an unusually large proportion of highly nitrogenized organic matter. The composition of the water as it passed on to the spongy iron filters is stated to have been:

Total solids (mostly dissolved)...................... 21 parts in 100,000.
Organic Carbon....................................... 0.623
Organic Nitrogen.................... .... 0.219
Ammonia... 0.028
Chlorine (combined)................................. 1.8
Hardness—temporary .... 4.6°
    "   permanent............................... 6.9°
    "   total................................... 11.5°

The water in this condition was very unpalatable.

"The aggregate effect produced by one filtration through spongy iron was as follows:

Total percentage reduction.
Total solids... 41.3
Organic carbon...................................... 60.9
Organic nitrogen.................................... 74.9
Ammonia.. —
Total combined nitrogen........... ... . 77.3
Chlorine .... 0.
Temporary hardness................................. 13.0
Permanent   " 35.3
Total   " 27.0

" The nitrogenous character of the organic matter was diminished from the initial proportion, nitrogen to carbon = 1 : 2.84, down to 1 : 4.4. By boiling, the hardness of the doubly filtered water is reduced to 4.4 parts per 100,000, or 3° on Clark's scale.

" Lastly, from being muddy, unpalatable, colored and much polluted, the water of the Nethe was rendered colorless, bright, palatable and fit for dietetic and domestic purposes."

Wood-charcoal is often used in filters of small size, mixed with sand. Practically, however, it adds nothing to the efficiency of a properly managed sand filter. One way in which charcoal is used is illustrated by the works of Marshalltown, Iowa. Here a filter basin, 32 × 16 feet, was built of masonry ; and a filter floor of two-inch plank was supported on joists laid crosswise. The floor was pierced with three-fourth inch holes, and covered with wire gauze. On this there is a layer of charcoal four inches thick, and above this 14 inches of clean gravel and sand. At Clinton, Iowa, a number of boxes, 16 in fact, filled with charcoal, gravel, and sharp sand, rest upon the conduit. The water flows on to the boxes, and through the material into the conduit. The boxes can be raised one at a time for cleaning. In case of fire, however, the water is taken into the conduit without filtration. Sponge, which is much used in filtering water for manufacturing operations, such as paper-making, has been used to a limited extent in connection with sand and gravel, even on the larger scale of a town supply. Alton, Ill., pumps from the Mississippi River ; and the water is filtered through sponge contained in a cast-iron filter box of 54 cubic feet capacity : this box fits into a tight chamber in the aqueduct leading from the river to the pump-well, and can be raised by machinery. The box can be raised, the sponges renewed, and the box replaced, in three hours. The amount of water filtered is about 150,000 gallons a day. When the river is muddy the sponges are cleaned every three or four weeks : sometimes, when the river is clear, not oftener than once in three months. An attempt was made at one time to filter the supply of the village of Malone, N. Y., through a filter of soft brick, but it was not found practicable to filter with sufficient rapidity.

Many other water works, in this country, make some attempt to " filter " their water by passing it through broken stone, gravel, or gravel and charcoal, or even through sand and gravel. In general, the most that can be said of these arrangements is that they act with greater or less efficiency as *strainers*, removing some of the coarser matters; the infrequency of the cleansing showing that the work done cannot be very great.   As an illustration of this point, may be mentioned a locality where the filter beds were constructed as long ago as 1853.   They are built with sloping sides and measure 50 × 60 feet.   The filtering material, which consists of sand, gravel, and pebble stones, has an entire thickness of 24 inches, and filtration is carried on under a head of from 10 to 15 feet.   The beds are not used in winter, but when in use the amount of water filtered daily is 1,500,000 gallons. The beds are cleaned not oftener than once a year.   This is an extreme case, but inadequate area and infrequent cleansing are the common faults of many so-called filters.   Of course, occasionally, the character of the suspended matter which is to be removed is such that a very simple straining process is all that is required: this is the case with some of our streams on which are a number of saw-mills, and where the comparatively coarse particles of sawdust comprise the main part of the impurity.   In such a case, as, for instance, at Bangor, Me., simple passage through a limited amount of sand is all sufficient.

Household Filtration.

In localities where there is a public water supply, it is, without doubt, the duty of the water board or company to deliver the water to consumers in a condition fit for domestic use.   If the source which is, on the whole, the most available for the water supply is such that filtration is absolutely necessary, the water should be filtered on the large scale by the authority controlling the works.   Practically, however, in the case of most existing water supplies, the water as delivered to the consumers may be appreciably improved by filtration ; household filtration is also often necessary in country residences and in the smaller towns where there is no public supply, and where it is necessary to use rain water which has been stored in tanks or cisterns.

For filtration on the household scale, numerous devices have been made and patented, and the greatest variety of material has been proposed : many sorts of porous stone, sand, powdered glass, bricks, iron in turnings and other forms, vegetable and animal charcoal, sponge, wool, flannel, cotton, straw, sawdust, excelsior and wire-gauze—these are some of the substances which are used. A filter suitable for household use must be made of a material which cannot communicate any injurious or offensive quality to the water which passes through it; it must remove from the water all suspended particles, so as to render the water bright and clear; and it must either be readily cleaned, or the filtering material must be such as to be readily renewed. In addition to these *requirements*, it is of great advantage if the filter is able to remove a noticeable amount of the dissolved organic matter which most waters contain.

As to the filtering material, the author[*] is satisfied that there is nothing, *on the whole*, better than well-burned animal charcoal (bone-coal). This material, as is well known, possesses great power in removing organic matter from solution, and is used in the arts to decolorize colored solutions : on many organic substances it acts, not simply by *adhesion*, but apparently by bringing them into contact with oxygen, and thus absolutely destroying them. Its power does not last indefinitely, and a bone-coal filter, like a filter of any other material, requires cleansing and renewal at proper intervals. Other materials to be mentioned render good service, and in certain sorts of filters, as, for instance, those made for attachment to ordinary cocks or faucets, the bone-coal possesses no essential advantage.

We will consider first the filters of small size, intended to be attached to the faucet, where the water is brought in pipes either from the service-mains of a general supply, or from a tank in the building; second, the portable filters intended to occupy a more or less permanent position, and to be filled with water, either by some ball-cock or other similar arrangement, or by means of smaller supplies continually renewed; third, the more permanent and fixed devices which are inserted or built into underground and other cisterns, or are introduced into the course of the service-pipes so that all the water used in the house passes through them.

Considering the volume of water which must flow through an extremely limited amount of material, no filter capable of being screwed on to an ordinary water-tap can act in any other way than as a strainer, and all that can be required of such a filter is that it shall remove suspended particles and be readily

---

* See Nichols : Filtration of Potable Water. New York, Van Nostrand.

cleansed or renewed at trifling expense. The older forms of filters, which could be cleaned only by unscrewing from the tap and reversing either the whole apparatus or some inside receptacle of the filtering medium, were all open to objection, and no one of them was to be recommended as superior to the primitive and unpatentable device of attaching to the faucet a bag of cotton-flannel to be frequently washed and renewed. At present, however, there are certain forms of filter in the market which can be reversed without removing them from the tap, and which are superior to anything previously in use for the purpose. Figure 32 shows such a filter. The water passes through the wire gauze at E and

FIG. 32.

the filtering material F. By means of a handle, the stem of which is shown in the figure, the ball may be turned over and the sediment collected on E be carried away with the first rush of water. By turning the handle half way, water may be drawn directly without passing through the filtering-ball.

We come now to the larger forms of filters, to those which are portable, but which are intended to occupy a permanent position in the room, or in some cases to be placed in the tank from which the supply is drawn. The material which, next to simple sand, has probably been used as long as anything for the purpose, is stone. Some varieties of sandstone are particularly porous, sufficiently so to allow of the use of slabs of the stone as filters; other similar substances, such as pumice stone or unglazed earthenware, have been employed; the most common arrangement being to insert the stone as a horizontal partition in a small tank or vessel: the action is, in the main, mechanical, and the sediment which collects upon the upper surface of the block is removed by washing and brushing. A material which is used to a considerable extent in England is the so-called silicated carbon: it is the residue of the distillation of a certain variety of bituminous shale. Thus it is a coke mixed with mineral matter, and is compressed into blocks for use. In the common form of household filters of this make, the block is cemented as a partition into an earthen jar, and is not readily cleaned, but there is no doubt that, until the filter becomes clogged, it is very efficient in purifying water even from the dissolved organic matter.

FIG. 33.

As a type of the better class of tank filters, we may take that much employed in England and manufactured by the London and General Water Purifying Company; this filter* is shown in elevation and in section in Figs. 33 and 34. The earthenware filter box is filled with animal charcoal, in the form of charred bones, broken into small pieces, and freed from dust. There is no chamber for storing filtered water: the water is filtered at the time it is drawn off for use. The filter is readily cleansed and the charcoal renewed. The water passes *upward* through the filtering material, in order that matters spontaneously settling down may not be deposited upon the filtering material, and may not, therefore, help to clog its pores; and, further, that the suspended matters strained from the water, being separated as they

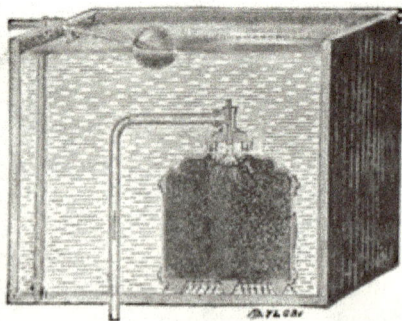

FIG. 34.

---

* A very similar filter made in Boston, England, is on sale in this country.

always are, mainly at the surface of the filtering material, may fall away from it and deposit elsewhere ; the consequence of this is, that the filtering material requires less frequent cleansing.

Bone coal is also used compressed into cylindrical blocks with an aperture in the center into which the delivery pipe is inserted, and one or more of these may be placed in the tank from which the water is taken. As a rule, the previously described method of using the bone coal is to be preferred.

Another material which has lately come into use to a considerable extent in England, is what is known as "spongy iron," which has already been alluded to in the description of the filtration works at Antwerp. The portable filters are constructed in various forms, but on the same general plan. Fig. 35 represents one form, where the water is supplied from an inverted bottle, which must be refilled as often as empty. In other forms the reservoir of unfiltered water is kept full by being connected with the service pipe by means of a ball-cock attachment. The vessels are of earthenware, but the spongy iron is also furnished in filters which can be inserted in tanks or cisterns.

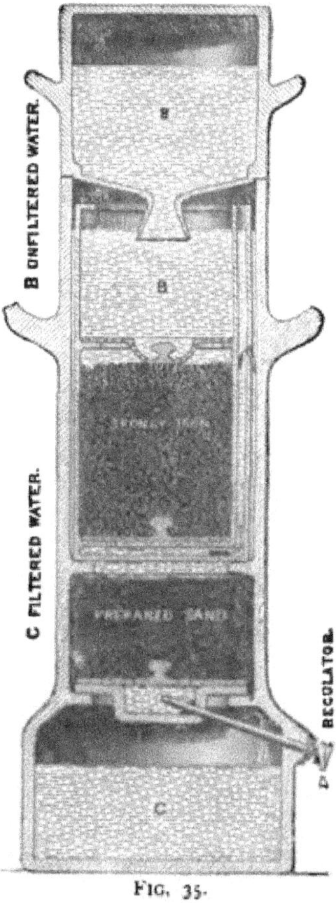

Although, at any rate with the smaller forms of filter, it is difficult

FIG. 35.

or impossible to obtain a water free from iron, there is no doubt that a considerable portion of the dissolved organic matter is removed, and it is claimed that bacteria and bacterial germs are completely removed. These claims are borne out by the experimental investigations of Bischof,[*] Hatton,[†] and others, and give

* Proc. Roy. Soc., xxvii, p. 258.
† Journ. Chem. Soc., xxxix, p. 247.

to the material a great theoretical advantage. Practically, however, it is extremely doubtful whether in the ordinary use of the spongy iron in filters such results can be obtained ; and at the best, the water must pass very slowly through the filter in order that purification may take place. Like other materials used for the purpose, it affords a means for improving an undesirable water, and for lessening the risk in using a doubtful water : it does not afford an excuse for employing a water known to be impure, on the ground that possible danger will thus be certainly averted.

Wood-charcoal is sometimes used in household filters, but, practically, it has next to no chemical action. The author had occasion some time since to examine an American filter which is much used in certain sections of the country, and in which the filtering medium is wood-charcoal with clean quartz pebbles. The filtering material is arranged in an oak tub and the water is placed in a zinc pan at the top, and passes first through a handful of sponge and then downward through the pebbles and charcoal. The experiments extended over several months, and the water was examined by Frankland's and by Wanklyn's method. In the case of the Boston water, when the filter was in constant use, absolutely no effect was produced on the water—the water which issued from the filter containing exactly the same amount of organic matter as when it entered. If the sponge were taken out, thoroughly washed and replaced, there was for a short time a slight difference between the filtered and unfiltered water, but the effect was temporary and soon ceased. In spite of the bulk and weight of this filter (the smallest size of which weighs about 150 lbs.), the entire work with water of this character seems to be done by the handful of sponge at the top. The filter is one of a class which claim to be chemical in their action, but which cannot do more than remove suspended matter ; and the action on clayey waters, with which the filter is sometimes used to advantage, is probably largely due to the principle illustrated on page 153 (Fig. 30).

The following simple form of filter is described by Dr. Smart, and answers fully as well as many patented contrivances. " The filter is made of tin and consists of a modified funnel, the body of which rests on a tin bucket or receiver, while the tube projects downward to the bottom of the said bucket. The lower end of the tube is tied over with some filtering cloth. Three-fourths of its length is filled with granulated bone charcoal and the upper fourth with sand. The upper end of the tube projects about half an inch into the body of the funnel to permit of tying a filtering cloth over the top of the sand. The angle between this projection and the sloping sides of the funnel will serve to trap solid matter. To clean this filter, the filtering cloth guarding the top of the tube will have to be removed, washed, and replaced. At longer intervals, when the filter shows signs of clogging, half an inch of the upper layer of sand may be removed and replaced by fresh material. At yet longer periods, depending upon the length of time during which the charcoal retains its powers of oxidation, the whole contents of the tube may be dumped out and renewed. Earthenware is more durable than tin, and would preserve the water cooler during the warm months."

There are various filters in the market which are arranged for use where there is a public water supply, by being connected with the service pipes in such a way that all the water entering the building passes through the filter. By proper arrangement of valves it is possible to reverse the current and cleanse the filter from the collected impurities. In some cases the valves are so arranged that the filter can be cleaned by a reverse current of hot water or steam. The revolving filters, mentioned on page 171 as adapted to faucets, are also made on the larger scale for insertion in the service-pipes of houses and other buildings and for manufacturers' use.

We come now to the discussion of filters suitable for cisterns of considerable size, and especially for the underground cisterns in which rain water is usually stored. The collection of water from the roofs of houses involves the collection of dust and dirt more or less objectionable in character, especially in places where soft coal is burned. Although it is possible by automatic contrivances to avoid the collection of the first portions of the water coming at any time from the roof, yet these do not perfectly accomplish their intended object, and are not at all commonly employed. Moreover, the construction of ordinary cisterns is such that, after the water is once collected, it is liable to deterioration and to contamination by various foreign matters which fall into it, so that, if not absolutely necessary, filtration is certainly very desirable. Where the water is stored in tanks in the roof of the building, one of the various forms of filters just alluded to may be placed beneath the tank and so connected that all the water used shall pass through it. The outlet pipe from the tank should start several inches from the bottom, in order that the sediment may deposit itself as far as possible on the floor of the tank and not be drawn into the filter: the tank should, of course, be cleaned from time to time. The disadvantage of this method is the inability to command a sufficient head of water to properly clean the filter by reversing the current. The tank may be divided by a partition and the water be required to pass through a filter constructed in the tank itself and filled with sand and charcoal or bone-coal, or one of the patent tank filters already described may be employed. (See Figs. 33 and 34.)

With underground cisterns, it is not uncommon to construct them so that the water is not pumped directly from the cistern, but from a sort of pump-well, to enter which the water must pass through a porous partition wall made of bricks. These walls are constructed in various ways: one form is represented in the accompanying cut, taken from "Scribner's Monthly Magazine" for September, 1877.

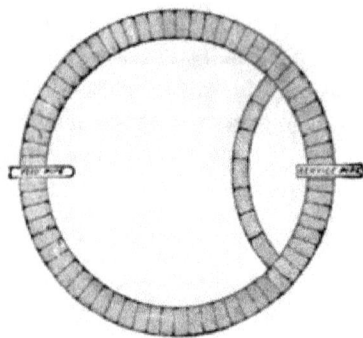

FIG. 36.

When the brick partition is new, it is undoubtedly of good service; but it soon becomes clogged, and covered on the outside with a deposit of organic matter, so that after a time the water which passes through the brick wall must first have an opportunity to leach out what it can from this mass of decaying matter.* As a rule, the interiors of cisterns are not very accessible, and when the cistern is relied upon as the sole or as a principal supply for the household, it is impossible to renew frequently the filtering wall, or even to thoroughly clean the outer surface. The best that can be done under ordinary circumstances is to clean the outer surface of the wall as thoroughly as may be with a stiff brush every few months,

---

* Some analyses of cistern waters thus filtered have been given in Table V, page 51.

and to renew the wall completely whenever the probability of a rainy season allows. If the body of the cistern be divided by a partition wall into two compartments which may be made to communicate or not at will, the two may be cleaned at different times and thus the danger of a water-famine be averted.

Other methods for accomplishing filtration in the cistern have been proposed. Filters of sand and charcoal, or of bone-coal, are sometimes constructed within the cisterns; but they are not easily reached for cleaning, and as a rule they are allowed to go uncleaned. Various devices

FIG. 37 (from Fischer).　　　　　　　　FIG. 38.

have been suggested for attachment to the suction pipe of the pump, two of which are shown in Figs. 37 and 38. Fig. 37 is a German device for using bone-coal compressed into blocks: Fig. 38 is an American device for taking the water as free from the sediment as possible. The cylinder contains silicious sand for the filtering medium and is buoyed up by an air-tight chamber at one end. The pipe has a swivel-joint which allows the filter

12

to accommodate itself to the level of the water in the cistern or reservoir.*

Still another method of accomplishing the desired object consists in placing the filtering material in a frame capable of sliding in a groove and of being readily lifted from its place. The filtering material may consist of porous tiles or of blocks of animal charcoal; and, if duplicate frames are provided, the grooves may be so arranged that a fresh frame can be lowered into place before the old one is taken away. Figure 39† represents a cistern constructed with such frames containing blocks of animal charcoal, as prepared by Atkins & Co., London. These blocks can be readily cleaned by scraping the outer surface (at some expense, to be sure, of the material of the blocks), and they can be renewed when necessary. They are made of various densities; the most dense permitting the passage of 30 to 40 gallons per square foot per day, while the most porous pass some 250 to 300

FIG. 39.

gallons. For use in ordinary cisterns tolerably porous blocks would probably answer well enough, and for such use as this the

---

* Scientific American, Jan. 10, 1830.
† This cut is taken from Fanning's Water-supply Engineering.

charcoal is more conveniently employed in this form of blocks than as fragments.

The arrangement which has been described is rather expensive for common use; although, if the necessary provision were made in the original plan for the construction of the cistern, it would, on the whole, be more satisfactory than other plans which involve less outlay at the start. The author is not aware that the blocks of compressed animal charcoal are prepared in this country, but there would probably be no difficulty in obtaining them if there were any demand.

There is one point worth noting in connection with domestic filtration, namely, that in this country we are in the habit of putting ice directly into the pitchers or small tanks from which drinking water is served. Natural ice is not always clean, and frequently, after the ice is melted, the water, even if clear at the start, will be found full of suspended particles, or having an abundant sediment. Filters are made so that the ice cools the water before the filtration takes place and the difficulty can also be obviated to a large extent by inclosing the ice in a clean flannel or cotton-flannel bag.

Filtration for Manufacturing Purposes.

For the majority of manufacturing purposes the object of filtration is accomplished if a thorough removal of suspended matter is effected. Sand, wood-charcoal, bone-coal, flannel and various other substances are employed as filtering media ; very good results are obtained by the use of sponge, and this material is employed to a considerable extent ; in some cases, the water is filtered through sand filters, similar to those used in connection with town supplies but on a smaller scale.

Two filters have recently been offered in the market to effect rapid filtration for manufacturing purposes and also for town supply. The " Multifold Filter," manufactured by the Newark Filter Company, may be of various sizes, and each apparatus consists of a number of shallow cast-iron pans ranged one above the other. Each pan has a false perforated bottom, on which rests a layer of sand, 6 inches or less in thickness, and each works as an independent filter. The water passes in the direction of the arrows shown in the cut under a greater or less pressure. The chief peculiarity of the filter consists in the ar-

rangements for cleansing. When the sand becomes clogged,
water is introduced under pressure through the hollow axis of the cylinder, and issues in fine jets from the radial arms, stirring up the sand and washing away the lighter substances. The arms can be revolved from the outside, so that the sand may be completely washed.

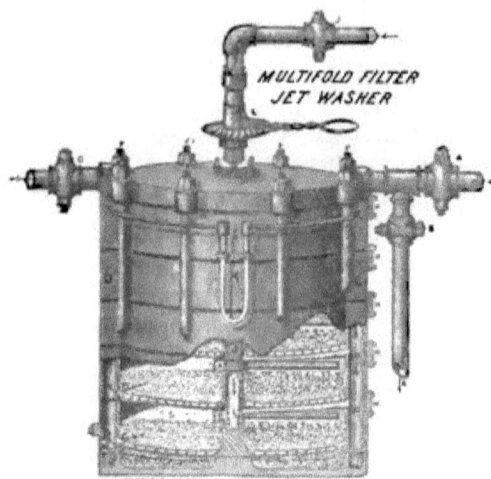

FIG. 40.

Another filter (system Piefke) has been recently advertised in Germany,* where the filtering medium consists of cellulose (vegetable fiber) which has been impregnated with some antiseptic substance. This material is disposed on a number of circular sieves arranged one above another in an apparatus somewhat similar to the preceding, and a thin layer suffices. The filter is cleaned by revolving the vertical axis of the apparatus, which is a rod to which scrapers are attached; the water continues to flow through the filters, and the material is kept in suspension until the impurities are washed away. This involves some loss of the prepared cellulose, but it is claimed that the filtration is efficiently and cheaply accomplished. No details from disinterested sources are at hand with reference to the practical value of either of these devices, which seem to possess certain merits.

* Journal für Gasbeleuchtung und Wasserversorgung, March, 1883. The apparatus is figured and described in the Scientific American, April 28. 1883.

CHAPTER IX.

The Softening of Hard Water.

As has already been explained (page 33), the hardness of water is generally due to the presence of compounds of lime or magnesia. While a moderately hard water may be perfectly well suited for drinking, for almost all the other purposes of a water supply a soft water is preferable, other things being equal. If common soap be added to hard water the water seems to curdle, but no permanent froth or lather is formed until, by the mutual action of the soap and the compounds of lime (and magnesia) on each other, the latter are completely converted into a lime (or magnesia) soap, an insoluble substance which forms the curd alluded to. After this point is reached, any additional soap becomes available for washing, but the curdy water is less effi-cient as a detergent. Hard water is, as a rule, much less desir-able for culinary purposes than soft water. Finally, hard water is also objectionable on account of the " scale " which forms in steam boilers in which it is used : in manufacturing towns this becomes a matter of great importance.

Temporary hardness.—The temporary hardness is due to the presence of *carbonate* of lime or magnesia : these compounds are soluble in water to a slight extent only, but are brought into solution by carbonic acid, as has been explained on page 9 : it will be convenient to consider them as existing in solution as *bi*carbonates. The temporary hardness of a water may be re-moved in various ways : in the first place, by adding soap, as is actually done when an attempt is made to wash with hard water —a method uneconomical on the small scale, and impracticable on the large scale on account of the expense ; in the second place, by adding ordinary washing-soda (carbonate of soda)—a method employed very generally on the small scale, but also impracticable on the large scale on account of expense. The chemical explanation of the second method is this: when *car-bonate* of soda is added to water containing *bicarbonate* of lime there result *bicarbonate* of soda and *carbonate* of lime; the former is soluble in water and remains in solution, the latter being insoluble separates as a fine powder. A simpler method still, as the explanation of the term "temporary" shows, consists in boiling the water for half an hour or more: the *bi*carbonate of lime (or magnesia) is decomposed, losing half its carbonic acid; this carbonic acid escapes as gas, and the simple carbonate of lime separates as a white powder. On account of this action, carbonate of lime is one of the chief constituents of boiler scale, and a similar deposit forms in the water-backs of kitchen ranges, and, in fact, in any vessel in which the water is boiled. Some natural waters are so highly charged with carbonate of lime that slight agitation suffices to drive off the "extra" carbonic acid and to allow the carbonate to separate; large deposits of carbonate of lime occur in nature which owe their origin to such an action. Fig. 41 (from the Scientific American) shows a portion of the feed-pipe of a boiler which was nearly choked up by the calcareous matter.

From a water which possesses temporary hardness, the carbonate of lime may be caused to deposit, and the water thus become softened, not simply by *expelling* the "extra" carbonic acid by heat or otherwise, but also by causing this carbonic acid to *unite chemically*

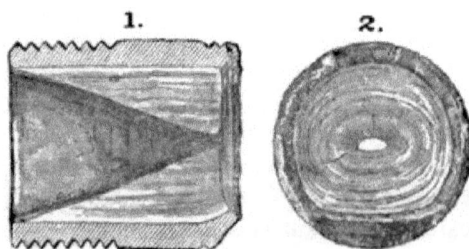

FIG. 41.

with some substance capable of thus decomposing the bicarbonate. Caustic soda or caustic potash will produce this effect, but the cheapest and most available substance is ordinary lime. The lime unites with the extra carbonic acid to form carbonate of lime, which settles out as a fine powder along with the carbonate originally held in solution. As carbonate of lime is not absolutely insoluble in water, a small amount remains in solution after the softening has been completed, not enough, however, to be seriously objectionable.

The use of lime was invented and patented about the year 1844 by Thomas Clark, professor of chemistry in the University of Aberdeen, but the patent expired long since. The process has been used in England at works furnishing as much as 1,000,000 gallons daily. The proper amount of lime is added in the form of lime-water or milk of lime. After thorough mixing the water is allowed to subside for from 12 to 24 hours, and drawn off from the sediment. The readiness with which the finely divided carbonate of lime settles depends somewhat upon the character of the water; and, as it settles, it drags down with it and removes from the water a not inconsiderable proportion of the organic matter present; if the water is colored by peaty matter, a very appreciable decolorization is effected. Experience, however, would seem to show that the process gives the best results with water which is naturally clear, such as spring water; and, in the case of turbid river waters, the softening process should be followed by filtration.

The economy of the process and the advantage of softening a hard water on the large scale, rather than by the use of soap in the household, is evident when we consider that, to soften a quantity of water requiring one hundred-weight of quicklime, the expense of materials would be (approximately):

1 cwt. of lime, say.............................$ 0.50
5 cwt. of sal soda (at 1.2 cents per lb.).............. 6.00
20 cwt. of soap (at 6¼ cents per lb.)................ 130.00

Of course, on a large scale the cost of labor, and especially of handling the sludge, may make the actual difference less than the theoretical, but, in any event, the saving in soap by the use of the softened water is very great.

On account of the difficulty with which the carbonate of lime settles in waters containing much organic matter, of the length of time required and of the necessarily large area of settling-basins, the process is seldom carried out according to the original plan. There are various modifications of the process which aim to accomplish the object with greater economy of time and space, using, however, the same material. These modified processes involve some form of filter by which the precipitated carbonate of lime may be removed at once without waiting for the subsidence to take place. It will suffice to describe one of these processes.

In England a number of manufacturing establishments and several towns have introduced Clark's process as modified by J. H. Porter, C. E.* The lime is employed in the form of a saturated solution, and the mixing with the bulk of the water to be softened takes place in a separate tank from that in which the solution is prepared. When thorough mixture has been effected, the liquid is at once filtered through cloth. The arrangement and construction of the tanks varies with the quantity of water

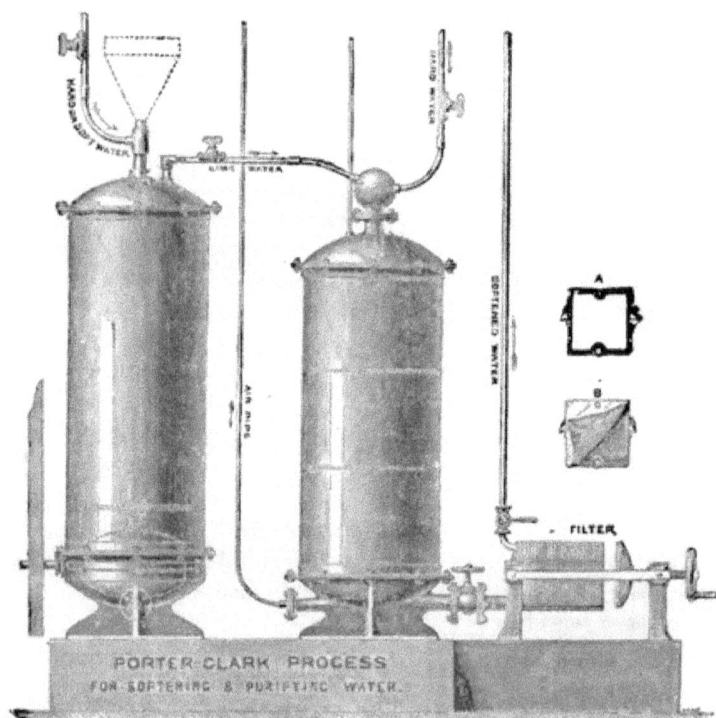

FIG. 42.

to be softened. Fig. 42 represents an apparatus for treating 300 gallons of water per hour. The preparation of the lime-water

---

* The Porter-Clark Process for the Softening, Purification and Filtration of Hard Waters, by John Henderson Porter, London.

takes place in the left-hand cylinder, which is furnished with a mechanical stirrer; the mixing takes place in the right-hand cylinder; the other details of the apparatus are evident from the figure. The filtration of the mixture may be accomplished by any one of a variety of filter presses; that employed by Mr. Porter is shown in Fig. 42 and more plainly in Figures 43, 44 and 45. Fig. 43 shows a portion of the filters used by the Lon-

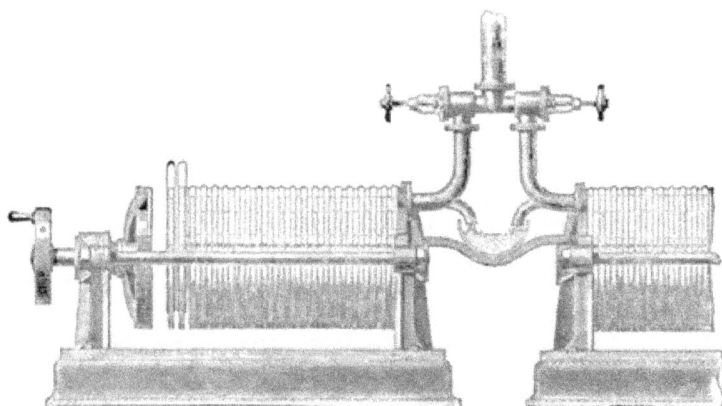

FIG. 43.

don and North-western Railway Company at Liverpool, where over 200,000 U. S. gallons of water are softened daily. Each filter is made up of a series of cast-iron plates and cast-iron open frames of the form shown in Figs. 44 and 45. "Over these filtering

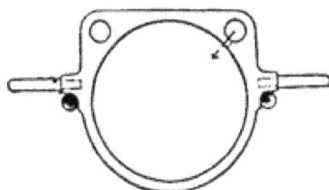

FIG. 44.

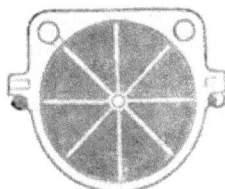

FIG. 45.

chambers, of about 1 inch in thickness, is dropped (as a towel plac-ed upon a towel-horse) a cloth of superior quality of cotton twill, having worked in it holes to correspond with the holes through the upper corners of both water-space frame and filtering chambers. When these alternate water spaces and filtering chambers with the cloths are tightly pressed together by a powerful end screw, it will be seen that the holes become, collectively, tubular channels of the length of the 'battery,' the channel of the one side admitting its chalky water to the circular water-spaces, whence, being inclosed and under pressure, it can only escape through the adjoining cloths into the concentric and radiating grooves which conduct it by a small outlet to the channel on the other side."

In the figure (Fig. 43) the left-hand filter is represented as unscrewed and with two of the cloths raised for purposes of cleaning. The cloths are readily removed and replaced by a fresh set as often as may be necessary—how often depends upon the amount and the character of the impurity, other than the chemically formed chalk, present in the water. At Liverpool and other places where the waters are from deep wells in the chalk or red sandstone, the filters run for 15 hours without changing the cloths and the labor of one man is found sufficient to cleanse cloths, and filters and to attend to other details of the process in softening 150,000 to 180,000 (imperial) gallons for the day's work. In other places, where the water contains a larger proportion of magnesia or surface impurities, the filters may not run for more than 6 or 7 hours without cleansing.

From the application of Clark's process, in whatever form, there results a large quantity of chalk or "whiting," more or less pure according to the amount of impurity in the water softened. If the water contains organic matters, a portion is precipitated along with the chalk, together with any sediment which the water may contain. In some localities there is a market for the whiting which tends to offset the expenses of the process. A portion might be burned into lime and used over again in softening a fresh portion of water, but being in a fine powder it could not be burned in ordinary kilns.

Permanent hardness.—The permanent hardness is usually caused by the presence of the sulphates (or other soluble salts) of lime and magnesia, gypsum (sulphate of lime) being the most common; the action on soap is the same as that of the bicarbonates, which has been discussed under temporary hardness. Water containing sulphate of lime may be softened by adding carbonate of soda, and this is the method commonly employed in the laundry The chemistry of the process is this: when carbonate of soda in solution is mixed with sulphate of lime in solution, there are formed carbonate of lime (which settles out in the solid form) and sulphate of soda (which remains dissolved); a similar action takes place with other soluble compounds of lime and magnesia. The expense of this treatment makes it impracticable to soften, in this way, the entire water supply of a town, a large portion of which is used for purposes where the hardness of the water is a matter of indifference. We have seen (page 5) that sulphate of lime becomes insoluble in water at high temperatures and contributes to the formation of scale in steam-boilers; hence, for technical purposes, it is desirable to remove the sulphate, and the process just indicated, or some other method, may be employed to advantage.

Treatment by other Chemical Processes.

On the large scale, attempts are seldom made to improve a natural water except by processes which have already been described; there are, however, a number of substances which may be used to advantage in purifying the small quantity necessary for drinking in localities where no really drinkable water exists. One of the longest used and best known substances is common alum, which is often added to a turbid water. Where the water contains carbonate of lime in solution, a chemical action takes place between it and the alum, resulting in the formation of sulphate of lime, which remains dissolved, of carbonic acid, which escapes as gas, and of hydrate of alumina, which separates out as a solid. As the hydrate of alumina forms and settles down, it entangles and drags down with it the finely divided suspended matter to which the turbidity is due: in fact, it enters into some sort of chemical combination with some of the dissolved organic matter which is thus removed. When the water does not contain enough carbonate of lime or other substance capable of decomposing the alum, the addition of the alum may be followed by the addition of a proper amount of carbonate of soda. Perchloride (or other soluble persalt) of iron acts very similarly to alum. Instead of hydrate of alumina, it is the hydrate of iron (ferric hydrate) which is formed, and this also, in settling, carries with it some organic matter. It was at one time proposed to treat the water of the Seine at Paris with alum, and the use of perchloride of iron and carbonate of soda were talked of for rendering potable the water of the Maas in Holland.

Another substance which has more recently come into notice is permanganate of potash. The action is the same as that described when discussing the use of this substance as a means of determining analytically the amount of organic matter present in a water. (See page 37.) In attempting to purify an impure water by this means, the highly colored solution of the permanganate must be added in quantity sufficient to impart a pink color, which remains permanent for from five to ten minutes. The permanganate, in destroying the organic matter, is itself decomposed, and oxide (or hydrate) of manganese separates as a finely divided solid. This may be removed by filtration, or it may simply be allowed to settle to the bottom of the tanks in which the water is treated. Other permanganates may be used as well as that of potash. For the treatment of the water which the British army was likely to meet with upon the Gold Coast, Professor Crookes,[*] in 1873, recommended a mixture of

> 1 part of permanganate of lime,
> 10 parts of sulphate of alumina,
> 30 parts of fine clay.

He stated that this mixture, when added to London sewage in the proportion of 20 to 10,000, afforded a very satisfactory purification.

The most simple manner of treating a water known or suspected to be impure is to boil it, although it is by no means certain that immunity from harm is thus, in all cases, assured. There is, however, evidence to show the value of the treatment; if, after the boiling, the water is iced, it becomes, of course, more palatable. It is stated that the Chinese and Japanese drink no water that has not been boiled ; and when we consider the unsanitary conditions which exist in those countries and the character of the water used, it seems as if boiling the water must prevent ills that would otherwise befall the people.

In some instances lime has been added to water which is used for domestic supply—the lime being added for purposes other than the softening of a water containing the bicarbonates. Thus, in Australia, at Sandhurst, Victoria, the impounded surface water

---

[*] Chemical News, xxviii (1873), p. 244.

which is used contains at times as much as 30 or 40 grains of yellowish-brown clayey matter in the (imperial) gallon, *i.e.*, say about 50 parts in 100,000. Here it was found that sand filters did not thoroughly intercept the clay in suspension, and that the water, after filtration, still remained cloudy and opalescent. Lime was added at the rate of 7 grains to the (imperial) gallon, and after standing 10 hours the water became clear : five-sevenths of the added lime went down with the precipitate, the other two-sevenths remained in solution in the water, and of course gave it a slight hardness. At several other works lime is used in the same proportion, and this treatment is, in some cases, followed by filtration, in others not. The capacity of one of the works where this treatment is employed is as great as 1,000,000 imperial gallons per day.*

Distillation.

The ordinary process of distillation is sufficiently familiar. When water is boiled, the gaseous substances which it holds in solution are expelled almost completely, either while the water is heating up to the boiling point, or with the first portion of the steam : the dissolved solids, on the other hand, remain behind while the water evaporates. If the water be boiled in an

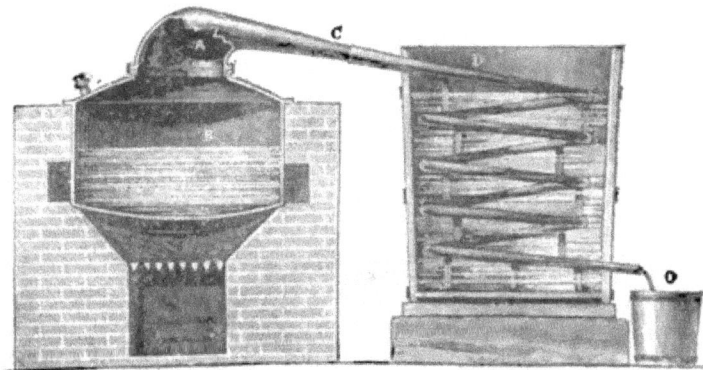

FIG. 46.

ordinary still—such, for instance, as is shown in Fig. 46—and the steam be subsequently condensed, the water which issues from the condenser will be tolerably pure, especially if the first

* Brady : Proc. Inst. Civ. Eng. Gr. Br. lvi, p. 134 and foll.

portions be rejected and the evaporation be not carried too far.
Distillation is, of course, a somewhat expensive process, for besides the cost of the necessary apparatus, each pound of water
evaporated requires the consumption of from one-twelfth to one-
seventh of a pound of coal, according to the quality of the coal
used and the efficiency of the boiler employed. On this account,
distilled water for drinking, cooking, and other domestic uses is
seldom prepared on any considerable scale except on shipboard.
Here, the steam is usually taken from one of the boilers used to
generate steam for the motive power of the ship, and the different systems consist in differences in the condensers (aerators and
purifiers), although the term "distiller" is often applied to this
part of the apparatus. The condensers are of various forms—
the ordinary worm, the flat worm or zigzag, and the tube condenser, consisting of a cylinder with tubes inside running vertically, the steam passing through the tubes and the water being
on the outside, or *vice versa*.

Ordinary distilled water has a flat and nauseous taste, owing
partly to the fact that the dissolved gases, notably oxygen and
carbonic acid, have been expelled, and partly to the presence of
certain volatile organic compounds which have been formed
during the distillation. This is often remedied by allowing the
water to remain for from 10 to 15 days in partly filled tanks
where it will be exposed to the air and more or less agitated by
the motion of the ship. A number of devices have been con-
trived and patented which aim to accomplish this aeration and
oxidation at once, and thus to produce a distilled water fit for
immediate use.

In the United States navy, a condenser invented by Passed
Assistant Engineer G. W. Baird is largely used. The essential
feature of this system is the introduction of air into the apparatus
in such a way that it mixes with the steam, and the water which
forms is condensed in the presence of an abundance of oxygen,
and thus becomes fully aerated. It is further claimed that the
air so introduced oxidizes the organic matter carried forward by
the steam.   This it no doubt does, if not at once, at least when
the water, thus aerated, is subsequently passed through a filter
of purified animal charcoal. Fig. 47 represents the condenser in
section. The steam enters at *a* and, on the principle of an
injector, draws air in through *b;* the mixture of air and steam

enters the system of cooling pipes B, where the steam is condensed. The pipes are usually of cylindrical section and are

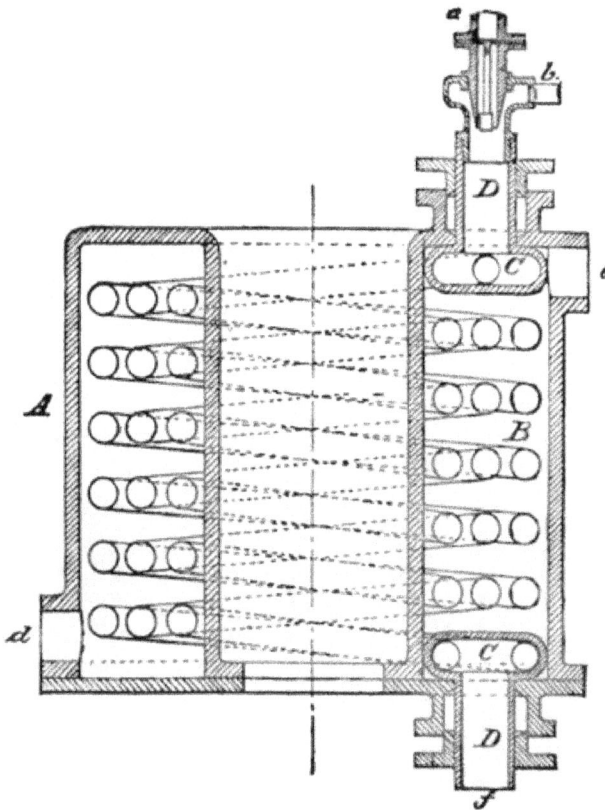

FIG. 47. — BAIRD'S CONDENSER.

made of tin or tinned copper; they are coiled into helices, the ends terminating in the common T-heads, C, C, at the upper and lower ends respectively. The refrigerating water enters at d and is discharged at e, and the condensed water flows out at f and thence passes to the filter. In the U. S. navy the water is not salified and is regarded as perfectly wholesome. It is stated * that in the Russian navy there is added to each 1,000 liters of distilled water a mixture consisting of 4.8 grams salt, 3.4 grams

---

* Fonssagrives : Hygiène et assainissement des villes ; Paris, 1874, p. 316.

sulphate of soda, 48 grams bicarbonate (*sic*) of lime, 14 grams bicarbonate of soda, and 6 grams carbonate of magnesia.

The British navy uses Normandy's system, and essentially the same apparatus is used in the German navy, as shown in Figs. 48 and 49.[*] The apparatus consists essentially of two cylinders, the two sectional views of B being taken at right angles to each other. Steam is generated in a separate boiler and enters the cylinder A through the pipe *d*, and passes into the sheaf of tubes *b* which are surrounded by water which is to be distilled. The water

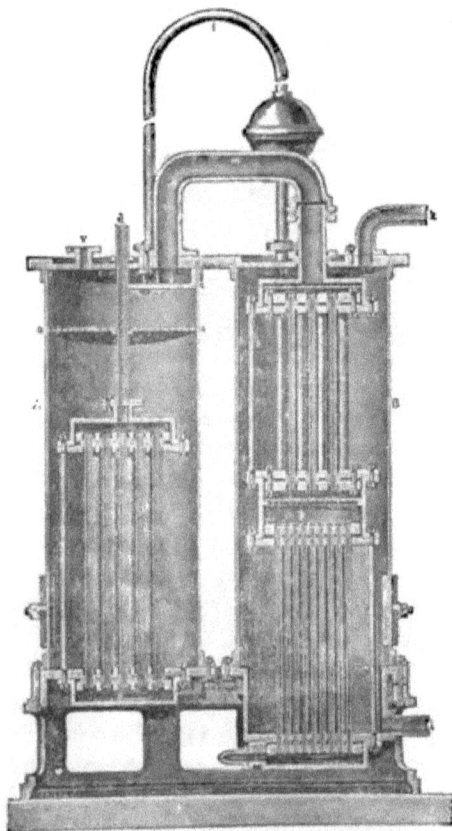

FIG. 48.   FIG. 49.

formed by condensation collects in the reservoir *e* at the base of the sheaf of pipes, and from here it flows into the vessel *g*, shown only in Fig. 48; if the water is required warm, it may be

---

[*] Fischer : Chemische Technologie des Wassers, p. 205 and foll.

drawn from *g* directly, otherwise it flows through a connecting pipe into the lower sheaf of tubes in the cylinder B. The level of the water in A—which flows in from B—is so regulated that the steam which is formed may free itself from any salt water which it carries mechanically, by passing first through the perforated copper plate *a*, and then by striking against *c*, before it passes through the pipe *m* into the sheaf of tubes *n* in the upper part of the cylinder B. The water which is here condensed flows, for further cooling, into the lower sheaf of tubes in B, into which the water condensed in *b* also flows, and which is the set of tubes with which the cooling water entering at *i* comes in contact. The water, thus fully cooled, is either discharged directly through the tube *r*, or is conducted through *s* to a simple filter filled with animal charcoal. The water used in cooling enters through the tube *i* and flows off through *k*, except so much as is necessary to keep the level of the water in *A* at the proper height. The air which escapes from the water as it becomes warm is conducted through the tube *t* into the steam space of the distilling apparatus, in order that the water, as it condenses, may dissolve it again and thus become more palatable. By means of the connection *y* the return steam from the steam pump may be allowed to enter *A*, to be utilized in the production of distilled water. Finally, when the water in the distilling apparatus, A, becomes too concentrated, it may be withdrawn by means of a cock not shown in the figures.

While distilled water is seldom prepared on a large scale except on shipboard, there are some localities where drinking water cannot otherwise be procured, and distillation must be resorted to. For example, the island of Walcheren, in Holland, is dependent for its supply of fresh water for drinking on the rainfall, all other water being brackish. For the supply of ships leaving the harbor of Flushing (Vlissingen), it has been necessary to have recourse to the condensation of steam, as being the only available source of fresh water independent of rain; Normandy's apparatus is employed. It is stated * that the plant cost 20.000 Dutch florins (about $12,000), and that 18 kilograms of distilled water are produced for each kilogram of coal burned, the water being distilled at the rate of one cubic meter per hour and being of satisfactory quality.

---

* Proc. Inst. Civ. Eng. Gr. Br., lxii, p. 408.

CHAPTER X.

SOME GENERAL CONSIDERATIONS.

Quantity and Waste.

WHATEVER source may be chosen for the supply of a city or town, it is essential that the quantity of water should be sufficient for the needs of the population for a number of years. The experience of many places has been similar to that of New York City. Within eight years after the completion of the Croton aqueduct, the New York Water Department wrote: "This Board warns the City Council, and through it every citizen, that every drop of water which the works in their present state can supply is now being delivered in the city." What is, however, a sufficient quantity? The following table gives the amount of water per head of population consumed in certain European cities:

TABLE XXVI.—CONSUMPTION OF WATER IN EUROPEAN CITIES.

CITIES (1880). *	DAILY AVERAGE SUPPLY PER HEAD, IN U. S. Gallons.	Litres.	CITIES. †	DAILY AVERAGE SUPPLY PER HEAD, IN U. S. Gallons.	Litres.
Glasgow	60	227	Karlsruhe	154	581
Paris	50.2	190	Bonn	76	289
Edinburgh	48	181	Hamburg	63	237
Dublin	45.6	172	Dresden	60	228
Hull	39.2	148	Frankfurt a. M.	59	223
Birmingham	30	113	Cöln	53	200
Blackburn	30	113	Altenburg	43	163
Leeds	27.9	107	Braunschweig	41	154
Liverpool	27	104	Bamberg	39	148
Manchester	24	91	Kassel	33	124
Sheffield	21.6	82	Hannover	31	116
			Altona	31	115
			Leipzig	23	86

The estimates of European experts as to the amount of water necessary for an adequate supply must be received with

---

* Brackett : Journ. Assoc. Eng. Soc., I (1882), p. 261.

† Grahn : Journ. f. Gasbeleuchtung u. Wasserversorgung, xx (1877).

some caution as applied to American circumstances, owing to difference in a variety of conditions. The following table shows the actual consumption in a number of American cities:[*]

TABLE XXVI.—CONSUMPTION OF WATER IN AMERICAN CITIES.

AMERICAN CITIES.	YEAR.	POPULATION.	Average Daily Consumption. Gallons.	Gallons per head per day.	Litres per head per day.
Fall River	1881	49,430	1,448,247	30.1	114
Providence	"	102,500	3,716,937	36.3	137
Lowell	1880	59,485	2,252,197	37.9	143
Cambridge	1881	52,880	2,472,108	46.7	177
Brooklyn	1880	566,689	30,744,590	54.2	205
Philadelphia	"	847,542	57,707,082	68.1	257
St. Louis	1879	346,000	24,958,000	72.1	273
Cincinnati	1850	256,708	19,476,739	75.9	287
New York	"	1,206,590	95,000,000	78.7	297
Boston	1881	416,000	38,214,900	92.	348
Chicago	1880	503,304	57,384,376	114.	431
Detroit	1881	118,000	17,926,377	151.9	574

From this table it is evident that there is a great difference in the amount of water consumed in different places, and if from 30 to 50 gallons suffice in certain cities, the use of 90 or 100 gallons in others presupposes a considerable waste: in fact, it is generally agreed by those in charge of water supplies that from a quarter to one-half of the water furnished is actually wasted. Mr. Thos. J. Whitman, of the St. Louis water works, said, a few years ago, that it cost the city fully $300,000 annually in fuel alone to simply supply the waste, and similar statements come from all large cities. For domestic and household uses 20 gallons per person per day is a sufficient allowance: taking into account the water used for manufacturing and mechanical purposes, that necessary for street sprinkling, extinguishing fires, for use in stables, etc., 60 gallons per day for each inhabitant is a liberal quantity in the case of large cities and manufacturing towns. In the case of the smaller, non-manufacturing towns 35 or 40 gallons should suffice. Mr. Dexter Brackett, in a valuable paper on the waste of water, from which Table XXVI and a part of Table XXV have been taken, considers 50 gallons per head as sufficient to provide for all the demands of the largest cities of the country.

The great waste which takes place being acknowledged, the

[*] Brackett: Journ. Assoc. Eng. Soc., I, p. 261.

question arises how to prevent, or at least diminish it.   There
are two general methods which suggest themselves.   The first is
a rigid system of inspection in order to detect all leakage from
the pipes and from imperfect fixtures, as well as all unlawful use
of the water; the second is the general and compulsory introduction of meters.   With reference to the first method, although
the authorities in charge of the distribution of water reserve the
right to inspect the fixtures at any time, yet such inspection is
annoying and repugnant to the average householder, and the
system admits of abuse.   A modification of this system, which
obviates the necessity of entering the building except in cases
where abnormal use of water is already known to exist, is that
devised by Mr. G. F. Deacon, Borough Engineer, Liverpool,
England.*   The following description of the system is taken
from a report on waste of water made to the City Council of Boston, Mass.†

"In the Deacon system the waste-water meter is used to locate
sources of waste.   This meter does not, like the ordinary meter,
record the number of gallons consumed, but it indicates the rate
of flow at any given time, and whether the discharge is due to
steadily flowing waste, or to intermittent and ordinary use.   It
therefore enables the observer to determine, by observations
taken at those hours when no water, or a very small quantity, is
used for legitimate purposes, whether waste is going on.

"The meter (Fig. 50)‡ consists of a hollow cone, having its
small end upwards, and containing a composition disk, of the same
diameter as the small end of the cone.   A vertical spindle, attached
to the upper surface of this disk, is suspended by a fine German-
silver wire, which passes, practically water-tight, through a small
hole in the top of the chamber, over a pulley, and supports a
weight.   This weight is so adjusted as to retain the disk at the
top of the cone when the water is at rest.   When any water is
drawn through the meter, the disk is pressed downward towards
the bottom of the cone, its position depending upon the amount

---

* A valuable report of Mr. Deacon is reprinted in the Report of the Cochituate
Water Board of the City of Boston, for the year ending April 30, 1874. City Docu-
ment No. 55, pages 84-112.
† Report on Waste of Water (May 25, 1882). Boston City Document No. 78, 1882.
‡ Figure 50 is reduced from a plate in a paper on The Constant Supply and
Waste of Water, by Geo. F. Deacon, in the Journal of the Society of Arts, May, 1882.

FOUR INCH DEACON WASTE WATER METER.

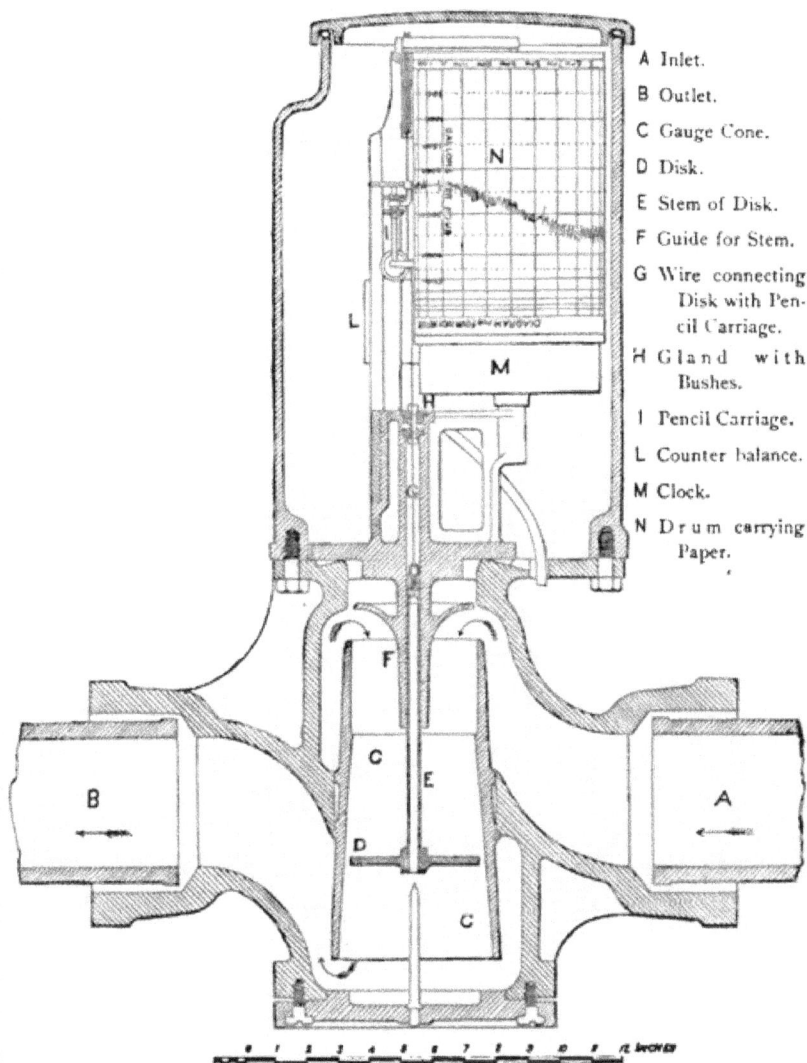

A Inlet.

B Outlet.

C Gauge Cone.

D Disk.

E Stem of Disk.

F Guide for Stem.

G Wire connecting Disk with Pencil Carriage.

H Gland with Bushes.

I Pencil Carriage.

L Counter balance.

M Clock.

N Drum carrying Paper.

FIG. 50.

of water passing through the meter. By means of a pen-cil attached to the wire the motions of the disk are record-ed on a drum, which revolves by clock-work, once in 24 hours.

"A fac-simile, about one-fifth full size, of a dia-gram drawn auto-matically by a waste-water meter, is shown in Fig. 51. It is obvious that when water is being drawn off for use the rate of flow from minute to minute must be va-riable; and this is accordingly shown by the irregular vertical lines from noon to midnight, and from 4 A. M. to noon. When con-tinuous—that is, preventable, waste alone is taking place —the flow must evi-dently be uniform; and this condition is indicated by the comparatively uni-form and horizontal line from 1 to 4

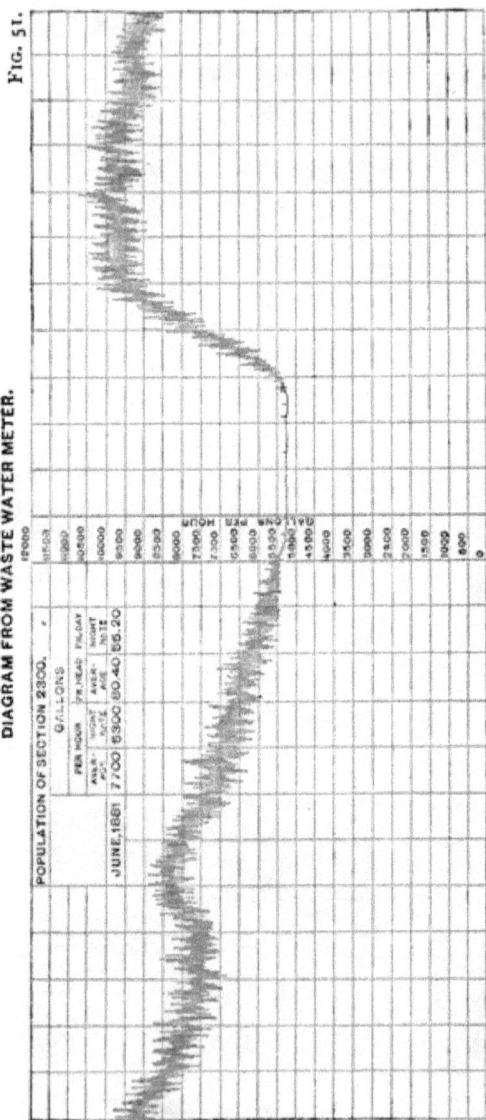

A.M., only occasionally broken by vertical lines, caused by persons drawing water during the night.

"The meter is placed in a box under the sidewalk or roadway, and so located as to control the flow of water supplied to a certain district, the limits of which have been previously determined. All the water used in this district is drawn through the meter, and the quantity and rate recorded. After a few diagrams have been taken, to show the ordinary rate of consumption, inspection is commenced. Every service pipe is provided with a stopcock, which is accessible from the sidewalk by means of an iron wrench about seven feet long. When this wrench is applied to the stopcock the sound caused by water passing through the service pipe can be easily distinguished. When no noise is heard, with the stopcock fully open, it is partly closed, and the increased velocity always causes a distinct sound, although the quantity of water passing the stopcock may be very small. A night inspector begins his work about midnight, and tests, by means of his shutting-off wrench, each service pipe. If he discovers any flow through the service pipe, the stopcock is closed, and a note made of the time and the number of the house. He continues this operation through the district until about 4 A.M., when he retraces his steps, and opens all the stopcocks he had found wasting. During this time the meter is recording the consumption, and the diagrams show the amount of water wasted by each of the service pipes that were closed, the time the inspector began and finished his work, and the time each stopcock was closed. The day inspector receives the night inspector's report, visits the premises where waste was noted, and ascertains the cause. In cases of waste from defective fixtures the owners are notified to repair the same, and the visits are continued until the notices have been complied with.

"The economy of this system, as compared with house-to-house inspection, is apparent. The attention of the inspector is at once directed to the place where the waste is going on, and the time lost in indiscriminate inspection is saved."

The Deacon system has given very satisfactory results wherever tried. The chairman of the Liverpool Water Committee, in his address in 1879, said :

"We have given the city a constant service * of water, with a

---

* Before the introduction of the Deacon system of inspection, the supply of Liverpool was an intermittent one, the water being on only 9½ hours out of the 24.

decline in the death-rate, and it now remains for me to show
what other effects have arisen from the change of system.   In
the year 1871 we delivered an average of 122,000,000 gallons
weekly ; in 1880 our deliveries will be about 115,000,000 gallons ;
and this, notwithstanding an increased sale for trade purposes
of 12,250,000 gallons weekly, and an increased population of
104,000.   The saving has been so great as to meet the increasing
demands of the city and district for eleven years.

" The change to constant service has already yielded nearly a
quarter of a million of money (£250,000), and the ultimate saving
to the rate-payers, when the 7,000,000 gallons per week yet un-
sold are absorbed, will be £50,000 per annum."

The conditions under which this system of waste detection
has been tried in Glasgow correspond more nearly with those
existing in Boston and other American cities, than do those of
other European cities where the system has been used.   The
supply furnished is constant and ample, and the proportion of
water fittings to the population is larger than is common in most
European cities.

The following table (Brackett) shows the results obtained in
Glasgow from an inspection similar to the one made in Boston :

TABLE XXVII.—WASTE WATER INSPECTION IN GLASGOW.

NUMBER OF DISTRICT.	NUMBER OF SUB-DISTRICTS.	NUMBER OF OCCUPANTS AT NIGHT.	NUMBER OF PERSONS PER STOP COCK.	GALLONS PER HEAD PER DAY.			
				At starting of meters.		After first three inspections.	
				Total.	Night rate per 24 hours.	Total.	Night rate per 24 hours.
I	9	14,972	25.8	71.0	54.0	40.9	21.1
II	6	10,002	22.4	79.0	72.2	50.4	33.0
III	3	4,986	35.4	73.7	62.4	44.2	21.7
IV	6	7,629	30.6	79.0	57.0	50.5	24.3
V	7	9,815	37.8	55.1	36.8	37.7	17.3
VI	8	12,614	39.7	37.2	29.5	27.1	17.8
VII	2	4,132	25.5	45.5	30.6	41.9	25.8
VIII	3	6,306	37.1	44.9	27.5	33.6	15.1
IX	4	7,821	32.1	44.9	31.7	30.8	15.2
X	2	3,012	34.6	44.2	33.4	25.0	12.8
Totals and averages.	50	81,289	30.6	55.8	45.2	38.4	21.0

The results of a trial of the Deacon system on a portion of

the water service of the city of Boston, Mass., are shown in the following table (Brackett).

TABLE XXVIII.—Waste Water Inspection in Boston, Mass.

Number of Section.	Estimated population.	Number of persons per stop cock.	Gallons per Head per Day.				Percentage of Reduction.	
			Before inspection.		After two or three inspections.			
			Total.	Night rate per 24 hours.	Total.	Night rate per 24 hours.	On total.	On night rate.
1	2,810	9.2	53.5	39.1	26.4	10.6	50.7	72.9
1 and 1 A	3,675	9.1	52.	39.0	34.1	13.7	34.4	64.9
2	2,170	8.1	49.9	33.1	36.7	13.2	26.5	60.6
3	2,030	6.2	71.8	43.2	45.1	20.2	37.2	53.2
4	1,880	5.9	68.4	42.2	47.8	22.3	30.1	47.2
5	1,790	5.9	72.7	53.3	47.8	17.8	34.5	66.6
6	1,875	7.2	60.	44.6	35.3	15.1	41.2	66.1
7	2,540	6.8	55.2	31.9	39.6	19.2	28.3	39.8
8	2,400	6.6	55.	40.8	37.9	18.5	31.1	54.7
9	2,150	5.5	62.9	40.1	36.2	13.7	42.4	65.8
10	1,790	5.6	52.3	28.1	46.1	18.7	11.9	33.4
11	2,800	6.5	43.7	17.5	25.7	9.5	41.2	45.7
12	2,300	7.6	80.4	55.2	31.2	12.5	61.2	77.4
Averages	....	6.86	58.5	37.5	37.7	15.8	35.6	57.9

From the above it appears that on the whole district covered by the inspection, containing a population of 21,760 persons, the average daily consumption was reduced from 58.5 to 37.7 gallons, a saving of 35.6 per cent, or 20.8 gallons for each person supplied, while the night rate was reduced from 37.5 to 15.8 gallons per head per day, a saving of 58 per cent. The Boston experiments being continued for a short time only, seem to have cost more than the value of the water saved; this is not the case where the system forms a part of the regular operation of the water works.

The Cincinnati Board of Public Works use a device invented by Mr. Thomas J. Bell, the Assistant Superintendent of the Water Works, which takes advantage of a fact long known, namely, that it is possible to detect a leak by taking advantage of the conduction of the sound caused by that leak through the metal pipes by some metallic connection, to the ear. Mr. Bell's device consists of a diaphragm inclosed in a hollow piece of wood, shaped like a telephone, and about the same size. A piece of iron extends through the middle of the neck of the "detect-or," one end projected and threaded, and the other communicating with the diaphragm. A threaded hole is bored in the top of the key used to turn water on and off at the cocks on the edge of the pavements, and, when it is desired to make a test, the detector is screwed into the top of the key and the ear applied to the detector. The least leakage or the smallest stream running from a hydrant can be distinctly heard. Inspections are made at night.

A waste-water indicator, invented by Mr. Benj. S. Church, resident engineer of the Croton aqueduct, N. Y., is thus described in The Sanitary Engineer, to the publisher of which we are indebted for the use of the cut (Fig. 52).

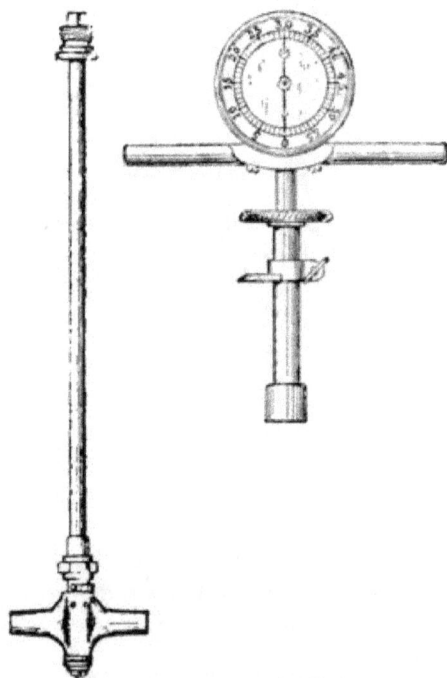

FIG. 52.—CHURCH'S DETECTOR.

"The device consists of a pressure gauge, with arrangements for attaching it to the pipe through which water is suspected of leaking. Its most extensive application is designed to be to service pipes from street mains to houses. For this purpose, a special stop-cock is placed on the service pipe under the sidewalk instead of the ordinary kind, and from it a pipe or hollow stem, instead of a solid rod, runs up to the stop-cock box. The shank of the key, also, is hollow, and has a pressure gauge attached at the top. By means of a coupling, turned by a wheel at its top (shown just below the handles of the key on either side of the gauge), an air tight connection is made between the stem and the key. When the cock is closed (by turning the cross-arms, and with them the gauge, which is fastened to them), a small 'port' in the stopcock plug establishes a connection between the street main and the gauge; the air of the stem is compressed, and the hand on the gauge indicates the hydrostatic pressure on the main. By turning the plug to another position, a second 'port' is opened, allowing the water to flow through, if there be any escape from the pipes in the house. If that be the case, the gauge will indicate a diminished pressure, depending on the amount of the discharge. The plug can also be turned to a third position, leaving it open to the house and closed against the street. By this means the approximate height of the leak (if such is found) is ascertained. The exact position of the ports is indicated on a scale with vernier, which slides up and down the coupling, to be clamped at the level of the side-walk for convenience in making reference marks thereon. The gauge is said to indicate a flow of five gallons an hour, and 're-veal the least leakage even to the size of a pin-hole.' The apparatus may also be applied to street mains to detect leaks in them." *

The second general method for checking waste is the universal introduction of meters. There can be no question of the justice and propriety of measuring the water used for manufacturing purposes or in hotels and other large establishments. It is, however, objected that the adoption of meters for private dwellings will cause an injurious economy in the use of water among the very class of the population where it is important that water should be used freely. This objection is obviated to a great extent, at least, in some places where meters are employed, by fixing a minimum tax—to be paid by all water-takers—which shall cover a certain quantity, based on a reasonable estimate of domestic needs. Water used in excess of this quantity is paid for by measurement, and special arrangements may be made for tenement houses and the dwellings of the very poor. It is further said that the cheaper meters are not very reliable, that it is often possible to pass a considerable amount of water without its being registered, provided the water be allowed to flow slowly, and that the meters are continually needing repairs and giving rise to dissatisfaction and complaint on the part of the water-takers.

Meters are in very general use in Providence and Pawtucket, R. I., and in Fall River, Mass., having been introduced with the water supply: Providence, with 9,780 services has 4,816 meters, and consumes 36.3 gallons per head of population; in Fall River

* The Sanitary Engineer, January 18, 1883.

60 per cent. of the services are metered, and the consumption is
30.1 gallons per head. The introduction of meters is, of course,
much more easy with new works than with works already established. No statistics have come under the author's observation
with reference to the matter of repairs in those American cities
where the use of meters is anything like general. The following
statistics are compiled from German sources:

In Magdeburg it was decided in 1879 to introduce meters
universally, and the water rate was fixed at 33 marks (say $8.00)
per house for any amount up to 300 cubic meters per annum
(about 215 U. S. gallons per day). Above this amount the
charge was made at the same rate, *i. e.*, 11 pfennige per cubic
meter. The introduction of meters was decided upon almost as
a necessity, but, according to subsequent official reports, has
been in every way successful. At the close of the year 1880
there were 2,792 meters in use. During the year 168 meters
had required repairs, and 70 had been tested at the request of
consumers. The meters are all tested before introduction, and a
record kept for future comparison. In Berlin meters are in universal use. Eighty-two per cent of the water supplied is
measured and paid for; the remainder includes what is used for
flushing the pipes, for extinguishing fires, for sprinkling streets,
etc., and also loss by leakage. Of the 15,853 meters in use in
1880–81, 2,093, or 13.2 per cent, were removed for more or less
serious defects, the number registering incorrectly or not at all
being 1,580, or ten per cent of the whole number in use. In
Breslau the number of meters in use in 1880–81 was 5,141; of
these, during the year, 1,085 were tested by request of the con-
sumer or at the instance of the inspector. Of the 1,085 tested,
740 were found to need repairs of some sort, 406 (*i. e.*, 7.9 per
cent) registered incorrectly or not at all. It should be said that
the error in registering is generally to the benefit of the con-
sumer.

Of the methods indicated to check waste, local considerations
must determine which shall be adopted. If a city " has at its
disposal 150 million gallons daily for a population which does
not consume 30 millions," as is stated to be now the case in Balti-
more, Md., there is certainly no occasion for introducing meters
at all; but in places where the available water is limited in
quantity, or where, without economy, the existing supply is

likely to prove insufficient in the immediate future, or in places where the rates are of necessity high, the introduction of meters would be advisable. The waste in Northern cities during the winter is enormous, as it is very common to leave the faucets open during the night, in order to prevent freezing. This cold weather waste can never be completely stopped until property owners are obliged to arrange their plumbing so that the water can be completely drawn from the pipes when liable to freeze. By the use of meters it can be largely reduced, as the waste would be reduced to the minimum amount required to prevent the pipes from freezing, and it would become a question to the water-taker whether it was economy to waste water or remodel his fixtures.

Next in importance to the special form of waste just alluded to, is that due to defective or improper fixtures. Such sources of waste may be readily detected by systematic inspection, and should be controlled by municipal regulation, as is indeed done in some cities. " Providence, New York, Brooklyn and other American cities license their plumbers, and to a certain extent inspect the fixtures used; but in English cities the ordinances and regulations are much more rigid than those in this country. Liverpool, Manchester, Glasgow and other English cities test and stamp all of the water fittings used. In Glasgow, during the year 1877, when this plan was first adopted, of 4,369 fittings examined, 14.6 per cent were rejected, while in 1880, of 27,517 examined, but 3.92 per cent were rejected. In the latter city certain varieties of fittings are proscribed. When any of these are found wasting water twice during three months, they are removed, and their use is not allowed at all in new premises.

" All cisterns are provided with overflow pipes, which are brought outside the building or made to discharge inside where they can be seen. The service pipes, except in special cases, are required to be of lead, and their weight is prescribed. No pipe or fitting can be covered until inspected, to see that it conforms to the regulations.

" Water-closets and urinals are not allowed to be supplied direct from the service pipe, but must be supplied from cisterns, so constructed, that in water-closets not more than two gallons can be used at a single flush, and in urinals not more than 1½

gallons, and so that they cannot be made to flow continuously
either by intention or neglect.

" The adoption of the above or similar regulations in American cities, while not in the least curtailing the legitimate use of
water, would be the means of preventing a very large proportion
of the present enormous amount of willful and useless waste." *

In view of the difficulty of supplying large cities with water
against which no complaints can arise, the question is often
raised whether it is not advisable, in some cases, to introduce a
double supply.   As the author has remarked elsewhere : † " It is
true that for many purposes, as for extinguishing fires and for
sprinkling streets, a water would answer which would not be
suitable for drinking, and such a supply might in many cases be
easily procured, while to procure an abundance of water well
suited for drinking would involve a large outlay.   To the double
system there is no (sanitary) objection, if the poorer water can
be drawn only from street hydrants, which are under municipal
control ; but it is not practicable to supply two sorts of water to
private dwellings, with any security that the distinction between
them will be regarded ; no domestic, and indeed no average in-
habitant, will fail to use for all purposes that water which is most
handily obtained, unless, indeed, it be actually repulsive to the
taste."   It should be said, moreover, that the introduction of a
second (inferior) water, where works already exist, would often
prove nearly or quite as expensive as the extension of the existing works and the increase of the supply of water fit to drink.

Conduits and Distribution Pipes.

Where the source of supply is at a considerable distance, the
water is usually carried by gravity in brick or other masonry conduits to a storage or distributing reservoir.   Open canals are disadvantageous, especially on account of the liability of pollution,
but also as giving opportunity for considerable changes of temperature and for vegetable growths.   The water in passing
through a long conduit has some action on the mortar or cement,
and may become slightly harder ; generally, however, the volume
of water is so great that there is very little perceptible effect.
Except in this respect, the water undergoes almost no change.

---

* Brackett, *loc. cit.*   † Buck's Hygiene, vol. i. p. 215.

Even the change of temperature in a properly covered conduit with constant flow is small, Thus, Kerner found, in the hottest days of the summer of 1875, that the water of the Frankfort supply increased in temperature from 9° C. to only 10° C., in flowing from the source to the main reservoir, a distance of 82 kilometers. In passing through the city mains, a further distance of six kilometers, the temperature increased 2°.75 C.* (Compare page 93.) Where the source of supply is a river or pond, a considerable growth of the fresh-water sponge is often found on the walls of the conduit for some distance. For this and other reasons, such conduits should be subjected to periodical cleansing, if inspection shows it to be necessary.

The distances of the sources of supply of various cities is as follows:

Altenburg (springs)	15.5 miles.	Munich (springs)	24.9 miles.
Danzig (springs)	12.4 "	Paris (River Dhuis)	81.4 "
Frankfort a. M. (springs)	52. "	Paris (River Vanne)	107.2 "
Glasgow (lake)	36. "	Vienna (springs)	60.3 "
Gotha (springs)	20.5 "		
Boston (Lake Cochituate)	16. "	New York (Croton River)	40.6 "

From the distributing reservoir, or directly from the source of supply, the water passes into the main distribution pipes, which are usually of cast iron. Although there are some waters which experience has shown to have almost no action on cast iron, with most waters the pipes soon begin to rust. The rust often begins at numerous isolated points, or nuclei, forming "tubercles," which increase in size, become merged together and finally—aided by the collection of sediment from the water—nearly choke the pipe. The presence of iron in the water, either in solution or in suspension, can hardly be regarded as deleterious to health, but the water is sometimes rendered unfit for washing and cooking. The presence and growth of the deposit of iron-rust, has, however, a very serious effect on the flow of the water, and it becomes necessary to remove the deposit by scraping the inside of the pipes. Several special tools have been devised for this purpose. The following tables (Tables XXIX and XXX) will show the effect of the accumulation of rust in diminishing the

* Wolffhügel: **Wasserversorgung**, p. 227.

capacity of the pipe and the flow of water : they are the results of observations made in Aberdeen, Scotland.[*]

TABLE XXIX.—DIMINUTION OF AVAILABLE CAPACITY OF CORRODED PIPES.

No.	AGE OF PIPE. Years.	CHARACTER.	INTERNAL DIAMETER. Inches.	AMOUNT OF RUST PER LINEAR YARD. Cu. Inches.	CAPACITY OF CLEAN PIPE PER LINEAR YARD. Cu. Inches.	PERCENTAGE OF SPACE OCCUPIED BY RUST.
1	20	Uncoated.	3	63.84	254.44	25.0
2	29	"	3	86.94	254.44	34.1
3	38	"	3	110.44	254.44	43.4
4	29	"	4	182.37	452.37	40.3
5	22	"	4	244.37	452.37	54.0
6	14	"	5	180.	706.86	25.4
7	15	Coated.	7	190.	1,385.42	13.7
8	15	"	10	240.	2,827.44	8.4
9	40	"	15	1,320.,	6,361.74	20.7

TABLE XXX.—DISCHARGE FROM CORRODED PIPES.

No.	DIAMETER OF PIPE. Inches.	AGE OF PIPE. Years.	APPROXIMATE AMOUNT OF CORROSION PER LINEAR YARD. Cu. Inches.	HEAD IN FEET. Before Cleaning.	After Cleaning.	DISCHARGE PER MINUTE. Before Cleaning. Imp. Gallons	After Cleaning. Imp. Gallons
1	3	29	86.99	42	47	47	143
2	3	29	93.	54	56	79	158
3	3	29	93.	70	74	143	200
4	3	32	190.	77	82	16	150
5	3	32	190.	72	72	115	187
6	3	26	80.	56	62	35	220
7	3	26	88.	36	43	65	130
8	4	29	100.	40	45	69	115
9	4	29	100.	38	42	125	107

These results are the average gaugings of five different trials taken once a week on the same day.

On account of the action of most waters on cast-iron pipes it is usual at the present time to protect the surface in some way from corrosion. The process commonly employed is that devised by Dr. R. Angus Smith : the newly cast pipes, which must be free from rust, are heated to a temperature of some 500° Fahr., and then dipped perpendicularly into a hot bath of coal-tar pitch mixed with a small proportion of heavy coal oil. In this bath they are allowed to remain for a short time and then withdrawn. The coating thus formed is firmly coherent and is unob-

---

[*] M. B. Jamieson : The internal corrosion of cast-iron pipes. Proc. Inst. Civ Eng. Gr. Br., lxv (1881), p 323.

jectionable from a sanitary point of view. It does not afford absolute protection against rust, but it delays and diminishes the action of the water to a great extent. The first line of pipes of this description laid in this country was laid in Boston in 1858. In 1876–77 some of these (20 in.) pipes were removed. "As they were taken up their condition was observed. Their inner surfaces were not entirely free from tuberculation, but were very much more so than are the surfaces of uncoated pipes in this city after they have been laid but a few years. The tubercles were isolated, and were not in sufficient numbers or of sufficient size to very materially interfere with the capacity of flow of the pipes. They were very easily removed—more easily than from uncoated pipes—seeming to have very little hold upon the tar surface.

" Upon cleaning off the surface under a tubercle one would at first suppose there had been simply a deposit, that no action had been had either upon the iron or upon the coating ; but a more careful examination would show that under the center of the tubercle a portion of the iron, from the size of a pin head to that of a small pea, had been transformed into a black substance that could be easily cut with a knife, and had the appearance of plumbago. The inference drawn from the general appearance of the pipes was that they would have lasted for an indefinite period." *

Some time since Professor Barff, of London, proposed to protect articles of iron, among other things water pipes, from corrosion, by covering them with an artificial coating of the black oxide of iron. The coating is produced by exposing the metal to superheated steam at a high temperature, and when once formed it protects the iron from atmospheric and other agencies which would corrode it. The process has been somewhat modified and is now known as the Bower-Barff process, and promises to become a practical and valuable means of protecting cast-iron pipes. Some wrought-iron pipes of this description have been introduced as service pipes in Altona, and probably elsewhere, but it is too soon for definite statements as to their durability.

Cast-iron pipes are usually connected by the hub and spigot joint ; the joints are first packed with tow or jute and then

* First Annual Report of the Boston Water Board. City Document No. 57. Boston, 1877.

melted lead is run in and driven up firmly. It has been found that the tow sometimes gives an unpleasant taste to the water, and the Rivers Pollution Commission recommended that the joints of the larger mains should be pointed up with Portland cement on the inside to prevent the water from coming in contact with the tow.

The sediment which accumulates in the pipes, especially in low-lying districts, although it has generally a rusty appearance, is not simply iron rust from the pipes. With the iron rust there is always more or less earthy matter, and sometimes the sediment contains a large proportion of vegetable organisms, such as the *Crenothrix*, already described. The following results were obtained from the analysis of the rust in the Aberdeen pipes already referred to :

	From uncoated 4-in. Pipe 21 years in use.	From coated 10-in. Pipe 15 years in use.
Organic and volatile matter	16.62	18.05
Sulphuric acid (SO_3)	0.60	1.08
Phosphoric acid	Slight trace	trace.
Magnetic oxide of iron	32.47	0.36
Peroxide of iron	9.04	37.55
Insoluble sandy matter	41.27	42.78
Lime	trace	0.18

Wrought-iron pipes, coated with cement inside and out, have been sometimes used, generally from motives of economy. They are made by rolling up sheet iron and riveting the edges of the sheet together as shown in Fig. 54. A longitudinal rib is sometimes employed as shown in Fig. 53. The lengths of pipes may be telescoped together, but are usually connected by means of an iron sleeve, filled in with cement. The durability of the pipes is very different in different localities, owing mainly to difference in the quality of the workmanship. Where the pipes have been made

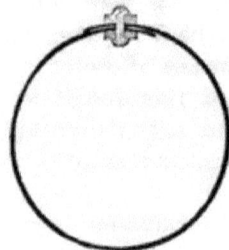

FIG. 53.

FIG. 54.

under the direction of the water department, by day labor, they have sometimes

proved very satisfactory, but where the work is done by con-
tract it is difficult always to obtain the best results.

In the extreme West, wrought-iron pipes are used for conveying water for hydraulic operations and for purposes of water
supply, sometimes under a very great head.   Water is conveyed
to Virginia City, Nevada, through such a main, the maximum
thickness of which is 0.34 inch, and which is exposed in some
parts of its length to a pressure of 1,800 feet head of water.   The
pipes are coated with asphaltum to prevent rusting.

Wooden pipes, generally bored logs, have been used more or
less for conveying water, and are still employed in some sections
of the country.   Detroit had at one time 130 miles of wooden
pipe, and 1½ miles were laid in 1880.   The logs used are sound
green tamarack, not less than 6 inches in diameter and 8 feet
long.   The joints are covered with iron thimbles, and the pipes
last for 16 years or more and cost (or did cost) only about one-
fifth as much as iron.

Service pipes.—The service pipes for house distribution in
connection with a public water supply are generally of lead, this
metal being employed on account of the facility with which it
may be worked.   Lead pipes are also sometimes used for conveying well or spring water to individual residences.   Various waters
act very differently upon lead, some corroding it rapidly, others
only to a very slight extent, under similar circumstances.   The
cause of the corrosion is to be sought in the dissolved oxygen,
of which all waters contain more or less, and in certain saline substances the presence of which determines a more violent action.
It is generally felt, for instance, that the presence of nitrates,
nitrites, and ammoniacal salts increases the action of water on
lead, while carbonates, sulphates, and notably phosphates, hinder
such action; but while certain general statements may be truth-
fully made as the result of laboratory experiment and from the
analysis of waters whose action on lead has been learned by
experience, it is a rather hazardous thing for a chemist to predict, *a priori,* what will be the effect of a particular water on lead
pipe under the conditions of ordinary practice.   Next to no value
attaches to experiments made by immersing strips of sheet lead
in open or closed vessels containing the water under examination.   In actual practice, many waters which would be pronounced dangerous on the strength of such experiments, prove

entirely harmless. The pipes very soon become covered with a naturally formed protective coating of difficultly soluble compounds of lead; and after a slight initial action, corrosion practically ceases if the pipes are kept constantly filled.

If it is felt necessary to make or to have made preliminary laboratory experiments, they should be made by imitating as nearly as possible the conditions of actual practice, and sufficient time should be employed. The following extract from the report on the examination of a soft surface water (where the time at disposal was somewhat limited), will serve as an example: *

"A coil of 100 feet of new one-quarter inch lead pipe was taken and filled with the water under examination. The pipe held 64 cubic inches of water, and the surface of lead was equal to about 900 square inches. The water was allowed to remain in the pipe for 50 hours and then removed, a fresh supply being introduced without allowing the air to come into contact with the inside surface of the pipe. The water as drawn was quite turbid, from the presence of the oxycarbonate of lead, and was found to contain (the lead being calculated as metallic lead):

	METALLIC LEAD.	
	Parts per 100,000.	Grains in U. S. gallon.
In solution	0.055	0.032
In suspension	1.257	0 733
Total	1.317	0.765

" At the end of 70 hours the water in the pipe was drawn out and found to contain :

	METALLIC LEAD.	
	Parts per 100,000.	Grains in U. S. gallon.
In solution	0.573	0.334
In suspension	0.137	0 080
Total	0.710	0.414

"The pipe was then thoroughly washed from any loosely adhering coating by allowing a rapid stream of Cochituate water to flow through for some time. The Cochituate water was then displaced by the water under examination, and this water was allowed to remain in the pipe for 30 hours. This water, when drawn, contained, both in solution and suspension, 0.157 part of metallic lead in 100,000, or 0.092 grain to the U. S. gallon. The

* Report on the Waters of Flax Pond, made to the City Council of Chelsea, Mass., 1875.

amount in suspension was not determined separately, as there was no very considerable quantity visible to the eye. A fresh portion was allowed to remain in the pipe for 40 hours, and then contained in solution and suspension 0.184 part in 100,000, or 0.107 grain to the U. S. gallon."

At the conclusion of the experiment the action on the lead had not ceased, even practically, but it had diminished very much, and there was no doubt that, in practice, the water would act very slightly on the pipes when in continuous use, as has proved to be the case in Boston, New York, Glasgow, Manchester, and many other places where the question has been discussed.

It may be said that, while with most waters the action on the lead *practically* ceases, it probably never ceases *absolutely*. The water of Lake Cochituate, as supplied in Boston, Mass., through lead pipes, always contains traces of lead in solution. The amount of lead taken up by the water in passing through some 150 feet of pipe which had been in use for some years, was found to be only 0.03 part in 100,000, or less than 0.02 grain in the U. S. gallon. Water which is allowed to remain in the pipe for some time, or is drawn from the hot-water faucets, may contain as much as 0.1, or even 0.2 part in 100,000 (from 0.06 to 0.12 grain in the gallon), and wherever lead distribution pipes are in use, it is safer always to run to waste enough water to clear the pipes, and never to use, for drinking or for cooking, water which has passed through the pipes while hot. A similar precaution should be used in the case of new pipes: the water should be wasted intermittently but freely for a number of days. There is great difference in the susceptibility of different persons to lead poisoning. It is thought that as little as one-fortieth of a grain to the gallon has caused sickness, but one-tenth of a grain is usually regarded as an outside limit. It is doubtful whether there are any well authenticated cases of lead poisoning from the use of the Cochituate water.* The Croton water supplied to New York city is similar to the Boston water in its action on lead,† although at least one case of poisoning has been reported, which was supposed to be due to the daily use for some time of water which had stood over night in the pipes. The practical experience in

---

* See Report of the Mass. State Board of Health, 1871.
† See Report of the Metropolitan Board of Health, New York, 1869, p. 420.

the use of lead pipe in the cities mentioned, and in many others, shows that, as a rule, there is no danger in using lead pipes for house distribution in connection with a public supply.

The most unfavorable situation for lead pipe is as suction pipes in wells. Here the corrosion is often very rapid, and it is rendered more violent by the fact that the continual changes of level expose a longer or shorter portion of the pipe to the alternate action of air and water. There are instances enough of lead poisoning from this cause.

It may be remarked, in this connection, that the lead pipe now in use, at least in the eastern part of the country, is much inferior in strength and durability, and apparently more readily corroded than that formerly in use. The lead now in the market has been desilverized by the zinc process, and this seems to give it a particular and disadvantageous character.

Other materials besides lead are used in the house service. To block tin or to tin-lined lead pipes, if the latter are properly made and properly put together, there is no objection on sanitary grounds. The corrosion of the tin by ordinary waters would result in the formation of insoluble and harmless substances. As to the suitability of the brass pipes which have been proposed, there seems to be no exact information. To the various sorts of "enameled" wrought-iron pipes which are in the market there is no sanitary objection. The coating or enamel is generally some preparation of coal tar, with or without linseed oil, and this sort of pipe is particularly adapted for use in wells, where a portion of the outer surface is exposed alternately to the action of air and water; unfortunately, the coating is not always perfect, and when the original surface of the pipe is exposed, rusting begins. Zinced or "galvanized" iron, as it is called, is fully as bad in respect to rusting. The pipes are prepared by dipping the iron, previously well cleaned by means of dilute acid, into a bath of melted zinc. The zinc adheres firmly to the surface of the iron, and penetrates it to a certain extent, so that we do not deal with a simple coating, such as we have on tinned iron, or on the various forms of enameled pipe. The idea is that the zinc shall protect the iron by virtue of a galvanic action between the two metals, and it does protect the iron for a time. When the pipes are exposed to the action of water, corrosion begins at once: at first, the action is on the zinc alone, provided the original iron was free from rust, and the treatment with zinc was thorough ; but after a time the zinc which remains will cease to protect the iron, and iron rust will begin to form. As regards this action, it is simply a question of time. Water that has passed through zinced pipes will be found almost always, if not invariably, to contain zinc compounds, either in solution or in suspension ; the amount, however, is generally very small. As to the effect of such water on health, there is some difference of opinion, but it is generally believed that the pipes may be safely used.*

One of the best materials for service pipes is wrought iron protected by the Bower-Barff process, provided practical experience justifies the theoretical expectations. To such pipes, coupled without the use of red or white lead, there can be nothing superior from a sanitary point of view, and for use in wells and cisterns they will supply a very serious want. Ordinary wrought-iron pipes, although possessing many advantages, have the great disadvantage of rusting very readily : the iron rust is harmless but unsightly in drinking water, and may render the water unfit for culinary purposes and for use in the laundry.

---

* For a full discussion of this subject, see Dr. Boardman's paper in the Report of the Mass. State Board of Health for 1874.

BIBLIOGRAPHY.

THE following list of books makes no claim to being exhaustive. It includes most of the works referred to in the preceding pages, and may perhaps be described as a list of such works as would together make a fair nucleus for a library of water supply, other than from a strictly engineering standpoint. Papers in periodical publications are not included.

I.—WORKS OF A GENERAL CHARACTER, MAINLY FROM AN ENGINEERING POINT OF VIEW.

Fanning, J. T.: A Practical Treatise on Water-Supply Engineering, etc. 8vo, pp. 650. Van Nostrand, New York, 1877.

Grahn, E.: Die städtische Wasserversorgung. 3 vols. 8vo. Vol. I. München, 1877. [Contains Statistik der städtischen Wasserversorgung: Beschreibung der Anlagen in Bau und Betrieb.]

Humber, William: A Comprehensive Treatise on the Water Supply of Cities and Towns, etc. Folio, pp. 378, and many plates. London, Crosby, Lockwood & Co., 1877. [An American edition was published by Geo. H. Frost, Chicago.]

II.—WORKS OF A GENERAL CHARACTER, MAINLY FROM A CHEMICAL OR SANITARY POINT OF VIEW.

Buck: Hygiene and Public Health. 2 vols. 8vo. New York, Wm. Wood & Co., 1879.

Denton, J. Bailey: Sanitary Engineering. 8vo, pp. 429, with many plates. Spon, London, 1877.

Fischer: Die chemische Technologie des Wassers. 8vo. Braunschweig, 1878–80.

Fodor: Boden und Wasser. Braunschweig, 1882.

Great Britain: Report of the Royal Commission on Water-Supply, with Minutes of Evidence. Parliamentary Documents. 4to. London, 1869–70.

Great Britain: Sixth Report of the Commissioners appointed in 1868 to inquire into the Best Means of Preventing the Pollution of Rivers. Domestic Water Supply of Great Britain. 4to. London, 1876.

[This report contains, besides complete statistics of the water supply of Great Britain, considerations and accounts of experiments on the following topics:

On the alleged self-purification of polluted rivers.

On the propagation of epidemics by potable water.

On the alleged influence of the hardness of water upon health.

On the superiority of soft over hard water in cooking.

On the softening of hard water.

On the improvement of potable water by filtration.

On the deterioration of potable water by transmission through mains and service pipes.

On the constant and intermittent systems of water supply.]

Lefort, Jules : Traité de Chimie Hydrologique. 8vo, pp. 798. Deuxième édition. Paris, 1873.

Lersch, Dr. B. M. : Hydrochemie oder Handbuch der Chemie der natürlichen Wässer, 2 Auflage. 8vo, pp. 718. Bonn, 1870.

Parkes, E. A., M.D.: Manual of Practical Hygiene. Fifth edition. 8vo. London and Philadelphia, 1878.

Reichardt : Grundlagen zur Beurtheilung des Trinkwassers. 3te Auflage. 8vo, pp. 107. Jena, 1875.

Sander, Dr. Friedrich : Handbuch der öffentlichen Gesundheitspflege. 8vo, pp. 503. Leipzig, 1877.

Wolffhügel : Wasserversorgung. [Aus dem Handbuch der Hygiene und der Gewerbekrankheiten, von Pettenkofer und Ziemssen.] 8vo, pp. 244. Leipzig, 1882.

III.—ON THE POLLUTION OF STREAMS.

Great Britain : Rivers Pollution Commission, appointed in 1865. Three Reports. Parliamentary Documents. 4to. London, 1866-67.

Great Britain : Rivers Pollution Commission, appointed in 1868. Six Reports. Parliamentary Documents. 4to. London, 1870-74.

Massachusetts : Seventh Annual Report of the State Board of Health, containing a special report on the pollution of streams, etc. 8vo. Boston, 1876.

Paris : Assainissement de la Seine. Épuration et Utilisation des Eaux d'Égout. Documents administratifs ; Enquête ; Annexes. 3 vols. 8vo, with plates. Paris, 1876.

IV.—ON FILTRATION, GROUND WATER, WELLS, ETC.

Belgrand, M. : Les Travaux souterrains de Paris. Études préliminaires. La Seine. Régime de la Pluie, des Sources, des Eaux courantes. Applications à l'Agriculture. 8vo, pp. 612, with atlas. Paris, Dunod, 1875. [Especially chap. vii, Des nappes d'eau souterrains, and chap. xxvi, Du filtrage des eaux, etc.]

Berlin : Vorarbeiten zu einer zukünftigen Wasserversorgung der Stadt Berlin. Ausgeführt in den Jahren 1868 und 1869 von L. A. Veitmeyer. 8vo, pp. 368, with atlas. Berlin, Reimer, 1871. [Especially pp. 109-130—experiments on the ground water in the neighborhood of the Tegeler See.]

Berlin : Reinigung und Entwässerung Berlins. Berichte über mehrere auf Veranlassung des Magistrats der königl. Haupt- und Residenzstadt Berlin Versuche und Untersuchungen. 12 Hefte, with 3 Anhänge. 8vo. Berlin,

Hirschwald, 1870-76. [Especially Heft v, "über die Grundwasserverhält-
nisse," with a great number of profiles.]

Brooklyn, N. Y. : The Brooklyn Water Works and Sewers. Prepared
and printed by order of the Board of Water Commissioners. 4to, pp. 159,
with 59 lith. plates. New York, Van Nostrand, 1867.

Darcy, Henry : Les fontaines publiques de la ville de Dijon. 4to, pp. 647,
with atlas. [Especially Appendix D, Filtrage.]

Dresden : Das Wasserwerk der Stadt Dresden erbaut in den Jahren 1871-
1874, von B. Salbach. 8vo. In three parts, with atlases containing many
plates. Halle, Knapp, 1874-76.

Dupasquier, A. : Des Eaux de Source et des Eaux de Rivière comparées,
etc. 12mo, pp. 414. Paris et Lyon, 1840.

Dupuit, J.: Traité de la Conduite et de la Distribution des Eaux, etc.
Suivi de la Description des Filtres naturelles de Toulouse par D'Aubisson.
4to, with atlas. Paris, 1854.

Fischer, Dr. F. : Das Trinkwasser, seine Beschaffenheit, Untersuchung
und Reinigung unter Berücksichtigung der Brunnenwässer Hannover. 8vo,
pp. 63. Hannover, 1873.

Göttisheim : Das unterirdische Basel. 8vo, pp. 72. Basel, 1868. [2d
Edition, 1873.]

Grahn and Meyer : Reisebericht einer von Hamburg nach Paris und London ausgesandten Commission über künstliche centrale Sandfiltration zur
Wasserversorgung von Städten, und über Filtration in kleinen Massstabe.
Von E. Grahn und F. Andreas Meyer. 8vo, pp. 153. Hamburg, Meissner,
1877. [Especially Anlage 3, "Historische Notizen über künstliche Filtration
im kleineren Massstabe."]

Grimaud, de C ux : Des Eaux publiques, etc. 8vo, pp. 348. Paris, Dezo-
bry, 1863. [Especially chap. xiv, "de la clarification des eaux publiques."]

Halle : Das Wasserwerk der Stadt Halle, erbaut in den Jahren 1867 und
1868. Von B. Salbach. Folio, with atlas. Halle, Knapp, 1871.

Kirkwood, J. P. : Report on the Filtration of River Waters for the Supply
of Cities, as practised in Europe. 4to, pp. 178, with 30 plates. New York,
Van Nostrand, 1869.

Munich : Berichte über die Verhandlungen und die Arbeiten der Commission für Wasserversorgung, Canalisation, und Abfuhr. Erster Bericht, 1874-
75 : Zweiter Bericht, 1876, und Anhänge, 1877. 4to, with plans and profiles.
München, Mühlthaler, 1876, 1877.

Nichols, W. R. : On the Filtration of Potable Water. Reprinted from the
Ninth Annual Report of the Mass. State Board of Health. 8vo, pp. 93. New
York, Van Nostrand, 1879

Pietke : Mittheilungen über natürliche und künstliche Sandfiltration, nach
Betriebsresultaten der Berliner Wasserwerke vor dem Stralauer Thor. 8vo,
pp. 75. Berlin, 1881.

Schorer, Th. : Lübeck's Trinkwasser, 8vo, pp. 284. Lübeck, Seelig, 1877.
[Especially pp. 248-257, describing the deterioration of water by vegetable
growth and decay, etc.]

Spon, Ernest : The present Practice of Sinking and Boring Wells. 12mo, pp. 216. London, Spon, 1875.

Ward, F. O. : Moyens de créer des sources artificielles d'eau pure pour Bruxelles. 8vo, pp. 106. Bruxelles, Decq, 1853.

Wiebel, Dr. F. : Die Fluss- und Bodenwässer Hamburgs. Chemische Beitrage zur Analyse gewöhnlicher Lauf- Nutz- und Trinkwässer sowie zu der Frage der Wasserversorgung grosser Städte von sanitären und gewerblichem Standpunkte. 4to, pp. 152. Hamburg, Meissner, 1876.

Wolff : Der Untergrund und das Trinkwasser der Städte. 2te Auflage. 8vo, pp. 60. Erfurt, 1873.

V.—ON THE SANITARY EXAMINATION OF WATER.

Eyferth, B. : Die mikroscopischen Süsswasserbewohner in gedrängter Uebersicht. 8vo, pp. 60. Braunschweig, 1877.

Fox, Cornelius B., M.D. : Sanitary Examination of Water, Air and Food. 8vo, pp. 508. London, 1878.

Frankland, Dr. E. : Water Analysis for Sanitary Purposes. 12mo, pp. 139. London, Van Voorst, 1880.

Hassall : Microscopical Examination of Water Supplied to the Inhabitants of London, etc. London, 1851.

Kubel, Dr. Wilhelm : Anleitung zur Untersuchung von Wasser, u. s. w. 8vo, pp. 184. Zweite Auflage von Dr. Ferd. Tiemann. Braunschweig, 1874.

Macdonald, J. D., M.D. : A Guide to the Microscopical Examination of Drinking Water. 8vo, pp. 65 and 24 plates. London and Philadelphia, 1875.

Neuville: Des Eaux de Paris. Essai d'Analyse micrographique comparée. 4to, pp. 63. 15 plates. Paris, 1880.

Schützenberger: On Fermentations. 12mo, pp. 331. Intern. Sci. Series. New York, 1876. [This contains a description of Schützenberger's method of determining dissolved oxygen, pp. 108 and foll.]

Wanklyn, J. A. : Water Analysis: a Practical Treatise on the Examination of Potable Water. By J. A. W. and E. T. Chapman. 12mo, pp. 182. Fifth edition, re-written by J. A. Wanklyn. London, 1879.

VI.—MISCELLANEOUS.

Boston, Mass. ; Report of Cochituate Water Board, 1874. [Contains a reprint of a report by Geo. F. Deacon, Borough Engineer, Liverpool, Eng., on the subject of " Waste."]

Boston, Mass.: Report on Waste of Water (May 25, 1882). Boston City Document No. 78, 1882.

Bowditch: Public Hygiene in America. 8vo. Boston, 1877.

Deacon: The Constant Supply and Waste of Water. A paper read before the Society of Arts, May 19, 1882. 4to, London, 1882.

Magnin: The Bacteria, translated by Dr. Geo. H. Sternberg, U. S. A. 8vo, pp. 227. Boston, 1880.

Nägeli: Die niederen Pilze. München, 1877.

Nägeli: Untersuchungen über niedere Pilze. 8vo, pp. 285. München und Leipzig, 1882. [This contains Buchner's paper referred to on page 21.]

De Rance: The Water Supply of England and Wales. 8vo, pp. 623. London, 1882.

Kuessner und Pott: Die acuten Infectionskrankheiten. 8vo, pp. 460. Braunschweig, 1882.

Parry: Water, its Composition, Collection, and Distribution. 12mo, pp. 184. London, 1881.

Rowan: Boiler Incrustation and Corrosion. 18mo, pp. 48. New York, Van Nostrand, 1876.

Wilson: Treatise on Steam Boilers. Third edition. 12mo, pp. 328. London, 1875.

TABLE XXXI.—*For the Conversion of Degrees of Fahrenheit's Scale into those of the Centigrade Thermometer.*

Fahr.	Cent.	Fahr.	Cent.	Fahr.	Cent.	Fahr.	Cent.
0	− 17.7	54	12.2	107	41.6	160	71.1
1	− 17.2	55	12.7	108	42.2	161	71.6
2	− 16.6	56	13.3	109	42.7	162	72.2
3	− 16.1	57	13.8	110	43.3	163	72.7
4	− 15.5	58	14.4	111	43.8	164	73.3
5	− 15	59	15	112	44.4	165	73.8
6	− 14.4	60	15.5	113	45	166	74.4
7	− 13.8	61	16.1	114	45.5	167	75
8	− 13.3	62	16.6	115	46.1	168	75.5
9	− 12.7	63	17.2	116	46.6	169	76.1
10	− 12.2	64	17.7	117	47.2	170	76.6
11	− 11.6	65	18.3	118	47.7	171	77.2
12	− 11.1	66	18.8	119	48.3	172	77.7
13	− 10.5	67	19.4	120	48.8	173	78.3
14	− 10	68	20	121	49.4	174	78.8
15	− 9.4	69	20.5	122	50	175	79.4
16	− 8.8	70	21.1	123	50.5	176	80
17	− 8.3	71	21.6	124	51.1	177	80.5
18	− 7.7	72	22.2	125	51.6	178	81.1
19	− 7.2	73	22.7	126	52.2	179	81.6
20	− 6.6	74	23.3	127	52.7	180	82.2
21	− 6.1	75	23.8	128	53.3	181	82.7
22	− 5.5	76	24.4	129	53.8	182	83.3
23	− 5	77	25	130	54.4	183	83.8
24	− 4.4	78	25.5	131	55	184	84.4
25	− 3.8	79	26.1	132	55.5	185	85
26	− 3.3	80	26.6	133	56.1	186	85.5
27	− 2.7	81	27.2	134	56.6	187	86.1
28	− 2.2	82	27.7	135	57.2	188	86.6
29	− 1.6	83	28.3	136	57.7	189	87.2
30	− 1.1	84	28.8	137	58.3	190	87.7
31	− 0.5	85	29.4	138	58.8	191	88.3
32	0	86	30	139	59.4	192	88.8
33	0.5	87	30.5	140	60	193	89.4
34	1.1	88	31.1	141	60.5	194	90
35	1.6	89	31.6	142	61.1	195	90.5
36	2.2	90	32.2	143	61.6	196	91.1
37	2.7	91	32.7	144	62.2	197	91.6
38	3.3	92	33.3	145	62.7	198	92.2
39	3.8	93	33.8	146	63.3	199	92.7
40	4.4	94	34.4	147	63.8	200	93.3
41	5	95	35	148	64.4	201	93.8
42	5.5	96	35.5	149	65	202	94.4
43	6.1	97	36.1	150	65.5	203	95
44	6.6	98	36.6	151	66.1	204	95.5
45	7.2	99	37.2	152	66.6	205	96.1
46	7.7	100	37.7	153	67.2	206	96.6
47	8.3	101	38.3	154	67.7	207	97.2
48	8.8	102	38.8	155	68.3	208	97.7
49	9.4	103	39.4	156	68.8	209	98.3
50	10	104	40	157	69.4	210	98.8
51	10.5	105	40.5	158	70	211	99.4
52	11.1	106	41.1	159	70.5	212	100.0
53	11.6						

TABLE XXXII.—*For the Conversion of Degrees of the Centigrade Thermometer into Degrees of Fahrenheit's Scale.*

CENT.	FAHR.	CENT.	FAHR.	CENT.	FAHR.	CENT.	FAHR.
0	32.0	26	78.8	51	123.8	76	168.8
1	33.8	27	80.6	52	125.6	77	170.6
2	35.6	28	82.4	53	127.4	78	172.4
3	37.4	29	84.2	54	129.2	79	174.2
4	39.2	30	86.0	55	131.0	80	176.0
5	41.0	31	87.8	56	132.8	81	177.8
6	42.8	32	89.6	57	134.6	82	179.6
7	44.6	33	91.4	58	136.4	83	181.4
8	46.4	34	93.2	59	138.2	84	183.2
9	48.2	35	95.0	60	140.0	85	185.0
10	50.0	36	96.8	61	141.8	86	186.8
11	51.8	37	98.6	62	143.6	87	188.6
12	53.6	38	100.4	63	145.4	88	190.4
13	55.4	39	102.2	64	147.2	89	192.2
14	57.2	40	104.0	65	149.0	90	194.0
15	59.0	41	105.8	66	150.8	91	195.8
16	60.8	42	107.6	67	152.6	92	197.6
17	62.6	43	109.4	68	154.4	93	199.4
18	64.4	44	111.2	69	156.2	94	201.2
19	66.2	45	113.0	70	158.0	95	203.0
20	68.0	46	114.8	71	159.8	96	204.8
21	69.8	47	116.6	72	161.6	97	206.6
22	71.6	48	118.4	73	163.4	98	208.4
23	73.4	49	120.2	74	165.2	99	210.2
24	75.2	50	122.0	75	167.0	100	212.0
25	77.0						

METRIC SYSTEM OF WEIGHTS AND MEASURES.

Weights.

1 Milligram	mgm.	= 0.001 gram.		1 Gram	grm.	=	1 gram.
1 Centigram		= 0.01 "		1 Dekagram		=	10 grams.
1 Decigram		= 0.1 "		1 Hectogram		=	100 "
1 Gram	grm.	= 1.0 "		1 Kilogram	kilo.	=	1000 "

Measures of Length.

1 Millimeter	m.m.	= 0.001 meter.		1 Meter	=	1 meter.
1 Centimeter	c.m.	= 0.01 "		1 Dekameter	=	10 meters.
1 Decimeter	d.m.	= 0.1 "		1 Hectometer	=	100 "
1 Meter	m.	= 1.0 "		1 Kilometer	kilom.	= 1000 "

Measures of Volume.

1 Cubic Centimeter	c.c. or $\overline{c.m.}$	=	0.001 liter.
1 Cubic Decimeter	$\overline{d.m.}$	=	1.000 "
1 Cubic Meter	$\overline{m.}$	=	1000.000 "

TABLE XXXIII.—EQUIVALENTS OF VARIOUS MEASURES OF VOLUME.*

Name of Measure.	U. S. Gallons.	Imperial Gallons.	It's Equivalent in				
			Liters.	Cubic Feet.	Cubic Meters.	Cubic Inches.	Pounds avoirdupois (of water).
1 U. S. gallon............	1.	0.833111	3.785203	0.135681	0.0037852	231.	8.3388822 †
1 Imperial gallon........	1.20032	1.	4.543457	0.160459	0.0045434	277.274	10.
1 Liter..................	0.264866	0.220097	1.	0.035317	0.001	61.0271	2.204737
1 Cubic Foot............	7.480152	6.232102	28.315289	1.	0.028315	1,728.	62.37916
1 Cubic Meter..........	264.18657	220.096714	1,000.	35.316600	1.	61,027.0963	2,204.737
1 Cubic Inch...........						1.	0.036009

* This Table is taken from Kirkwood's Filtration of River Waters, p. 167.

† The exact number of pounds or of grains in a gallon is differently given by different authorities, the discrepancies arising from a difference in the value assigned as the weight of a cubic inch of water. The weight of a cubic inch of water is usually stated to be, according to the English standard, 252.458 grains, at 62° F. and under 30 inches barometric pressure. The English imperial gallon contains 277.274 cubic inches of water, the weight of which is taken to be 10 pounds avoirdupois or 70,000 grains. The old wine gallon of 231 cubic inches, according to this standard, would contain 58,318 grains, but some authorities give the amount as 58,333.3. The United States standard gallon of 231 cubic inches, contains, at 39° 83 F. (the temperature of the maximum density of water adopted by Hassler), and under a barometric pressure of 30 inches, 58,372.175 grains of pure water : this fixes the weight of a cubic inch of water, at that temperature, as 252.6933 grains.

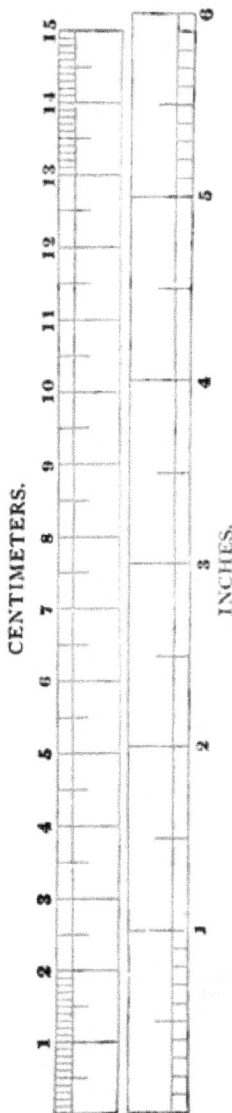

CENTIMETERS.

INCHES.

TABLE XXXIV.—*For Facilitating Approximate Calculations from one Denomination into another.*

FEET.	METERS.	POUNDS AVOIRDU-POIS.	KILO-GRAMS.	U. S. GALLONS.	IMPERIAL GALLONS.	LITERS.	CUBIC METERS.
1	0.30	1	0.45	1	0.83	3.79	0.0038
2	0.61	2	0.91	2	1.67	7.57	0.0076
3	0.91	3	1.36	3	2.50	11.36	0.0114
4	1.22	4	1.81	4	3.33	15.14	0.0151
5	1.52	5	2.26	5	4.17	18.93	0.0189
6	1.83	6	2.72	6	5.00	22.71	0.0227
7	2.13	7	3.18	7	5.83	26.50	0.0265
8	2.44	8	3.62	8	6.66	30.38	0.0303
9	2.74	9	4.08	9	7.50	34.07	0.0341
3.28	1	2.20	1	1.20	1	4.54	0.0045
6.56	2	4.41	2	2.40	2	9.08	0.0091
9.84	3	6.61	3	3.60	3	13.63	0.0136
13.12	4	8.82	4	4.80	4	18.17	0.0182
16.40	5	11.02	5	6.00	5	22.71	0.0227
19.69	6	13.23	6	7.20	6	27.26	0.0273
22.97	7	15.43	7	8.40	7	31.80	0.0318
26.25	8	17.64	8	9.60	8	36.34	0.0363
29.53	9	19.84	9	10.80	9	40.89	0.0409

MILES.	KILO-METERS.	KILO-METERS.	MILES.				
1	1.61	1	0.62	0.26	0.22	1	0.001
2	3.22	2	1.24	0.53	0.44	2	0.002
3	4.83	3	1.86	0.79	0.66	3	0.003
4	6.44	4	2.49	1.05	0.88	4	0.004
5	8.05	5	3.11	1.32	1.10	5	0.005
6	9.66	6	3.73	1.58	1.32	6	0.006
7	11.27	7	4.35	1.85	1.54	7	0.007
8	12.87	8	4.97	2.11	1.76	8	0.008
9	14.48	9	5.59	2.38	1.98	9	0.009

TABLE XXXV.—*For the Conversion of Parts per* **100,000** *into Grains per Gallon, and vice versa : also, for Comparing Degrees of Hardness.*

Parts in 100,000	Grains in U. S. Standard Gallon.	Grains in Imperial Gallon.	Degrees of Hardness.		
			French: Parts CaCO₃ in 100,000.	English: Grains CaCO₃ in imp. Gallon.	German: Parts CaO in 100,000.
1	0.5837	0.7	1	0.7	0.6
2	1.1674	1.4	2	1.4	1.1
3	1.7512	2.1	3	2.1	1.7
4	2.3349	2.9	4	2.8	2.2
5	2.9186	3.5	5	3.5	2.8
6	3.5023	4.2	6	4.2	3.4
7	4.0861	4.9	7	4.9	3.9
8	4.6698	5.6	8	5.6	4.5
9	5.2535	6.3	9	6.3	5.0
1.7131	1	1.1992	1.4	1	0.8
3.4262	2	2.3983	2.9	2	1.6
5.1393	3	3.5975	4.3	3	2.4
6.8524	4	4.7967	6.7	4	3.2
8.5655	5	5.9958	7.1	5	4.0
10.2786	6	7.1950	8.6	6	4.8
11.9917	7	8.3942	10.0	7	5.6
13.7048	8	9.5934	11.4	8	6.4
15.4179	9	10.7925	12.8	9	7.2
1.4286	0.8339	1	1.8	1.2	1
2.8571	1.6678	2	3.6	2.5	2
4.2857	2.5017	3	5.4	3.8	3
5.7143	3.3356	4	7.1	5.0	4
7.1428	4.1695	5	9.0	6.3	5
8.5714	5.0033	6	10.7	7.5	6
10.0000	5.8372	7	12.6	8.8	7
11.4286	6.6711	8	14.3	10.0	8
12.8571	7.5050	9	16.1	11.3	9

INDEX.

www.ingramcontent.com/pod-product-compliance
Lightning Source LLC
Chambersburg PA
CBHW030407270326
41926CB00009B/1313